Earth to Moon

Earth to Moon

A Memoir

Moon Unit Zappa

∴

DEYST.

An Imprint of William Morrow

DEYST.

HarperCollins books may be purchased for educational, business, or sales promotional use. For information, please email the Special Markets Department at SPsales@harpercollins.com.

FIRST EDITION

Designed by Alison Bloomer

Library of Congress Cataloging-in-Publication Data has been applied for.

ISBN 978-0-06-311334-3

24 25 26 27 28 LBC 5 4 3 2 1

FOR JETT, FOR MY FATHER, AND FOR ME

Since my house burned down I have
a better view of the moon.
—Mizuta Masahide

CONTENTS

Good morning!
Well It's Christmas Day,
I'm Moon and guess what
I got! A rabbit fur coat,
a ten speed bike, roller
skates, earings and a
Lot more! I will call you
Golden Anagan Well I
might write later?
Moon

TO
LIZ
MOON
XMAS
77
FROM
yer
ol
MOM
N
DAD

Hello and Welcome to My Book

Growing up I was just like you—I had a rock star for a dad, was told to call my parents by their first names, had two invisible camels for playmates, and daydreamed about my future following in Frank's footsteps by helping people and making them laugh, only I'd be dressed like a nun.

I admit I was also tempted to be barefoot and in charge behind the scenes like my fertile, bossy mother. One hundred babies sounded about right for my temperament since I already adored helping Gail raise my three younger siblings. Ninety-seven more of what I already loved seemed like a dream. Plus that episode of *The Little Rascals* where they took care of all those babies by gluing them to the floor and feeding them cake really cracked me up.

. . . Of course, the children-acquisition details were hazy since I didn't want to have a husband. Who wants a man who leaves all the time and stays away too long?

Luckily, destiny had something else in mind for me altogether.

As they say, man plans and God laughs. Or gives you an unconventional celebrity family and a random hit single when you're not even a musician. Or psychologically, emotionally, professionally, and legally kicks you in the taint until you rock-bottom your way back to life among the loving living, or whatever the expression is.

But I'll get to all that . . .

I GOT MY FIRST JOURNAL when I was five, for Christmas, then every year after, I'd get a new one. They were hardbacks bound in black leather with gold embellishments on the cover and along the paper edges. So fancy. These books felt important. I believed I had a responsibility to do excellent work in them, to match their external beauty and honor the dead trees I held in my hands, a concept my mother had recently illuminated along with explaining that hamburgers were deceased cows. Plus, the diaries were from Gail *and* Frank, my mother *and* my father, with the inscription to me in *his* handwriting, so I put undue pressure on myself to turn these blank nothings into weighty somethings, as I saw my idol dad doing on his large, butter-colored music paper.

When I wasn't writing short stories about my imaginary camels, T'mershi Duween and Sinini, or about aliens or ballerinas or nuns, or alien ballerina nuns, I'd report on the happenings in the house or the world at large. I was political and wrote a letter to President Ford to ask him to stop men from clubbing baby harp seals. I was ambitious and practiced signing my autograph in various handwriting styles. I was complimentary and wrote a letter to Tina Turner to let her know she was almost as good a dancer as me. I was boy crazy for Shaun Cassidy and scrawled my married name "Moon Unit Cassidy" everywhere in loopy cursive. I used my journals as a secret best friend I could tell anything to: "I'm sad. I wish my dad would take me with him to Europe." When I still lived at home and had no privacy, I'd write in code about really secret stuff so I had somewhere safe to be the real me, to vent my feelings with impunity.

Or draw penises.

As time went on, I loosened the reins on my dad-comparing and perfectionism in my journals. And in life. I had no choice. Rightly or wrongly, I believed I would never be as good as my dad, so I had to learn to live with plain old me.

This book is a collection of memories, reflections, drawings, photos, actual journal entries, and some overheard stories as I recall them. Some names and identifying details have been changed to protect the privacy of those mentioned.

I partly wrote this memoir as a reclamation, to tell my version of what happened in my childhood and early life as a gift to myself, as a map that charts how and where I ended up as an adult. I also wrote this book to entertain, so I hope you find something funny or of value here.

If you choose to only read this wee introduction, I hope you can embrace my big takeaways: Love yourself, love yourself, love yourself. Growing up doesn't end when you become an adult. Outrage is the appropriate response to deception and betrayal. The way out is through. Make peace with what hurts and head toward joy. Run with the people who love you, lift you, and make you laugh. Write your future with the ink of today.

May you go farther sooner.
Xx Moon

PART I

Earth

Countdown

1967-1980

CHAPTER 1

Moon Unit

First, some context:

It's America in 1967. The twentieth-century space race is on, Evel Knievel has successfully jumped sixteen cars, the Vietnam War is growing in both number of troops and amount of pushback from the flower children protesting in Haight-Ashbury. In the same year Elvis surrenders his pelvis to marriage during the sexual revolution, I get born in New York City, instantly famous, to a Jean Shrimpton look-alike and a skinny icon with a big nose and notable mustache. Frank has already been dubbed a musical genius by fans, critics, enemies, and peers. My birth name—Moon Unit, no hyphen—raises eyebrows across the planet during a time when "longhairs" are as terrifying to "the establishment" as communists.

My first name, Moon, is weird enough at a time when girls usually receive more common names, like Lisa, Kim, Karen, Debbie, and Jennifer, but my middle name, Unit, polarizes people, either unhinging or enthralling normies worldwide. If, however, you knew my dad's softer side, you'd know my middle name was bestowed upon me because my arrival heralded our foray into becoming a family *unit*. I will automatically feel an unspoken, steadfast, ferocious loyalty to my family—the Unit part—and a pull to be like the actual moon, with no light of my own, just an ancillary object in the infinite reflecting of the light of the sun, a.k.a. the light of my heavenly father, Frank, orbiting his every need and expression.

The way it was told to me, my twenty-year-old mother, working as a secretary to the owner of the Whisky a Go Go on the Sunset Strip in 1966, first met my formidable twenty-five-year-old father at LAX, when she drove a coworker friend, his girlfriend, to pick him up. Insta sparks commenced between the club assistant turned chauffeur and the composer with "Freak Out" and "Absolutely Free" under his belt. Shortly thereafter, he ran into my mother at the bank. Flirtation on rocket fuel. He was the eldest of four, she the eldest of seven. Both his parents were second-generation Italians; his dad was a research scientist and metallurgist who spoke Italian to his stay-at-home wife. Gail's second-generation German American dad was a nuclear physicist and naval captain, her Honolulu-born mother of Portuguese descent also a homemaker but with movie star good looks.

Gail and Frank were both negatively impacted by constantly moving from town to town as kids. They both had an aversion to religion, the status quo, and being mislabeled as hippies. They both had a love of sex, civics, cigarettes, and self-expression. I am unsure if either of them was technically single when they met that second time, but Frank asked Gail out on an official date while waiting for his turn at the teller window.

They say you know everything on the first date and everything else on the second. Frank, a gentleman, made good on his reputation for being antiestablishment when he picked Gail up in his lemon-yellow station wagon and took her to a business meeting, where he blew his nose into her skirt. Gail was shocked but smitten, impressed by his dominance and humor, and high on being brought into his inner circle immediately. He was impressed that she was gorgeous, could keep up, and knew when to defer to him but could also speak her mind. Date two was accompanying him on his whirlwind winter tour in platform shoes and floor-length coats and never leaving his side, from what I can tell from old photos. Their fates were thus sealed.

In January 1967 my mother swore she felt my conception in Montreal, Canada. In early September of the same year, when my father was about to go on the road for many months, in anticipation of missing my birth, Frank gave my very pregnant mother two names to choose from—Moon Unit and Motorhead. Doe-eyed, lovestruck Gail, née Adelaide Gail Sloatman, made her selection.

The now twenty-six-year-old, Baltimore-bred Frank Vincent Zappa, realizing he would be leaving the twenty-one-year-old, miniskirt-wearing, military-brat model/secretary/fangirl from Philadelphia to fend for herself in a basement apartment on Jane Street in the West Village, offered something else—matrimony. I imagine my hypersexual maestro father must have known that due to cost, time differences, and leggy groupies in every city in Europe, he would likely not be checking in all that frequently, and, if he did so, it would be via expensive (therefore short), static-y, long-distance landline phone calls.

So, they tied the knot.

I like to think it was mutual true love, but perhaps it was a swirling mix of practical and conciliatory stressors along with some latent, good old-fashioned Catholic guilt that caused my father to hastily marry my mother in a New York City courthouse fourteen days before my delivery. Comically, he sealed the wedding offering (his second, her first) not with a ring, but with a ballpoint pen they'd used to sign the courtroom paperwork. No bouquet, just that pen clipped to her dress. The pen was promptly lost, a "sign" my mother must have considered, and my dad hopped on a plane in the smoking section to be fêted for his virtuosity.

Then, two days later, on September 16, 1967, twelve days before my birth, Gail's father died under "mysterious military circumstances" reported as "heart failure." I can only imagine that in utero, my system was *also* flooded with an abundance of grief hormones. In a photo, it appears Gail attended the funeral solo. It is easy to picture the new bride feeling doubly abandoned by the most important men in her life, deeply sad and helpless, wondering about the "government cover-up" she believed was related to her father's classified knowledge of UFOs. The navy captain grandfather I never met was buried at Arlington National Cemetery.

While mourning, broke, and friendless, my "rock widow" mother fought postpartum depression in a sunless, underground one-bedroom apartment. After a few intolerable, snowy months more or less trapped with a newborn attached to her nipple and a needy, talkative Siamese cat, Gail hit an all-time low. The isolation, exacerbated by the alarming smell of the "Great Garbage Strike of 1968," pushed my mother to express her misery. The only advice my absentee father gave was "Go west, young woman."

So, she did.

Their dollars stretched in the Golden State. Swaddled in cotton, satin, and velvet, the grieving but determined newlywed and new mom returned to California and the warmth of their holy meeting place, where she single-handedly settled the three of us into a Laurel Canyon landmark known as the Log Cabin. Long gone now, the all-wood mansion, resplendent with a bowling alley in the basement and boasting 1920s movie cowboy Tom Mix's horse buried beneath it, loomed large near the Canyon Country Store, a rock and roll hot spot that still stands today. Our spacious oasis had a swimming pool, a waterfall, and caves behind it that my parents would soon discover housed another burgeoning clan, the Manson family.

So, we moved again.

This time, Gail found a sun-drenched, two-bedroom, ranch-style fixer-upper in the windy hills above Laurel Canyon under canopies of eucalyptus, pine, royal palm, and Chinese elm. Do either of them have an inkling this will be their forever home? That here Gail will hone her penchant for color and the humble abode will eventually morph into an outer manifestation of her inner chaos and whimsy, a sort of Winchester Mystery House–like compound with a full recording studio in the basement? Do they realize that together they will plant roots and claim victory over childhood upheaval? That here my father will do the difficult, solo, quiet, internal work necessary to transcend his potential, cementing his stratospheric talents for the ages? That here they will raise and divide a family and breathe their last breaths?

I have no clue, but this home with all its raw potential is where my story begins.

CHAPTER 2

Dweezil

I love the word "skedaddle." It has the word "dad" embedded in it and sonically conjures a fast, cartoonish fleeing. I often wish escaping with Frank were an option, but I stay put on a street named after a dead president where I have my living and growing to do.

In 1969, the year of the moon landing, we are firmly ensconced as a family, baby number two is on the way, and Gail already has a couple of stories she takes pride in sharing about me. There's the time she was barefoot and hitchhiked to the Canyon Country Store with me on her hip, and I, not yet two, protected us by saying, "Fuck off, pervert," to the flirty creep who approached her. Then there's the one where I, not much older, was playing naked on the hard-wood floor in the living room. Apparently, while splaying my labia open, I called out to a visiting fellow, "Jerry, look at my pee pee." He glanced, then looked away. "JERRY!" I demanded. "LOOK. AT. MY. PEE PEE!"

"Moon just *knew* he was gay and had to confront his fear of vaginas," Gail would say, beaming, in the retellings.

Gail informs me I am an empath and my stomachaches, mysterious ailments, and emotional outbursts "belong to other people." Gail explains that, like her, I am psychic, with the ability to detect people's secrets and the presence of ghosts, especially their unrest. On numerous occasions she tells me that I "chose" her to be my mother before I was born and that "the younger you are, the more you understand everything about God and life, and the more you remember all your past lives."

◐

NO MATTER HOW MANY TIMES I hear Gail say this, I can't quite grasp the math that you "understand everything" when you are at your youngest, because she also says, "You understand everything at your oldest." My mind melts like candle wax; a lifetime on a straight line bends into a circle.

The God part is also confusing because Gail and Frank said they don't believe in God and are atheists because they were both raised Catholic. Now they are "pagan absurdists," which I think means they make their own rules up about what to believe and how to express their ideas in a funny way on any given day, but also something about oak trees and druids. Gail also says I am not allowed to go to church, but I am allowed to look at her collection of prayer cards and watch *The Flying Nun*. Gail's convinced I am a wunderkind after reading an article about spacing out being a form of genius. "Earth to Moon," she sweetly says to coax me out of my wall staring/other-side-transmission gathering.

In addition to my unusual "abilities" tuning in, I'm getting all kinds of otherworldly intel by osmosis, by eavesdropping on conversations, or from Gail directly. Gail loves talking, and I love listening and watching her every move while she cooks or cleans or smokes or talks on the phone or drives or makes tea for the drop-in freaks or sews or draws pictures for me. I pay close attention when she explains about spontaneous combustion, Area 51, UFOs, black holes, and how to spot friendly aliens versus the Greys. She also talks about karma, Stonehenge, dowsing rods, telepathy, reflexology, Tutankhamun and mummy curses, Bigfoot, Loch Ness, the Salem witch trials, the difference between good and bad witches, and how to cast white and black spells. I don't question Gail about any of this because I love her and she loves me. No one else challenges her either. This is all just taken as gospel and normal for life at my house.

When Gail isn't doing her Lamaze breathing or chain-smoking, we use the Ouija board to contact the dead. Gail also encourages my ESP and something called "remote viewing," which means seeing the past or future or something hidden or far away, training me with a deck of cards covered with triangles, squares, circles, and wavy lines. We playfully practice "sending" and "receiving." Then we play a memory-strengthening game called Concentration with a regular deck of Hoyle playing cards. This, alongside front-row seats to my dad's in-home enjoyment of vacuuming visiting women's titties instead of helping Gail clean the house and actually hoovering the dusty floor.

I love Gail's special attention and occult homeschooling, but some of what Frank and Gail do and say and the people and things they have around the house scare me. Like the orgy artwork on the walls or when Gail is mad or the moaning that comes from their room or the story about the crazy person who showed up at the Log Cabin with a gun. Apparently, my quick-thinking father suggested everyone step outside and toss what they had in their hands into a well on the property. It worked; the guy threw his weapon in. Then Frank said everyone had to leave so he could get back to the studio. That worked, too. The guy left.

When Tutu, Gail's mother, arrives from Hawaii, and Gail practices her breathing more regularly and Frank pays a little more attention to Gail, like standing closer to her or touching her arm more when she gets on and off of furniture, I know the baby is coming soon.

I'M RIGHT. ON SEPTEMBER 5, 1969, my brother Dweezil is born in Hollywood, California. His full name is Ian Donald Calvin Euclid

Dweezil Zappa. If people thought my name was weird, they lose it over his. It's hard to believe when I overhear Frank and Gail say the nurses at the hospital were so outraged by the name on his birth certificate that they refused to feed Gail after my brother's delivery. He gets the name Dweezil because he has the same baby toenails as Gail, which Frank has nicknamed "Dweezil toes" because the nail beds on her pinkie toes are so small. His other names come from the guys in my dad's band. In a few short years, my brother will ask for a legal name change to just Dweezil Zappa and get his wish.

I adore my quiet, cherubic baby brother to pieces. I love his curls, his green eyes, his long lashes, and watching him eat his feet when Gail gives him a bath in the kitchen sink. I love his full pink lips and all his drool. I am grateful he brings some temporary calm to our busy house. Everyone but me seems enthralled by Gail's declaration that she had the best orgasm of her life pushing Dweezil out of her vagina. I may not know exactly what she means, but it makes me feel wiggly.

By the time Dweezil is two I've already been grappling with a host of complications. Table surfaces are littered with R. Crumb comics, *Omni* magazines, empty tea and coffee mugs, and ashtrays with my dad's snuffed-out Winstons and my mom's Marlboro Reds. A diverse array of horny dreamers, oddballs, misfits, and sycophants freeload on heavy rotation. I still wear my pacifier around my neck for security, never knowing who's safe and who isn't, who my dad is humping and who he isn't. The house smells of pungent men and women who dance on our kitchen countertops. Our backyard is full of oleander, ivy, crabgrass, dog shit, and the remnants of old milk cartons and carnation-scented wax. I don't love seeing strangers in our yard cavorting or making candles in the nude, near my toys. My feet are just starting to heal from the time two ladies were supposed to be watching me and my feet got burned on the radiator.

Don't get me wrong, there are some great times, too. When my father is home, Gail hugs me tight and Frank draws bugs on my nose in between composing and editing, or he vibrates my chin with his strong, speedy guitar fingers or bounces me on his knee to make me sound funny when I talk or sing. I love when my dad plays 45s with spooky sounds like creaking floors, rattling chains, strange laughter, howling wind, or thunder. I study how gently and precisely my dad sets the needle into the album grooves. I look at the rectangle of gray felt on the record player lever and I listen as my dad adjusts the rate switch to show me how different the same record can sound. He also trains my ear to listen for whether the sound is real or how something else could be used to make a sound seem convincing. He also tells me about an art form called walla walla that is just for people who specialize in background sounds in movies.

Another time Frank shows us reel-to-reel black and white cartoons of Betty Boop and Felix the Cat through a projector on a screen in the basement. Sometimes Frank will draw something like he used to when he made sets and greeting cards before he became famous. He is very good at drawing funny things, like a monster made of snot, and once he painted the whole bedroom I now share with Dweezil black without asking Gail.

AT HOME IN OUR PURPLE kitchen, while Gail makes peanut butter toast, I love when my dad uses every curse word and laughs and encourages me to say them. He shows me all the finger gestures and other profanities that he learned on his travels all around the world, even the things he can't say on TV. I like the hand gestures from England and Italy the best. He says them all so funny and explains there is no such thing as a bad word, only a bad intent, and that any word can be a weapon.

I love listening in on Frank and Gail talking about people's hang-ups with him and Lenny Bruce or explaining about true lewdness and what a deviant really is. I love learning about my father's strict no-drug-use policy and firing people who disobey. Frank demands perfectionism and has long, rigorous rehearsals, but he also insists on improvisation. I also love hearing people talk about Frank performing nightly for a year at the Garrick Theatre and how he would do a show just as professionally for no one as he would for a full house. There was also the time the audience became the show and Frank sat and watched them bang around onstage instead. We still have an artifact from that residency in the basement, a naked, pink blow-up sex doll that's taller than me with an O for a mouth and a hole between its legs that my father liked to play with onstage. I don't really like it because it gives me the wiggly feeling. I wish my dad would play with regular dolls with me.

Another great thing is when Gail makes spaghetti and chicken cacciatore and beef stroganoff for my dad and we put it on a tray with a glass jar of cayenne pepper and we put it on the dumbwaiter and lower it into the basement so he can eat without having to stop working. I do not like that food because it's too wet and chewy, but I adore helping Gail help Frank. If Dweezil and I get lucky, Gail *and* Frank might take us to my favorite restaurant, Sambo's, for waffles, or into Hollywood to CC Brown's for a hot fudge sundae.

I also adore watching Gail do side bends by the pool to get her figure back, and I love watching her in the bathroom when she drops a bit of water on a tin of thick, black, cakey mascara, then dips a tiny brush in the tarry pool and blinks it onto her eyelashes. Dweezil can walk now, but when he says "up," Gail lifts him onto her hip. I wish she'd still carry me on her hip, but that's my brother's spot now. Since Dweezil's arrival I am getting used to new rules. Outside our house everything is about what my dad needs, like before, but inside our house everything is about my dad *and* Dweezil. Gail and I come last.

When my father is away, which feels like most of the time, the patterns and rules change. Gail hugs Dweezil way more and pays even more attention to him. It takes forever to leave the house and we go to boring places like the swap meet, where it's hot and dusty and crowded, or Pic 'N' Sav, where it's cold and the lights are too bright. When Gail pampers Dweezil, our cross-eyed Siamese and our cream-colored German shepherd named Georgie provide some comfort to me. Or one of the members of the band the GTOs, which stands for "Girls Together Outrageously," will hang around and might give me some attention I am missing—Miss Pamela watches me swim in our giant, freezing-cold pool, and Miss Sparky lets me smell her Mary Quant pot gloss and try on her slip-on boudoir shoes with real feathers. Once I even got to see where they each live—near Busch Gardens, where they sometimes take me. Dweezil and my dad and the drop-ins get the lion's share of attention, so I am glad to hog a small amount wherever I can get it.

The good part when Frank is away is that Gail lets us sleep in the bed with her. I treasure these times because Gail reads so many books to us: *Where the Wild Things Are*, *In the Night Kitchen*, *Snow White*, *Fletcher and Zenobia*, all the Richard Scarry picture books, and all the Pooh and Piglet stories. I could do without *The Pink Fairy Book* and all the other yucky ones in that series. I memorize the poem "Jabberwocky" and beg Gail to read the Brer Rabbit stories from *Walt Disney's Uncle Remus Stories* over and over again, especially the part where the willful, impatient rabbit gets stuck in tar. Gail is so hilarious when she reads, *and* she does every voice perfectly. I absolutely adore funny voices!

I admit I get very mad when everyone says Dweezil is so pretty. *I* am the girl, so I am supposed to be pretty. Everyone from the GTOs who comes over or people that we meet on the street or in a store says he has "bedroom eyes." How come Dweezil has good eyes and good hair that everyone loves, and I don't? I guess I am mad a lot because Gail makes me sign a contract she draws up to insist I stop biting people in perpetuity. It is my first binding family document, but as life unfolds it won't be the last.

Each time my dad comes back from touring, I have to get used to him all over again. It takes a little bit of time. Like his band practicing his new songs, we all have to learn how to play our new parts and count in yet another different time signature.

By the time I am four, Dweezil and I have a secret language and we name the messiest side of our house, with its shade and the ivy that no one waters, the Wild Way. There we sneak and eat bark and march through fallen leaves. We sometimes go to day care in Hollywood, where we nap on cots and I throw sand at the bullies who pick on Dweezil for his name and shyness. At playtime we talk on a fake phone and add salt to a bucket with a handle we take turns churning to make cherry ice cream from scratch. One time they give us a salad at snack and my mind is blown when I try something called "French dressing."

At home, Gail teaches us songs until we know them by heart and sing along to them, like "Lollipop" and "Witch Doctor" and other silly songs her mom and dad taught her about frogs and Eskimos, King Kamehameha, and a guy named Susanna who climbs over a garden wall. Sometimes Gail drives us to take Suzuki-method play-by-ear piano lessons. I love when she explains about the difference between puns and limericks and Gail and Frank's made-up jokes, like "Eggyhoog," which is "the celebration of cosmic awareness of egg-sistence," and "Gream, the weekday between Thursday and Friday." But the Dweezil-doting by her and absolutely everyone is wearing thin. Just because I am getting big, how come I can't have baby food and bottles, too? But also, why can't I have my own high-heeled shoes, and a Gypsy outfit with veils and a real crystal ball?

When I take matters into my own hands and try to cut Dweezil's eyelashes off, Gail catches me halfway through and I get yelled at *and* spanked. I decide I do not like my family or the house where we are living. Too many people. Too much nudity. Too smelly. Too loud. Too many cigarettes. Too many lima beans. Not enough plum Gerber's. Not enough attention.

I love the song "Hooray for Hollywood," so I decide to pack the things that matter most to me—a large hat, two statement rings, a dress with flouncy sleeves, a beach ball, and our dog Georgie—and run away from home to start my own life in Hollywood.

No one looks our way as Georgie and I head down the crumbling brick stairs. I have heard about Schwab's drugstore and getting discovered at the counter. I might want to go there. I want to be an actress so I can dress up all the time. I want a pink house like the one belonging to somebody named Rudolph Valentino that we see when we drive on the winding road. I want my name in a star on the sparkly street by the Chinese Theatre.

Outside our falling-down brown fence covered with bougainvillea, I smell eucalyptus. I see hill after hill with palm trees and elms, sycamores and pines. I see the blue sky and birds high above. My white sandals make a slapping sound as I wend my way to where our driveway meets the road. A decision is made for me about which direction to travel as Georgie trots left. But my rainbow-sherbet-colored beach ball slips through my fingers and rolls right. I watch it stop between two houses across the street. I trot after my ball and feel my arm scrape on the stucco. "Ow!" I yelp. Tears fly. I can't figure out how to get my ball, carry my little suitcase, get my dog back, *and* start my new life. Four things at once is a lot for a four-year-old. A neighbor hears me crying, and I'm taken back to Gail and Frank, who hadn't even noticed I'd gone missing.

Oh well, I think, *I'll try again later.*

🌑

MANY YEARS FROM NOW, WHEN I am a parent of a child I'd never leave alone and naked in a room with strangers, I'll wonder, *Could* *my spacing out have been overwhelm or the parasympathetic nervous system "freeze" response to a chaotic full-throttle household?* I'll ask Gail why she didn't protect me. She'll eye-roll like a bored teenager, defensively shaming me for being so uptight, and inform me that Jerry, the man I insisted as a two-year-old should look at my "pee pee," has since become a prominent elected official and an activist for gay rights, further proving her skill in recognizing my inherited gifts.

Potāto, potāto.

CHAPTER 3

Is It Luck?

H old still," says Gail.

"Ow," I say, even though she already sprayed Johnson & Johnson detangler into my hair.

We are in the echoey bathroom with the infinity mirrors. I am sitting on the metal chair with the squishy yellow seat my daddy has to use in the shower so his leg cast doesn't get wet. Frank was pushed into an orchestra pit by a "fan" and now he has to wear a cast from his ankle to his hip for a whole year.

"That doesn't hurt," Gail says, tugging my long, knotted hair with her black bristly hairbrush.

I want to look presentable because Gail is taking me to meet my idol. I think maybe she is being extra nice to me because my daddy is home again or maybe because I had my tonsils and adenoids out and stayed at the hospital all by myself and woke up during the anesthesia and saw giant tarantulas coming to get me, or maybe the niceness is because the braless lady my daddy was sleeping with in the basement finally went back to New Zealand for good, or all three, so I hold still. But Gail is always rough with my hair, like she is with hers. I inherited her fine, thin, easily tangled hair. Dweezil got Frank's long, silky curls. "Mason Pearson hairbrushes are the best," Gail explains as the brush makes a scratchy ripping sound as she drags it through my matted strands. "Better to buy expensive things you love that last forever than cheap, ugly things."

"Okay," I say.

When she tries to pull the brush through my tangles, my head drags back, too. To take my mind off my hair, I study a hexagonal jar half-full of glistening black sand from the Big Island, which is a plane hop away from Oahu with the white-sand beaches where my grand-mother Tutu lives. The black sand sticks to you and kind of looks like instant coffee, but finer and with diamond sparkles in it. Gail took me and Dweezil in a camper van to see the active volcano, which was fun and scary. My uncle Squidget told me the Hawaiian legend about bad luck when you take black sand, or anything, from the is-land without asking the island. Gail took some scoops anyway. Now I wonder if my dad's bad-luck leg is from Gail or from himself, or a curse. Gail knows how to do curses, so maybe other people do, too?

I hate that my daddy is hurt, but I am glad Frank is home earlier than expected and can't do his regular work, which means maybe he will let me try his crutches or sit on his lap in his wheelchair or try to ride in it all by myself. Now that Frank is home, Gail is happier and tries to make him even happier by cooking Chateaubriand and baked potatoes with butter and sour cream and strawberry shortcake for dinner instead of what we've been having—cold Colonel Sanders drumsticks and wings, or oatmeal with runny eggs snuck in. I decide when Gail is done brushing my hair, I am going to draw a picture for my daddy to make him feel better, too.

"Tell me again about what happened to Frank," I say.

"He was pushed off the stage by a fan," sighs Gail.

"But why would that guy hurt him if he is a *fan*?" I would like to act and make people laugh and sing like my dad or Cher or Carol Burnett, but not if my fans hurt me.

"The man was adamant Frank was looking at his girlfriend funny and lost his mind," says Gail, pulling my hair harder. Gail says it like she believes maybe Frank was doing something that made the man mad. Gail says girls always throw their panties onstage at my dad. I wonder if maybe that man's girlfriend is one of the thousands who throw my daddy their panties? Gail also told me a popular musician named Lou Reed publicly said the fan should have killed my dad, which makes the story more confusing to me. How is it possible some people are not sad my father got hurt or wish him more hurt? All I know is that Gail at her maddest screams loud and for a long time, but she would never push my dad. I would never push him either.

Frank never yells. Frank always stays calm no matter how much Gail yells. Even when Gail screamed "tour expenses," "manager," "money," "groupies," and "the clap," my dad stayed calm. He stayed calm even when Gail threatened to leave and take us with her, and when she threatened to leave without me and Dweezil. Sometimes Gail gets so mad she just drives away on her own. The scariest thing I can think of is Gail driving away and never coming back.

I want to ask Gail if "lost his mind" means from anger, or from drugs, or born that way, but she seems to be getting angry and impatient just talking about it, which makes me think either Frank did something wrong, or I did by asking, so I zip it.

I am pretty sure now it's too late to change the bad luck from the sand. I think maybe Gail would have to take it all the way back to Kona and apologize and maybe sacrifice something? She won't, so maybe we're stuck with that luck. Even if she went, I don't think she would right the wrong, because I have never seen or heard Gail ever say sorry or give anything back or swap or share. She is proud of how she takes what she wants, because she is the oldest of seven and she always had to share and babysit and now it's her turn forever.

I wonder, *Do I have bad luck now? Does Dweezil? Are we safe or can bad luck grab you anywhere? How many times can it get you? Can it ever be stopped? Can we ask the island permission now, all the way from California? Can I be the one to ask and say sorry if Gail won't?*

"Ow!" I say again when she starts in on the biggest knot.

"Look at this rat's nest!" Next thing I know Gail says, "This knot is too big. I have to cut it." But before I can scream no she has scissors in her hand and I hear the sound of snipping. I run my fingers into my hair to feel for the missing spot. "Watch your fingers!" Gail snaps, and my mouth quivers. I feel like I might burn up like Gail's friend Anja who starts fires with her mind.

"Stop crying," she says, "you can't even see it."

WE ARE IN THE CAR a long time, at least as long as one television show, but I am very excited because we are going to the house of the real Snow White! I love *Snow White*. My dad brought the movie home in a metal canister for us to watch in the basement. Gail read me all the books and I know the songs "I'm Wishing" and "Someday My Prince Will Come" by heart.

When Gail pulls up in front of a small house with a regular pointed roof instead of a castle, I am confused. Why would Snow White be here? She married a prince. This house is smaller than our house. Gail opens a little gate. I stay close to her. Gail takes my hand, and we cross a miniature bridge. "Oh, look," says Gail, "she has a wishing well!"

We knock on her front door. "Why hello," says a brown-haired lady, squatting to my height. "Who have we here? You must be Moon!" The voice of Snow White is coming out of the body of this small woman. I am baffled.

I look at Gail. "But where is Snow White? You said I would meet the real Snow White."

"This *is* the real Snow White," says Gail. I don't understand. Snow White is a beautiful girl with black hair, a red bow, and skin the color of snow. This lady is just a person.

"Hello, dear, I *am* Snow White," says the woman. I squint and scrunch up my face. She sounds just like Snow White but looks like a lady you'd see in a grocery store.

"She loves the wishing song," Gail says, and the lady begins to sing.

"Ha-ha-ha-ha-ha," she trills. "I'm wishing . . ."

I hide my face between Gail's legs to drown out the sound. I touch my mother's leg stubble. Even through the fabric the hair on her leg is short and sharp. Gail pulls me out from under her and nudges me forward. I back up again, pressing my nose into Gail's dress to breathe in the smell of her Calèche perfume. I look down at my mother's pretty feet in her platform Kork-Ease.

"That's all right," says the lady in a regular voice. "I'm very pleased to meet you. My real name is Adriana Caselotti. I am the *voice* of Snow White."

I am frozen on the spot. Inside, my brain is breaking. Wait . . . cartoons aren't real? Regular people make their voices? How many other cartoons aren't real? *All* of them? If cartoons aren't real, how many other things aren't real? What else do grown-ups pretend? Is anything real? I don't know it yet but I have just begun my initiation into sound, its influence and reverberations, and the power of the human voice.

"Would you like to throw a penny in my wishing well?" asks Adriana Caselotti in Snow White's voice again.

I don't want to. I want to run away and cry. I feel choked, but by what? The bad luck? I desperately want my favorite things to stay my favorite things without getting ruined or cursed, so I accept the penny, close my eyes, and compose my wish: *Dear Big Island, please, please do not be mad at me and my family anymore.*

—

CHAPTER 4

Secret Powers

S he has a real crystal ball," says Gail, standing in our purple
kitchen, trying to tempt me. She hands me half of a liver-
wurst sandwich with romaine lettuce, mayonnaise, and butter on Roman Meal bread, my favorite, and a cup of Typhoo tea with
milk and sugar. "You can have a reading, too."

"Ooh!" I say. "I'm going to wear my ballerina dress." It's black
with a velvet flower at the hip. I hop off the kitchen counter to get
changed and find my shoes, tea in one hand, sandwich in the other.

"Careful!" Gail says as the lettuce falls onto the floor next to
Dweezil and his Aquaman doll. I freeze.

Gail's face gets tight, her anger rising. We all watch Gorgo, our
Siamese cat with the kinked tail, saunter over to give the wilted leaf a
sniff and lick. A clicking sound pulls Gail's attention. "What's in your
mouth?" she asks Dweezil. He spits a razor blade into my mother's
hand. Her eyes go wide. My dad uses these to splice tape in his studio downstairs. Gail's fury unfurls. "*Never* put these in your mouth
again. Do you hear me? *DO YOU HEAR ME?*"

Gail turns to me. "You are supposed to watch him!" I see the
veins in her neck and temples bulge and swell. "I can't always be
there every little second!" she shrieks. I am five.

I suddenly feel I am hovering a few inches above my body. I don't
want Gail to be mean to Dweezil, so I accept her admonishments as

a booming reminder of my big-sister role and tether myself to the scene, and to my little brother, to protect him. I watch the shapes Gail's mouth makes, watch her lips curl, fold, widen, sputter in slow motion, and I make a physical barrier between her and my three-year-old brother and absorb her anger and loudness, even though my dad told me that people's eardrums can explode if they stand too close to a speaker at his concerts. I briefly pretend I am watching a TV show and mentally try to turn the volume down. I get the gist of Gail's words. Dweezil does, too, but he is unfazed by Gail's wall of rage because it is aimed at me, the shield and scapegoat. Spent, her fury passes. He looks up at her with his yellow curls framing his heart-shaped face, green eyes shining.

"Ice cream," he says in a calm voice.

Gail melts; immediately brushes past me and scoops him up, lifting him to her bosom; and begins hugging and kissing him. "Yes, yes," she says. "Yes, of course we can get ice cream. We'll go to CC Brown's for hot fudge sundaes." Her golden child is a small, warming sun in her arms. Relieved to have helped, I run to get my ballerina dress and sandals, excited for my "reading."

GAIL PARKS OUR ROLLS IN a lot behind a red brick building. My bare legs make a sucking sound as I unstick them from the leather of the back seat to look around. I like seeing the Hollywood sign in the distance, but now I hate Hollywood. It feels dirty. I don't know why a psychic would want to work here. Or anyone, for that matter. "Are we there?" I ask, crinkling my nose.

"Yes," says Gail.

"But this looks like a doctor's office. Are we getting shots?"

Dweezil's face contorts. He doesn't want a shot either.

"No, no shots," Gail says as she opens her car door, grabs her purse, and shimmies around to Dweezil's side of the back seat.

Gail holds Dweezil's hand as we walk past pawnshops and stores for tourists selling T-shirts and mugs and snow globes and miniature Academy Award statues and magnets in the shape of palm trees. Even though it's fun to pronounce the names of the stars on Hollywood Boulevard, there are lots of scary-looking people walking around the neighborhood that make it not fun. They look like the people at my dad's shows, which I know means they are on drugs, but dirtier, which means they probably have nowhere to live.

I wonder why my mom wants to see a psychic anyway. Maybe it's because of the groupies. Especially the one from New Zealand we just had living in our basement. I for one am so glad "the Auckland slut" is gone and my dad is back upstairs with us and sleeping in the right bed with Gail again.

"OH! YES," SAYS CAROL AS soon as she sees us. "Your kids are *definitely* Star Children," she coos. "They are very special, with a greater purpose." Carol is a short, smiley, round-faced woman with brown curly hair and a long peasant dress. She kneels to my height. "Moon, how old are you?"

"Five," I say.

"Yes," says Carol, "you're an Indigo all right."

Gail beams. "I knew it." Gail and Carol smile at each other. I get the sense this is good news but have no idea what they are talking about. I stare at them and brush my tangled hair out of my face.

"Come in," says Carol warmly, motioning to all of us.

Gail corrects her. "The kidlets can wait in the hall," she says, and pulls paper, crayons, and Pentels out of her purse for Dweezil and me. My curiosity is piqued. *What can't Gail say in front of us*, I wonder.

"Maybe you two can draw me something," offers Carol.

"I will!" I say.

"The great thing about Star Children," says Carol, guiding Gail into her office, "is they are always protected by grace because of their larger destinies." I try to get a good look inside the dark room, but she closes the door fast, and suddenly Dweezil and I are waiting in a hallway all by ourselves. I press my ear to the door, but now I can only hear our mother and Carol speaking in whispery voices.

Soon enough, though, we're bored, so Dweezil and I smooth the hallway carpet one way, then dig our fingernails into the synthetic wool to make shapes, then smooth the wool the other way so the images vanish. Then we take our shoes off and try to pick up the Crayolas and markers with our feet. Then we race and slide and get rug burns. A man with hair like a friar comes out of another office and shushes us, so instead of racing we try to walk with all our toes curled under or on the outsides of our feet. That's what I'm doing when Gail finally comes out. Our mother looks ashen, moves slowly, stares at the ground. I can tell she wants to leave and not keep her promises about ice cream and me getting a reading, too.

"You can have a reading the next time," says Gail, bending down to tie Dweezil's shoelaces.

"That's not fair!" I yelp when her words confirm my suspicions.

Gail is suddenly on one knee grabbing me by both shoulders and shaking me. "Earth to Moon, life's not fair." When Carol appears in the doorway, Gail stops.

"How about a short one?" says Carol.

"I have to pee," says Dweezil.

Gail sighs.

INSIDE CAROL'S PSYCHIC ROOM IS a squishy couch with patchwork fabric and sparkly artwork on black velvet—posters of silhouettes of bodies surrounded by white light with rainbows shining out of their middles. In the corner there are two live plants and, on a small table . . . a real crystal ball!

I rush over to look at it. I can't see smoke or any images, just lines and cracks and bubbles. It looks broken inside, but when I turn my head, I can see opalescent rainbows.

"Make yourself comfortable," Carol says to me. I plop on the couch. My feet don't touch the floor. The carpet is greenish brown. Carol closes her eyes. "You can close your eyes, too."

"Okay," I say, and I do. It looks like orange sherbet in my head. I feel woozy and warm, then a weightless feeling, like outer space. I open my eyes. I don't think I like this. I think I want to leave, but Carol is smiling with her eyes closed.

"Wow," says Carol. "I have only ever seen an aura like yours once before."

It's weird to watch someone talk with their eyes closed. I cover my mouth, so she doesn't hear me giggle.

"They are asking me if you know you are naturally in contact with all life-forms at all times. From your Earth home to deep space to your star home." My eyebrows knit together. I am wondering if "they" means ghosts or angels or aliens or invisible friends and if "they" are friendly. "They are asking me to remind you that you always have access to the akashic records and can be star seeded any time you need. They want you to know it's like an all-access backstage pass at your dad's concerts, except this gives you access to everything, everywhere, that ever existed or will ever exist at any time. Do you understand?"

The akashic records? "That sounds like a forever library."

She opens her eyes and stares at me with a frozen smile. "Yes," she says, nodding slowly, "it is exactly that, a library that never closes." I smile back, hoping I said the right thing. Carol nods. "It means you can always ask for help and help will always come."

"I have a library card for the real library," I say. "Is yours invisible or real?"

"It's both," she says. "But you already know that." Carol winks at me, then closes her eyes again.

I close my eyes again, too. Now I feel like little sparkles of light are everywhere inside of me and outside, too. Am I making this up? I remember Gail said I am an "empath." I wonder if I am in Carol's body or mine. Are these her mind pictures or mine?

"Are you aware of any recent messages and who brings them?"

"Well . . . ," I say, trying to read what she wants of me, "my dog Georgie died, and she came to me in a dream with my grandfather I never met and some other people were there and they all said they'd be waiting for me when I die. Do you mean like that?"

"Yes, good, they are guides you can summon. Anything else?"

What does she mean? "Well . . . we have ghosts in our house. Once Gail told me she was minding her own business in the bathroom brushing knots out of her hair and suddenly she had ectoplasm all over her head. Gail said that's what happens when ghosts cross from their side to ours."

"Yes, that can happen when spirits pass through the veil that separates the living from the dead."

"I wouldn't like that to happen to my hair. Oh! Once someone saw a ghost in a pinstripe suit in the garden and chatted with him as he passed her on the steps."

"Go on," says Carol.

"And we also have a ghost animal in the living room who bit my aunt Mariel on the ankle. Gail said she saw two little puncture wounds in her ankle, and it was not Gorgo because our cat was asleep in the sun when it happened, and the marks weren't the shape of Gorgo's teeth. And another time something slapped me in my sleep, and it left a red mark on my cheek. Gail said that was also a ghost."

Carol coughs, then takes a small sip of water. "Have your guides mentioned anything about your purpose here or shown you any of your talents?"

"Uh . . . no . . . I don't think so, but I can do almost all of the things in the Swami Satchidananda yoga book at our house except pull a rope through my nose and swallow it, and whenever I get stomachaches Gail tells me I am picking up on someone else's stomachache. I asked her who they belong to if they aren't mine and how come they feel real to me and if they aren't mine how come I have to feel them . . ."

"Did your guides ever mention the word 'bodhisattva'?"

"No . . . ," I say, "I don't think so." I feel a sinking feeling, like I am guessing all wrong.

"They have very special talents, almost like secret powers, and they come here to save the world by unselfishly staying behind to end the suffering of others instead of advancing themselves. Bodhisattvas have huge hearts."

"Oh!" I say. "Well, I've always wanted to change my name to Beauty Heart!"

"Really? Where did you hear that name?"

"Nowhere," I say, puzzled by her question. "I made it up."

Carol opens her eyes and stares through me now. "Can you do what I'm doing? Can you read people and see things?"

I don't think I like this.

I can't lie, so I say, "I'm not sure, but maybe I will be a writer because I love to read, and I have a very good imagination. Or an actress like Cher because I look like her and I love her show and I also have an innie belly button."

Carol smiles, so I smile back.

ON THE DRIVE HOME, SAFE in our familiar car, I think about what Carol said: I have powers. What she said *must* be true because she is someone who doesn't know me at all who is saying the same kinds of things Gail already tells me about myself in private. Now that I *know* it is *extra* true, maybe I can help Gail more. I can help her not be sad. If she's not sad, then she won't be mad, and if she's not mad, maybe we can have a happier house.

I wonder if my daddy knows I have powers like Tabitha on *Bewitched*. "I'm gonna tell Daddy what that lady said and make a special outfit!" I say proudly.

Gail's eyes go big in the rearview mirror. "You will do no such thing!" says Gail, hot and fast. I don't understand why she doesn't want Frank to know, but I do understand that's the voice Gail uses when I am not allowed to question her or talk back. She sounds like my grandmother Tutu when they fight. I sigh a big exhale through my nose.

I sing the snake charmer song to Dweezil. I keep my voice low and say to Dweezil, "I'm gonna charm cobras and sleep on a bed of nails."

"What did you say?" says Gail sharply.

"Nothing," I say to her. "I'm singing." Dweezil's eyes flicker with recognition, then disinterest. He studies the webbing of his fingers. I sing and sway in my seat anyway as we wind our way up through the twisty canyon, past the houses on stilts and the road too skinny for two cars.

Unselfishly staying behind to end the suffering of others. It sounds like a big responsibility. I swell with self-importance. I have *powers*. "Bodhisattva," I whisper to myself, "bodhisattva."

LOOKING BACK, I WONDER WHAT Frank thought about everything I was being spoon-fed. Did he even know? Now, as a grown woman and parent myself, I think my wildly imaginative, lonely mother must have shared all of this stuff with me when Frank was away, when I was a captive audience and she had no one else to talk to. Whether my father knew or not, I was on my way to becoming an odd, compliant, anxious, and hypervigilant child who'd glimpsed the future.

CHAPTER 5

A Rehearsal

Frank stands at the stove stirring his cream of rice while Gail paces and talks on the phone, listening with mounting agitation. "Go fuck yourself and the horse you rode in on," says Gail, slamming the phone down in a crescendo. Dweezil and I look up from our cinnamon toast. "That's *it*," announces Gail, stomping around the kitchen. Frank turns off the fire and grabs a spoon to eat from the pan. In go cream, butter, and brown sugar.

My heart is in my throat. "What's the matter?" I ask.

"Bokiki," says Dweezil, my insider baby word for "telephone." I smile.

"Calm down," says Frank, slurping his runny breakfast.

"They said your son is 'retarded.'"

"What's 'retarded'?"

"They're retarded for thinking he's retarded," thunders Gail. "Dweezil is a genius." Gail glares at Frank. "Aren't you going to say something?"

"What's their proof?"

"They said he never says anything. Which is bullshit because he talks to Moon all the time."

Dweezil crosses his eyes and does his impression of a mosquito. I laugh.

"He can talk, Frank, he's probably bored," says Gail.

Frank shrugs. "So don't send him back." He reaches for his Winstons.

My heart is wild horse hooves. Sure, I hate the school, with its dirty slide and sandy yard and mean bullies who pick on Dweezil. Sure, I bite or throw rocks at them to protect my brother and shut them up. Sure, I prefer the books Gail reads at home over the terrible baby books and the nap mats and rough blankets on the floor. I definitely hate when they bring the TV in and offer us *Mister Rogers' Neighborhood* or *Sesame Street* or *Davey and Goliath*. But I don't want to go without Dweezil.

"They can't get away with that," fumes Gail. "And I can't pull him out without pulling Moon out, too." He's chewing smoke now as she drones on at him, hammering other grievances. "What about me? What about *me*, Frank? I do everything around here."

Frank snorts a long sigh out of his nose, then calmly stands with a rigid body to silently say this conversation is done. Before he can descend into the studio, Gail has her car keys in her hand and she's racing out the front door with no shoes on. "Gail," Frank calls with a firm voice.

"You deal with this shit," she shouts from halfway down the stairs.

"Gail-Gail!" Dweezil cries out.

"Gail!" I call out, rushing to the door and the sound of speeding tires.

I am scared and crying. Arrangements are made for someone to watch us so Frank can work.

When Gail finally returns, it's almost time to pick my dad up from rehearsal. I am flooded with relief that she came back and isn't gone forever. Gail is quiet and just gets Dweezil and me dressed like she always does, like the bad day was just a bad dream. But I know it was real because my face is still salty. Gail washes my face with a warm washcloth and the scary day turns invisible but not gone.

THE STARRY NIGHT AIR OF California is brisk. "It's a city but it's also a desert," explains Gail as we turn onto Yucca. She tells us about Native American plants like the century plant, which blooms every hundred years, and about aloe and how you can use the inside for a burn, or you can use sugar crystals or honey but never butter. Then Gail is driving slow and parking, and before long Dweezil and I are each holding one of her firm hands as we approach the rented soundstage. Three steps for us for every one of her platform strides. I can hear my dad's distinctive music coming from inside the building. Even when it's muffled, I can pick out the separate, sharp, bumpy, colliding sounds of horns and vocals, marimbas, vibes, drums, bass, guitar, all racing and weaving and rising. I feel happy I am getting to see my dad at work. I look up at Gail. She is staring straight ahead in her big nighttime glasses and walking fast, like we are late. Gail lets go of my hand and pulls the heavy door open. I get a blast of her clean smells—her lemon cream shampoo from London and her yummy French "green" perfume.

Inside the rehearsal hall, the music is an erupting volcano with notes exploding to the rafters. The big room has soft walls and bunchy padding sticking out. The place smells like cigarettes, sweat, and damp. There are people and wires and amps and lights and instruments everywhere, faces I recognize and those I don't. Some of them smile when they see us. Frank doesn't even look over.

I watch my skinny father in his stripes and tall shoes. He smokes, brushes his silky black curls out of his face, and conducts at the same time. He punctuates the air with his pointy cream-colored baton, silently explaining the tempo to watching eyes. His small movements become big sounds. Then he rests one hip on a stool and moves his fingers up and down the neck of the yellowish-brown guitar he wears on a strap across his body. I look at Gail's approving face warmed by the colored lights, watch her sway and move rhythmically in time. Though no one explains anything to me, I understand they are running through a series of songs that will be performed as a show, and that we are standing in a darkened part of the room that is where the audience will be when they take it on the road to the concert venues. All the songs are familiar, but I don't know any of the names since I usually only hear them in pieces from the intercom in our house or when I bring Frank coffee or cayenne pepper for his food.

"Moon, Dweezil, come here," says my dad into the microphone when he finally sees us, "come say something into the mic." Before Gail can say anything, I run straight for him. The band peer at me from over their instruments and give smiles and waves. My dad holds three fingers under my chin and vibrates it as he holds the mic to my mouth. He doesn't have to tell me to sing a note. This is our at-home bit—I sing and he wiggles my chin faster than he can strum. To my surprise, the amplification of my nonsensical sounds in a large space makes me feel expansive and jolted by live-wire electricity. But I also feel exposed. The band laughs. Frank makes his "plooking" sounds into the mic with exaggerated facial and body language. We all laugh, including me, even though I don't like his sound-effects version of fucking. He hands the mic back to me to copy him. I scrunch up my nose and press my head into his side out of shyness. Gail and Dweezil inch closer. "Go on," he says, "say something, then it's Dweezil's turn." I can't think of anything to say or sing under the pressure, so I go for some copycat facial clowning and make some warbles and oinks and hums. Frank smiles at me and pats my head like he's cracking an egg. I let the invisible yolk cover me like a love barrier shielding me from the dead air of missing laughter for my awkward, exploratory efforts. Then Dweezil's hands are on the microphone and he gets his turn having a sonic chin wobble into the dark, wide-open space where the future awaits and the imaginary audiences will be.

CHAPTER 6

—

Nothing Is Fair

Why does Dweezil get to have his birthday first?" I say, crossing my arms. Frank is away. Again. It's August and it is too hot and I am mad because Dweezil always goes first. Unless Frank is home, and then *he* does. It doesn't help that I do not yet understand the concept of the calendar. Gail, barefoot and knee-high in laundry, ignores me as she folds, sweat sticking to her. Her and Frank's towels and sheets go on the forest-green carpeted steps, and Dweezil's and my stuff goes on top of our shared bunk. "It isn't fair!" I persist. "He is younger than me!"

I look over at Dweezil peacefully sitting on the floor playing with his Justice League dolls, then back at Gail folding Dweezil's dungarees with care.

I stomp my feet. "He gets everything!"

She accidentally kicks over a pile of just-folded clean clothes. "Moon! Stop it!" Gail screams. "Dweezil's birthday is at the beginning of September. Yours is at the end. *That's* why his birthday is first."

"But I was born first," I shout back. Then I lie down on the floor and slam my fists on the ground and kick my legs.

"Do you want a cold shower?"

I keep kicking. Then Gail's feet are coming toward me, slap, slap, slap, and her arms are under mine. She lifts me; I sail up. Gail is stronger than the wind at the Nuuanu Pali on Oahu, where my grandmother lives. Gail grips me tight. "No!" I scream at the top of my voice. Flailing, I accidentally hit her in her big tits.

"Ow!"

Then we are in the echoey bathroom. Gail drags me into the shower fully clothed, puts the water on cold, and holds me under. I scream. Water gets in my mouth and eyes. The cold and wetness are in my hair. I cough. She won't stop. "No!" I fight. My dress is sticking to me and water is running down my legs. Gail will hold me under the water until I can be calm. Gail can wait a long time. When I am silent she turns the water off. My teeth are chattering. Gail helps me take off my wet clothes, then she dries me off like she loves me again.

"Go get changed," she says.

I run to my room.

"Slow down!" she shouts. "You'll slip and crack your head!"

I put on a T-shirt that has my name on it. It says "Moon Unit, Twentieth Century Fox." It is my favorite shirt. I want to be an actress and work for that company someday. The shirt is warm and smells like detergent. When I am all dressed, I watch Gail pile my wet clothes into the dryer. Her face still has some mad in it.

Dweezil is chewing on the nipple of his Evenflo filled with cold milk tea. He takes a long sip, then sets his bottle down next to Aquaman. He adjusts the scuba gear Gail made earlier for his Batman and

Robin dolls out of cardboard tampon applicators wrapped with tin-foil.

I decide to play with my Raggedy Ann doll and dance in the mirror. But when I look in the mirror, I notice my name on my shirt now says "nooM." My heart starts beating fast. I feel lightheaded. I pull the shirt off to look. When it's lying flat on the wood floor it says "Moon" just fine. But when I put it back on and look in the mirror again, it says "nooM" again. Maybe something is wrong with my eyes. Maybe something is wrong with the mirror. Or the world. I feel my chest get tight.

"Gail," I call out. "Something's wrong!" I am still mad at her, but I am also scared and I need her help.

She rushes out of the laundry room. "What? WHAT?"

"My name is backward!"

She looks at me and my shirt. Then she laughs. "There is nothing wrong with the shirt," she sighs, "the mirror flips the image." I still don't get it. I am certain she doesn't either. I take my shirt off again and show her the problem.

"On the floor it's right," I say, "but now look . . ." I pull the shirt back over my head and show her my reflection.

"Yes, Moon, I just told you, everything is reversed in the mirror."

I look at myself in the mirror and at Gail, too. "But . . . ," I stammer, "you look the same." She is laughing harder now. "What?" I scream in protest. "I don't understand!" Now I'm not just scared and mad, I'm seething with fury at Gail. "It's not fair!" I bellow.

"Okay," she repeats, "it's not fair." She has a funny look on her face, like she's giving up on me and keeping a secret all to herself. She starts walking away.

I take my shirt off and throw it on the floor. "I'm never wearing that shirt again!" I open my dresser drawer and pull out my rust-colored ice-skating dress.

Gail spins and rushes at me. She gets her face next to my face. "Earth to Moon!" she shouts. "You think the world revolves around you, but it doesn't!" She picks up my shirt and drops it in the garbage can by the door, then storms out. Dweezil looks up but says nothing.

I shimmy into my dress and flop onto my bunk bed. My throat feels choked and my body feels fiery hot. I wipe my nose with my arm. I stare at my Raggedy Ann and Raggedy Andy dolls. I am soothed by their blank, forever-happy stares. I like that they are united even though I don't know if they are brother and sister or married. I sit up and walk to the mirror. They look exactly the same. Then I get my T-shirt out of the garbage. I keep it wadded up so I can't see my name reversed. Then I climb onto my top bunk and hide it in my pillowcase.

I am trying to get used to what makes Gail maddest, but I can't always guess. I want her to be nicer, like she is when Frank is home.

Soon enough Dweezil and I are in another fight. He pulls my hair and I pinch him hard and he cries very loud. Gail yells, "Stop it!" from the other room, but we don't stop. I hear fast running. Gail is suddenly standing above us with handcuffs in her hand. She forces a metal loop on one of his ankles and the other metal ring on mine and clicks them closed so we can't get away. We both scream at her instead of each other as she drags us across the floor into the bathroom. Our shouting bounces off the cold tile. Sweat flies from her face. "Gail-Gail," Dweezil cries.

"I want my daddy!" I scream.

Then she stands up and slams the bathroom door.

"No!" we scream in unison. She comes back with a tape recorder. She sets the small black machine on the floor and presses record. "No!" we scream louder. Her eyes are wild and blank. "I hate you!" I shriek. My face is red and hot. Dweezil's hiccupping with tears.

"See how you like it!" Gail blazes on like a fire.

She presses rewind. The garbled sound of our voices is loud. Gail presses play. We hear our screams back. We stop crying. We are still. Frozen. Dweezil is shaking. The corners of my mouth turn down. I don't look at Gail. I silently make a promise to myself: *I will never be like her.* Then I stare at her straight in the eyes.

"When Daddy gets home, I'm going to tell on you."

WHEN MY BIRTHDAY FINALLY COMES, Gail goes all out even though it's just me and her and Dweezil. Gail hangs colorful paper lanterns and decorates jewel-toned plastic cups of fruit punch with tiny umbrellas. We have my favorite dinner—greasy egg rolls, chow mein, fried rice, and fortune cookies. Gail gives me a turquoise kimono with frog buttons and a new journal. Best of all, she makes my cake from scratch, a white one that she covers with cream cheese frosting the color of the ocean in Hawaii. Then Gail gives me a birthday card. It has a drawing by one of our favorite illustrators, Sandra Boynton, of a mischievous-looking monster. On the outside the monster on the card says: "You can have any wish you want granted on one condition . . ." I flip to the inside: ". . . you must never open this card."

I blush with embarrassment at having been tricked. I feel stung. I look up at Gail. Her face is frozen with hyena-like glee. I stare back with puzzlement. I hate this card, but something inside of me tells me to save it anyway. I tuck it in my new journal as a reminder to myself.

But of what?

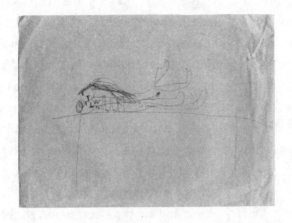

CHAPTER 7

Aliens

On the TV in our living room, Bugs Bunny is fighting with a little Martian about uranium PU-36. Dweezil and I are sitting cross-legged on the floor. I am wearing a short yellow top with embroidered flowers and my ruffly underwear and no shoes or socks. Dweezil is wearing a striped shirt and cords and no shoes. We are having as much TV and chocolate milk and fruit punch and snacks as we want because Miss Sparky, Miss Pamela, Miss Lucy, Janet, and Jackie are over. They all smoke and twirl and flutter around and say "Hi, doll" to me when they get here. I can see them in the kitchen and half listen, which means Gail can do the same with us.

Even though they are all around Gail's age, none of these women seem as grown-up as her. All of these women wear short skirts and silk slips and feathers and beads and bloomers and see-through tops and different patterns of eye makeup and fragrant pot gloss that stains their lips the color of boysenberries. Not Gail. She wears dungarees or long dresses and no makeup. Some of them are in the GTOs. Not Jackie. Gail said she is Frank's manager's girlfriend and "straight," which means boring and not a performer. One time there was a blackout, and Gail and Miss Sparky got flashlights and candles and we had a surprise go-go party on the kitchen counter, and another time Jackie gave me a bunch of her old slips so I could dress up. Sometimes they come over when they are hungry or to talk about who they "sail for" or who their "fave-raves" are. Miss Pamela and Miss Sparky smile the most and are the nicest to me, so they are my fave-raves. I have wiggly teeth. I am almost six.

Miss Cinderella and Miss Christine used to be my fave-raves, but Gail said they went away, meaning forever, but I don't know why. Sometimes the others chortle with laughter and sometimes they sing lines from songs they know in unison or copy words Gail uses, like "hideous." Gail says the draft and murder and hurting animals are "hideous." Miss Sparky says BO and having pimples all over your face and back are "hideous." Gail looks friendly on the outside, but I can see her concentration and stiffness underneath when these women come over. Gail hides the butter now because once one of them ate a whole stick of it straight from the refrigerator.

Today Gail is seated like a queen and giving them all advice and reading to them from a blue book with an eye and a black ring on the cover. The book says I am a Nine of Hearts and that I have a bad future ahead, so I hate that book, which is confusing since the psychic said I have powers and that should mean a good future. Gail is a good card, the King of Spades, so she loves the book.

"Your tongue is pink," I say to Dweezil, then take another gulp of my fruit punch.

"You have a mustache," Dweezil says.

I wipe my mouth on my arm. Sticky pink comes off.

I watch Gail serve everyone Typhoo tea with milk and sugar. We get all the drinks delivered from the Alta Dena milkman. The plain milk comes in glass bottles that Gail showed me how to open by sticking my elbow in the foil top so it's easier to pull off. Chocolate milk and fruit punch come in plastic jugs that I still need her help to open. For our snack we get baked beans and hot dogs on our melamine Make-A-Plates.

When the GTOs come over, the house smells like cigarettes and perfume and old fabric and burnt coffee. "A nose circus" is what my daddy calls rooms with too many smells. I want to go to a real circus. Gail promised to take us to Barnum & Bailey's, and I can't wait. I want to see acrobats and sideshow freaks. I also want to go because Gail usually only takes us to a stinky carpet store or to get groceries or to pick my dad up from rehearsal in the middle of the night because he doesn't drive.

I look over at Gail telling them all their futures, then dab some of my punch on my lips. "Look," I say to Dweezil, "I made lip gloss." He glances at me.

The Martian's voice in the cartoon is really funny. I can copy it perfectly. Ever since I met Snow White I pay extra attention to the voices. Everyone says I am a perfect mimic and have an ear for accents. I can do Popeye's laugh, Olive Oyl when she calls for help, Snagglepuss when he says "Heavens to Murgatroyd," Foghorn Leghorn when he says "Boy I say boy you're about as smart as the little end of nothing sharpened," and Cher.

When the GTOs and other ladies visit Gail, what they really want to know is whether they will marry a rock star, too. They are listening to Gail because she is married and they aren't. But I can tell they are also jealous of Gail, especially Janet and Miss Lucy and Miss Mercy, because they get very wiggly around my dad, and they are frequently taking their clothes off and laughing when he pinches their nipples to say hi. I don't think my dad is very nice to Gail when he does that, and I don't think the ladies are very nice to Gail when they let my dad do that, but Gail keeps her face plain. She chain-smokes Marlboros and pretends everything is fine.

I don't want any boobs when I grow up. I certainly don't want my dad or anyone to see my boobs or think about my boobs. My dad says, "More than a mouthful is a waste." He also says, "No one wants to ride an ironing board." If I do have to have boobs, I want mine to be like Miss Pamela's. Everyone says she has the best ones because they are "egg boobs." That means the nipples are in the right place on top of the boobs with no lumps on the areolas, like in the *Playboy* and *Oui* magazines we have lying around.

I am half practicing the Martian's voice and half spying on everyone talking about the Sunset Strip, who gets the credit for giving Alice Cooper his look, who they are sailing for in the Yardbirds now, and what clothes they all like.

Gail is great at sewing. Her sewing room is on the other side of the TV room. It's a very messy, special, tiny room that only she's allowed to go into, stacked with fabric in case she wants to make something for herself or for my dad.

My favorite things in Gail's sewing room are the old, round metal tins that used to have butter cookies from Europe in them. Now they are filled with zippers and buttons, bobbins and seam rippers, real silver thimbles and feathers, sequins, ribbons, rhinestones, and lace. Sometimes Gail makes things for us, like when she made Dweezil a Thor costume for Halloween, and Shazam another year. I've been a dinosaur, the bride of Frankenstein, a genie, and Morticia Addams with black tentacles at the bottom of my dress, stuffed with pillow foam to keep their shape.

Tutu taught Gail to sew. Everyone in Hawaii has a tutu. It means "grandmother." Her real name is Laura Nettie Freitas Sloatman and she insisted on matching and looking fancy so no one could tell they were poor. My daddy is the oldest of four and he was poor and forced to wear matching things, too. I saw a photo with him and his family in matching hats. Gail and Frank hate matching. Now they both wear anything they want, even if that means wearing nothing. I wish I could wear a matching outfit with someone, and I also wish Gail would teach me to sew.

Gail also knows about other things, like regular and Chinese astrology, the I Ching, runes, acupuncture, mythology, Atlantis, the aurora borealis, Mensa, Freemasons, the Tower of London, the Dark Ages, the Vatican, healing with your hands, healing with your mind, exorcisms, ley lines, the evil eye, Chaucer, answer and callback doo-wop, dreamtime, Uluru, aqueducts, Bath, and Stonehenge. These are just some of the things she tells me and Dweezil and the GTOs about. The GTOs always nod their heads and agree with everything Gail says, but Gail only agrees with what Frank says or yells at him about the stuff that makes her mad.

The GTOs never see any of that. No one does. Just me and Dweezil and Gail and Frank, but Dweezil is still too small to say anything much. Gail told me we must always be "discreet," which means keep secrets. "The only people you can trust are us," she says, meaning her and Frank and Dweezil. "We are like foxes in a den." I just adore picturing us curled up and squished together in a burrow underground like the photo of me, Dweezil, Gail, and Frank in the basement. When the phone rings, I watch Gail write a phone number on the wall in permanent ink next to the door where she measures our changing heights. I hate when she puts other people on the height wall who are not our family. I don't want them to butt in on us.

I am not scared of Gail's sewing room during the day, but I am scared of the room downstairs next to my dad's studio during the day and the night. There are little stairs that lead into a tiny, dark room where we store my dad's suitcases. I am convinced something bad lives in there, like a ghost or a monster or an alien. Because of Gail's father I never met and how Gail said he died, I *know* aliens are real.

I never sleep with my arms or my feet out of my blankets if I can help it, because I am scared. Luckily, I have my two invisible camels, Sinini and T'mershi Duween, who can warn me about danger. When I told my dad about them, he wrote a song about T'mershi. It makes me feel good that he likes something from my head, though I am a tiny bit mad that he took something that belonged to me. The song is long, with no words, and sounds like a fast, bumpy, tilty camel ride. I would love to ride a two-hump camel, maybe even get one. Or a koala, the very cutest bear. They are from Australia and fall out of trees when they eat eucalyptus, which we have in the yard, so mine would have plenty to eat.

I want to go to Australia and New Zealand and all the other places Frank has been, but I'm still mad about all the ladies who have tried to steal my father and break up our family. I can't believe women do that, try to take other people's dads and husbands. Gail would never do that and neither would I.

I am not so sure about the GTOs, so I keep a close watch.

It seems like the whole world wants my daddy. We all want his attention and we don't want to wait until there is an emergency. If there was an emergency, I don't think he could really do anything. Unless it was about a guitar. And he's always traveling to Europe. But if there's a bad fight between Dweezil and me, or Gail and me, he can immediately make it stop with his silent anger. Stopping is the only solution because you can't take up too much of his time.

I wish Frank's silent anger could make Gail and him stop fighting.

My dad is at rehearsal tonight. Or somewhere. I only know he isn't here. If he were here, we would hear his music coming through the intercom or traveling up the dumbwaiter in the kitchen.

Now Gail and the others are talking about a lady named Cynthia Plaster Caster who makes plaster-cast statues of famous musicians' cocks. They are listing all the ones she has and agreeing, "Jimi Hendrix is her best one." I think maybe she has one of my father, but I am not sure how.

⊕

LATER, GAIL AND FRANK HAVE a fight and Gail rushes me and Dweezil into the car and we drive away. Gail says she is taking us to the circus. It is sudden, but I am excited. I want to see the Barnum & Bailey acrobats and the elephants, but we only get as far as a wide street with enormous houses. I don't see any circus tents where Gail pulls over and parks.

"Are we here?"

Gail just stares.

"Gail," I say.

"Gail-Gail," says Dweezil.

She is frowning with faraway eyes that say not to break her concentration.

⊕

BACK AT OUR HOUSE, IN the room I share with Dweezil, Gail reads us *Lorenzo*, *The Little Red Fish*, *Tikki Tikki Tembo*, and *The Orchard Cat* to make up for no circus after all. When Frank comes in the room, she tucks us in. "Good night," he says, pinching our noses and saying "Moo waa." Gail flips the light off. I hug my Raggedy Ann and Andy dolls in close.

"Keep the door open," I say as they leave, "I don't like it too dark."

"Okay," says Gail, opening it back up a little. The door creaks. I make sure my arms and legs are inside my blanket so monsters and aliens won't get me. I close my eyes, picture my happy camels, and listen to the sounds of night birds and Dweezil's soft breathing. Soon I am fast asleep, but before I know it, I wake up to the sound of moaning and my vagina feeling fizzy, an alien sensation. The moaning turns to high-pitched screaming—Gail's. It sounds like someone is hurting her. I jump out of bed and rush toward her cries coming from my parents' bedroom. Standing in the open doorway, I can't understand what I am seeing. My mom is on her back with her legs in the air and my dad is over her, pressing on her, with his black hair flopping in his face. Both of them are naked. "Stop hurting her!" I yell, and my dad jumps off of Gail. He is standing now. Gail is staring at me, breathless and sweaty. They are both looking at me.

Gail slides herself off the bed with her arms outstretched and moves toward me. I step back. "It's okay, Moon, did you have a bad dream?" She puts an arm around me. She smells like my dad. My dad comes closer to me, too. I don't want either of them to touch me or hug me. But I also do. I feel mad but I don't know why. "Do you want to sleep in here with us?" Gail says.

"No," I say. Gail stays naked and walks me back to my room. Dweezil is still sound asleep. I climb into my bunk bed. Gail tugs the blanket up to my chin. This time when she leaves, she closes the door all the way. I reposition Raggedy Ann and Andy so they aren't touching. Outside my windows the sky is getting lighter. *At least the Greys won't come*, I think.

The bad aliens never show up in daylight.

CHAPTER 8

—

Gifted?

I have my first glimpse of mortality when I am seven. I have seen dead insects and rats and crawling maggots, but until second grade I had not considered how a lifetime is bookended by a birth and a death, and therefore a before and an afterward, edges and finite parameters within a larger whole that stretches, possibly endlessly, in both directions.

Dweezil and I are eating puffed wheat at the kitchen table. I am watching Gail pump espresso for my dad. Even though the sun is up, it's almost Frank's bedtime just as our day is starting. I notice Dweezil's hair looks funny from sleep and is full of knots. Gail is packing our lunch boxes and telling Dweezil the same thing she always tells me about the number zero: "It represents a hole and a whole," she says, "nothing and everything, full and empty, unity and infinity."

"Mmn," Dweezil says, nodding.

Then she places a Dole fruit cup in my Holly Hobbie lunch box and one in Dweezil's *Emergency!* lunch box and readies bread for peanut butter and guava jelly. Then Gail tells me, "You've been asked to be part of a program at Carpenter Avenue called 'Gifted.' When you are at school you will be escorted to another classroom with only a few other students."

I stiffen. My puffed wheat plops back in the bowl. Panic begins rising in my body. Am I in trouble? I like Miss Brock. Did I do something wrong? "Why?" I ask.

"Because you are exceptional, and when Dweezil goes to Carpenter they'll see that about him, too." She says it like it's a fact and she's the reason.

"What's 'exceptional'?" I ask.

Her brow furrows. "Look it up in the dictionary," she says, putting Frank's tiny cup of hot coffee on its matching saucer.

"Fine," I say. I can tell she's not gonna budge on this. "How do I spell it?"

"Look it up," she repeats with mounting annoyance.

"How can I look it up if I don't know what it means or how to spell it?" Dweezil decides this is a good time to try making tornado milk, stirring his spoon as fast as he can.

"Shit, I have to get you two to the bus stop," she says huffily, then rushes toward the stairs to the basement carrying Frank's coffee.

IN THE GIFTED CLASS I know a few of the other students: the drama teacher's son Danny, who wears ties, and a French boy with blue eyes and hair the color of a ginger snap. We are each given a whole raw chicken and told to take it home and boil it. We are going to remove all its fat and meat and examine it as a skeleton, like dinosaur bones in a museum. It is taped up tight in brown paper from a butcher shop. It is heavy and cold to the touch.

When I get it back home, I put it on the kitchen counter. When I open the brown paper, the bald chicken flops open. A small bit of thick, dark liquid squirts out where its butt is. "Ew!" I scream.

"What!" says Gail, running in from another room.

"It pooped!" I say, pointing.

Gail examines the chicken. "That's normal," she says. "You just run it under cold water."

"How can it poop if it's dead?" I say.

"Lots of things can happen after something dies. Your body can harden into rigor mortis, your fingernails and toenails and hair on your head continue to grow . . ."

"What!" I say, cutting her off. I cover my ears with my hands. "I don't want to be gifted!"

Gail helps me put my school chicken in a big pot. As it boils, I wait at the kitchen table next to Dweezil. I draw with colored markers and he rolls a tiny metal car around and makes it do jumps and twirls off stacked magazines. The chicken must cook, then cool, so I can look at just its bones. Gail is going to use the meat to make Chinese chicken salad for my dad and us. Gail heats safflower oil in a pan and drops in clumps of clear, dry mei fun noodles. They sizzle as they puff up into white, twisty worms. I wait, looking at the tilting piles of stacked magazines: *National Geographic, Life, Newsweek, Omni, Creem, Penthouse, Playboy, Hustler,* and *Oui.* The ones with naked ladies are called "smut." I open a smut one with a lady in white lace on the cover. She is squeezing her big boobs by pushing in her elbows. I do and I don't want to look at the ladies' naked bodies. The pages are shiny and slippery and sort of orange. Some words catch my eye: "corpse," "mortuary," "Marilyn Monroe." It is a story about someone who worked in the funeral parlor when Marilyn's dead body was brought in. He said that fans tried to break in and have sex with

her corpse. That she was so beautiful that men would take any opportunity to lie with her. I feel sweaty and dizzy. I fold the magazine
closed and shove it back into the pile. When Frank comes up from
the studio to get himself some food, he grabs my nose and Dweezil's
at the same time and says, "Moo waa," then he sticks his fingers under Gail's dress until she jumps.

"Grab some plates," says Gail, whisking sugar into rice vinegar
for the dressing.

But I feel sick. I don't want anyone to do anything to my body
after I am dead. Or when I'm alive, for that matter.

"Earth to Moon," says Gail, "bring the plates over to me."

I look up. Gail is dropping canned mandarin slices into the salad
and staring at me with "hurry up" eyes. I am standing in front of the
cupboard with the plates in my arms, glued to the spot. Tomorrow, I
have to take the bones back to school. I feel sad and weird, like when
you get a year older before you are ready.

THAT NIGHT, GAIL TUCKS ME in, but I can't sleep. My Empire State
Building night-light casts a pointy shadow on the ceiling. I turn on
my right side and rest my cheek on my folded hands on my pillow.
My pillowcase smells like creamy laundry soap. I pull my legs up to
my belly button and they get tangled in my nightgown. My tummy is
growling because I didn't have an appetite. I try my left side. Music is
floating in through the intercom. I sit up. The notes go forward, then
backward, then forward again. I can hear that my father is editing. I
tiptoe out of my room and follow his music down the hall to the door
that leads to his basement, where he is working. I know I am taking
a chance, because he does not like to be disturbed for any reason unless it's food or a phone call or someone is going to interview him or
take his photo or tell him news.

The only other time I remember bothering Frank was when Dweezil rubbed my favorite Honey Hill Bunch dolls' faces in dog shit and threw them over the neighbor's fence. My dad looked up with his "make it fast" face, and even after I explained what Dweezil did, my dad just stared with his brow pinched and said, "So, what do you want me to do about it?" I wanted him to punish Dweezil or make him say sorry and buy me all new dolls, but he just picked up his pen and went right back to his work.

Still, I risk it and go down the stairs past the orgy painting I hate, past the scary dungeon, and push open the heavy wooden door.

This time I say, "Daddy," to my father's hunched back. He doesn't hear me. I walk over to him and touch his shoulder with my finger, and when he turns I say, "I'm scared."

"What are you scared of?"

"Can I sit on your lap?" He exhales a "how long is this going to take" exhale through his nose, then lifts me onto his lap.

I bury my face into his neck. He smells good, like old coffee and cigarettes and sweat and scalp. "I'm scared about dying."

"Don't think about it," he says, kissing my head and then scooching me off his thighs.

"But . . ." I look into his eyes, twisting a piece of my nightgown around my finger. I know I have overstayed my welcome. "Are *you* scared?"

"No."

"Why?"

"I don't think about it." He lifts his cigarette out of the ashtray, taps the ash off the end, takes an inhale, then sets it down again. I sense that's my cue to go back upstairs, so I turn and close the big door behind me and walk up the stairs, already feeling like a ghost.

Back in my bed, my teeth chatter. I try to calm down. But how can I be calm when everything dies? I listen to my dad's repetitive music coming through the speaker in the hallway, forward, then back, then forward. I listen and pick out a single instrument and only follow where that sound goes. I follow its notes like they're bread-crumbs on a garden path.

I try to imagine what it would feel like to be my dad and not be scared. Outside I see the silhouette of our big tree. I think about its leaves falling, then mixing with the ground and bugs and dirt and worms and turning into fertilizer. I think about new seeds sprouting and the cycle continuing like a circle. I press my eyes closed tight and see the notes of the music my dad is playing in my head. I watch as they crash into each other and move away. I know his feelings by the instruments he picks and what he makes them do together before any words are added to the song. I listen and pretend he is telling me a story. I listen to the notes of his song-story and my breathing slows down. My body feels heavy now. My eyes close to the night and the dark. I keep listening and let my daddy's music wrap around me like tangled seaweed, and the music and my steady heartbeat inter-twine until sleep pulls me under.

CHAPTER 9

Family Time

My dad is standing in our living room, which used to have algae-colored carpet. "We got an echidna," says Frank, holding up a framed photo of something that looks like a cross between an anteater, a porcupine, a shrew, and a chewed-up hamburger.

"Ew," I say. "What *is* that?"

"Evelyn," he says.

A FEW DAYS LATER, DWEEZIL, Gail, Frank, and I are in the Rolls during the day, a rarity. Another rare thing is Gail's wild hair is down and brushed and she's wearing cake mascara. Rarer still, we are *all* visiting the Los Angeles Zoo.

Usually Gail takes just me and Dweezil all by herself to see the hot, dusty animals batting flies away or cooling their bodies in their man-made ponds. When Gail brings us by ourselves, we walk and walk until our legs are tired, then get ice cream sandwiches and ride the tram back to the parking lot. Today is different. Today is special because Frank is here, and because he and Gail are taking us to see "our" echidna that we "adopted." They donated money, so now Evelyn is our pet, but she lives at the zoo and we are going to meet her.

I can tell we are getting close when I see the skinny, swaying palm trees as we exit the freeway and pull into the parking lot. I hear the familiar and pleasing zoo sounds of peacocks and monkeys and water fountains as we pass through the large welcome gates and into the shade of the eucalyptus trees. We get looks from other zoo-goers, ranging from admiration to confusion to dismissal, based on my family's motley appearance.

Our greeter is a man in safari clothes. "Raise your hand if you are ready for a special tour!" he says in a chirpy voice. My hand shoots up. Frank and Gail share an eye roll. Dweezil shuffles his feet. Our overly enthusiastic docent hands us our passes and walks us past the flamingos and takes a right. We pause and I look on with wonder and disgust at the reptile and tarantula habitats. After a small lesson in how to spot poisonous snakes and spiders and the differences between their lairs and webs, he guides us all up a walkway to a small pen with no top. Our last name looks impressive in raised brass letters on the rectangular plaque on the bars of the outdoor cage.

"Hello, Evelyn," says Frank warmly to the spiny mammal.

"Echidnas are from Australia," says the docent. "Notice their front feet face forward and their back feet face backward, so when they dig, the dirt flies forward and back and they just sink!" He laughs, so I laugh and hope we get to see that in action. Dweezil looks at Frank and Gail, who nod in approval. My dad reaches for a cigarette.

"Oh, there's no smoking here," says our leader. "You'll have to go to the smoking section by the entrance." Frank gives him a look I recognize. It means we are leaving as soon as our visit with this ugly new family member is done.

"Can we pleeeeeease see the polar bears? And the orangutans?" I say, not wanting this day to end. "And can we take the tram and get ice cream sandwiches?"

"But first, how about a photo by your new addition?" Our guide pulls a Kodak Instamatic 20 out of his pocket. Gail looks at Frank.

"We'll take it from here," says Frank. That means "no photo and you can be on your way now." Frank's directness leaves no room for lingering or negotiation. The docent's smile fades. He retreats, calling, "Okay, well, if you need me I'll be in the front office where you found me."

"Daddy, pleeeeease can we stay just a little bit longer?" I beg.

Dweezil busies himself climbing on a little ledge and jumping off. Gail looks around to see what animals are close by. "I'll take them to see the sea lions," says Gail. "We'll meet you by the entrance." I can't tell if she's also disappointed. I want her to try harder to make him stay.

Frank heads in the direction of the parking lot and we venture the opposite way. The sea lion habitat is closed for cleaning, so we get a quick look at some boring old birds of prey.

When we find my dad, he and the docent and some other folks are smoking and laughing. The strangers get a photo next to my dad. How come strangers are allowed to get their photo taken with Frank but we aren't?

"Here," says my dad, pressing something hard and silver into my palm as we head for the car. I look. It is a little zoo souvenir from the coin-making machine. It says "Good luck" on one side and "Moon Unit Is Beautiful" on the other. I gasp. I love it so much. It is the first time my dad did something all by himself, without Gail, just for me.

"Thank you!" I gush, hugging him so hard. "I will always keep this forever," I say, holding it to my heart and skipping around. Frank smiles back at me with full-hearted eyes. I hope Frank made something for Dweezil, too.

All I can do is stare at my coin on the drive home. I smile with my whole body. My daddy thinks I am beautiful.

🌐

WHEN WE GET HOME, I notice an open box on the kitchen table. It has a satin ribbon lying beside it. The lid is set to one side, and inside tissue paper is a little white dress with the word "Peru" hand-embroidered on it.

"What's this?" I ask.

"It's a gift for the baby," says Frank. "If it's a girl we'll name her Peru."

"Now I know for certain it's a boy," says Gail.

"What baby?" I ask.

CHAPTER 10

Ahmet

Ahmet Emuukha Rodan is born on May 15, 1974. Dweezil and I are told our new brother is a preemie, which means born too early, so he has to stay in the hospital and have tubes in his heart. Gail has to stay there, too, because she had something scary called a "C-section," but Ahmet has to stay longer. I wish my dad could stay with us while we wait for Gail and Ahmet to come back, because we are never alone with just my dad. But I know he has to work "to provide for us." That's what Gail always says. Instead, we are home with my dad's brother Bobby.

Bobby was in the military and now he does a job with publishing books. When our uncle Bobby and aunt Marsha come over to watch us and help out, they bring my little cousin Jason, and Dweezil and I find out they have different family rules even though they are also Zappas. Three of their rules are: we eat at the table all together, we have to finish what we have on our plates, and we have to stay at the table until everyone is done eating. Our rule is: eat wherever you want, whenever you want, for however long you want. I think I would like Bobby and Marsha's rules of being cemented to my chair if my dad stayed at the table instead of them. I would eat extra slowly and I would not even mind eating SpaghettiOs instead of good, real spaghetti with Ragú.

When Ahmet comes home from the hospital, he has puffy, yellow, goopy eyes and Band-Aids on his chest. Gail says that's because he is still "jaundiced" and has "a high bilirubin count." I watch Gail change his diaper on the bed. Ahmet is so cute, with thin wisps of hair and longer eyelashes than Dweezil. My dad has two brothers and one sister. Gail has three brothers and three sisters. I now have two brothers and no sister. I am so excited because now we are a perfect family just like in the cartoon *The Aristocats*, with a mom and dad, two boy kittens, and one girl. Dr. Pressler said his eyes will be brown like Frank's and he may have allergies to pets. I hope not because I want to keep our cats.

Ahmet's name has a lot of parts to it. His first name comes from Ahmet Ertegun, who I think Gail worked for or dated before my dad. "Emuukha" is made up and fun to spell. And Rodan is a monster enemy of Godzilla. My dad loves Godzilla movies.

My dad says Ahmet is going to be a mogul. Maybe that's why someone even gave Ahmet a real silver piggy bank with his whole name engraved on it. My dad never says what I am going to be, but I wish he would. It seems like he thinks the only things girls can be are stewardesses, secretaries, groupies, and moms. In the Dr. Seuss book Gail and Frank gave me called *My Book About Me*, there are a lot fewer things for girls to circle about their futures than for boys, and boys' jobs sound like more fun.

When Ahmet is sleeping, Gail says, "Go outside," which I hate because we have an outside dog named Froonie that lives in the ivy and makes me feel sad. She is a black poodle with matted hair in some places and exposed, dry, bald skin in others. She scratches herself all the time and never gets a bath and poops everywhere. I don't want to touch her, but she wants to be touched. I know just how she feels. If I want to be hugged, I have to be the one who does the hugging. Luckily I want to hug my new baby brother all the time and he lets me and likes it! Way more than Dweezil, Gail, and Frank do, it seems.

ACCORDING TO GAIL, MY DAD'S family is bad, and hers is, too, but they are stuck with them because they are family. Frank and Gail don't have to see them, which means we don't, except when Gail needs something from them. All I know is my family is good and I *want* to be stuck with them and I will always love them, and Ahmet looks more like me than Dweezil every day, and smells as yummy as clean towels and bubble baths.

I wonder when Ahmet will learn our dad goes away for almost a whole year every year and that Gail yells a lot. Or that we are not allowed to join the military or become lawyers or Republicans, that stupid people and incompetent people and managers and record company people and the neighbor with the long driveway who lives behind us and union people in England are bad. I wonder if I am supposed to tell him. I wonder if Gail and Frank always hated all those things, or if someone taught them to hate them like they taught me.

CHAPTER 11

A Harp Lesson

Do you want to keep taking lessons or not? If so," says my dad, "Lou Ann says you'll need a bigger harp, and the bigger harp is a lot of money." His dark brown eyes meet mine. Gail is standing beside him in the doorway, with one hand on his chest and a catalog in the other. I am cross-legged on the floor playing with my remaining Honey Hill Bunch dolls. I brush my hair behind my ears, then trot a doll with flowery fabric legs and Velcro hands over to a tiny porcelain tea set.

"Earth to Moon, Earth to Moon. Come in, over," says Gail.

My dad makes a snorting sound that means he is annoyed and steps into my room in his snakeskin platforms. Gail tosses the slim, glossy catalog with a picture of a large gold harp on the cover onto my bed. She crosses her arms and follows him. I can't tell if my dad is mad at me or Gail for interrupting his work, so I make a red-haired doll pile into my left K-Swiss tennis shoe because that makes it a beach-bound convertible two-seater.

My dad is very tall, and Gail seems taller because, she says, she has a big "aura." Together they block my bedroom door, which is half wood and half stained-glass window. Gail let me design it, but now I feel tricked because anyone can just look in my room any time they want.

Gail is wearing a floral dress; enormous, tinted prescription sunglasses; and her candy-apple-red five-inch clogs. My dad has on a striped shirt with a boatneck and white painter pants with no underwear. I can see his cock hugging his left leg through the fabric. I really hate that my parents don't wear underwear, so I stare past them. Why do I even need a bigger harp anyway? I like the small, plain brown one I play. Even if I get taller than my harp teacher or taller than my dad, can't I still play the tiny, not-fancy one?

My dad takes a seat on the chair behind my Irish harp and tilts it toward his ribs. It looks small against his narrow body. I look at my collectible mice sitting on a crescent moon display above his head. Every time I learn a new song, Lou Ann rewards me with a toy mouse with real fur and a little costume. I have a ballerina mouse, a cowgirl, a chef, a doctor, a princess, a toreador, and a hula mouse. I can play "Twinkle, Twinkle, Little Star," "Frère Jacques," "Silent Night," "Greensleeves," a traditional Celtic jig, and a Japanese lullaby about cherry blossoms. I like to do the swirling roll down from the high notes to the low notes and back again. I like how the strings attach to these metal circles that look like crab eyes, and I like how the red and blue nylon strings look next to the ones of coiled gold and silver wire. My dad plucks a few strings that ring out clear and bright. He is better than me without a single lesson. He straightens my harp, puts it back in place, stands up, and heads for the catalog on my bed. I hate the idea of their spending money on the bigger harp when I have absolutely no idea if I am even any good at the harp.

Even though Gail and Frank have presented this as giving me the grown-up choice to keep playing harp or not, I do not think that is fair or very nice because I am not a grown-up and I know my real job here is to search my parents' faces and guess the right answer. Sometimes it is fun and easy to figure out what they want me to do or say or think or feel, but not now. When they ask me to choose whether or not I want a bigger harp, I guess they are really saying I have no talent or dedication and that I am not worth the cost of the instrument. Their faces and body language say they'd rather spend their money on stuff that matters, like my dad's equipment and rehearsal hall rentals or the fancy hotels he stays at with other ladies who are not Gail.

ONE OF MY RESPONSIBILITIES AS the oldest kid is to figure out what will make Gail and our dad calm down the fastest. When Gail stops yelling, that's how I know she's calm. I know my dad is calm when he goes back to work in the basement.

Another family thing I figured out all by myself is that if I succeed at something, my parents take all the credit. If I do well in a school play, the teachers and adults say talent runs in the family. If I sing a note with perfect pitch in the chorus, it's because I got my dad's musical genes. If I look pretty, I look just like Gail. What is weird is all their ideas and good qualities come from inside them, but mine also come from them, too. This does not make sense to me or seem right or fair. It makes me feel like an empty sock puppet, irrelevant unless someone else's hands do the work.

My dad holds up a picture in the harp book for me to see. I nod to show him I am considering it. He turns a few more pages of the glossy brochure, then hands it to me.

Gail stands, looking over my shoulder as I take a turn flipping the pages. I don't allow myself to be tempted by the intricate carvings. I like the one that looks like the front of a ship's bow decorated with a maiden with flowing hair, but that one has five zeros and a dollar sign.

Frank and Gail do not ask me if I love playing the harp or ask if I love music. They don't say it's important to stay with something. They don't say confidence comes from being good at something, and being good at something comes from practice and discipline and small successes over many years. And I don't tell them that what I like most about the harp is the plucked strings and that when the notes hit my body I feel awake all over, like fireworks are going off. I don't say why I wanted to start playing the harp is to be good at music, like my dad.

I look up at their expectant faces and remember we are a little den of foxes. Foxes stay safe by doing what's best for everyone. And then I remember: since girls can only become flight attendants and secretaries and wives and mothers, do I even need to play the harp?

"Moon!" Gail barks.

"Okay," I say, "we don't have to get the bigger harp."

"Okay," says Gail. "The reality is harps are heavy and expensive to buy, repair, replace, travel with, and insure." I am sad to stop playing my favorite instrument but relieved I've guessed right.

"I am going back downstairs," says my dad.

"Anyway," I say, "I want to be an actress."

CHAPTER 12

Music All Around

Soon I will be nine. I don't know if we have money or we don't, but Gail has made some changes to the house and the upstairs world where she and Dweezil, Ahmet, and I dwell.

The whole outside of our house is now royal blue with pale pink trim that "no one else has anywhere else in Los Angeles," according to the painters. The kitchen is bigger and has an "island" now, plus there's another laundry room and a new bathroom with a Jacuzzi for Gail and Frank, and instead of a screened-in porch, we now have a carpeted alcove with carpeted walls, carpeted storage benches, shelves for books and speakers, and a place for a turntable and all my dad's records.

One thing I like to do when I am in the new alcove is look in all the fancy books with colored fabric and gold lettering that belong to Gail and Frank. Gail's books are mysteries or have words like "intuition" or "occult" or "magic" or "goddess" in the titles. The books belonging to my father have strange words like "Sufism" and "Kabbalah," or long titles like *Scotch Rite Masonry Illustrated* or *Science: The Wealth of Nations* or *Science: Novum Organum*. The complete collection of the tall green science books about "achievement in learning" and "ethics" is from 1902, before any of us were born.

Besides my favorite big book of hairstyles that Frank's parents gave him, I adore a book called *Integral Yoga*, which has a man with a long beard and underpants like a diaper. I try to copy Swami Satchidananda and all the yoga poses in his book in our new alcove. I can do almost all the pretzel shapes quite easily, plus all his eye crossing, tongue curling, stomach flapping, and nostril closing. I am practicing tucking my legs behind my ears when my father quietly pads in and heads for his record player.

"Hello," I say, flopping out of the posture to see what has captured my father's attention enough for him to ascend to the upstairs world this time. It is lovely, melancholy music with no words that lures me in the way an animated character follows a cartoon aroma. "What *is* this?" I ask my father as I move closer to him to see the album in his hands.

"Satie." He hands me the album sleeve. I study it. The art is a bearded man with a bowler hat in magenta on gray, repeating over and over. "Erik Satie" is in block letters. I read other names and titles I can't pronounce. Reinbert de Leeuw. "Ogives," "Gymnopédies," "Sarabandes." We listen to the glum and gorgeous notes in silence. I try to hear what he hears. My mind opens up to take in the pauses, the pace, the individual phrases inside a longer grouping.

"You like Bach?" Frank asks, thumbing through his collection.

I know this is a rare moment I am spending alone with my dad, so I don't want to say the wrong thing. I don't want to be the reason this moment ends. I wish I could know exactly what to do to make it last forever.

"Yes," I say.

"Good," he says, nodding. "But only listen to the Philips recording of Glenn Gould's *Goldberg Variations*."

"Okay," I say.

He runs his fingers over some additional selections. I see names like Howlin' Wolf, Johnny Guitar Watson, Mahler, Varèse. Some of the covers with their colors and images of bridges or incense or instruments conjure travel to faraway lands and make me curious about whether the music will match or be strange or pleasing. "There are women in Bulgaria who practice singing by pressing their ears together—they can feel the vibrations and pitch of the notes in their cheeks and jawbones," he says with energy and wonder, "and there are singers who shout into each other's mouths and musicians who can play the notes between the notes." I am transfixed and transported.

"These are my old forty-fives," he says, opening up a cupboard below the turntable and the big albums. He shows me which of the small ones with the paper sleeves are songs, like "Monster Mash," and which ones are sound effects, like rattling chains and blowing wind. He explains the difference between 45s and seven-inches and how to see what the RPM is and how to set it on the record player and what happens if you have the settings wrong and how to carefully lift the arm and look for dust on the fragile needle. It is a lot to remember, but I concentrate as hard as I can to follow. I also notice he's slightly more fidgety and sense his pull to return to his work in the downstairs realm. Then he surprises me and says, "You can have all my old forty-fives if you want."

My eyes grow as big as the singles as I hug him as hard as I can and say, "Thank you!"

When my father leaves the room, I stay put and locate the spines of the selections he showed me. One at a time, I pull them out again and stare at the album covers of the music he liked best and burn the images into my mind.

CHAPTER 13

Water Is Thicker Than Blood

My favorite place at our house is the pool. It is a humongous rectangle with a light blue bottom, two sets of underwater steps in the shallow end, and a little seat with a handrail to get in and out of the very deep end. There are metal lounge chairs with stretchy yellow and white plastic seats and a cement and brick sidewalk that wraps all the way around that Ahmet and Dweezil use like a racetrack for their Big Wheels.

All the plants around the pool make it look like a jungle, with vines and succulents, flowering trees and shrubs that started off as clippings Tutu steals from everywhere. When I remind my grandmother stealing is wrong, Gail's mother says the plants give her permission. The only bad thing about the pool is Gail says it costs too much money to use the heater, and the solar panels don't work, so it's always freezing cold.

Even though Gramma Zappa is not allowed over here anymore, our uncle Carl, who lives with her, still is. Carl is my dad's youngest brother, and today he is our babysitter and lifeguard while Ahmet has a nap inside where it's quiet. I can do flips and giant cannonballs off the bouncy board with the sandpapery grip, or hang on to it with my hands with my eyes closed to be fair when we play Colors.

To play Colors, you have your back turned to the swimmers and you shout out colors. If you guess someone's color right, they try to swim across without being tagged by you. Otherwise they get a turn calling out the colors. "Red, green, aqua, burnt sienna, Naugahyde . . . ," I call out, but Carl and Dweezil swim across before I can catch them.

"Raspberry, lava, Jupiter, leather . . . ," I shout, then spin and splash and graze Dweezil's foot.

"Celery, celadon, copper, rust, cement, brick, wire, yellow-jacket . . . ," calls Dweezil.

When we play Colors, we laugh hard and try to outdo each other, feeling a Zappa pride in naming a rainbow of things we feel certain other people wouldn't consider. Same with drawing. Water and sky and sun and clouds don't always have to be blue and yellow and white. And we don't have to make anything stay inside the lines, even if teachers and grown-ups who are not our family tell us we do.

In our pool, we also have a longboard and sturdy plastic boats to play Shark. If you are the "fisherman," you paddle like crazy with your hands to try to tag whoever is the "shark." Gail hates this game and also hates when we use an overturned boat like a house on the water with a breathing space, because she says it's easy to get stuck underwater and drown if a boat flips. Gail says drowning is a silent killer and when we have swimming birthday parties we have to be extra careful so no one dies or sues us. That's another reason Gail and Frank don't drink or serve alcohol or let people bring their own alcohol—to make sure no one drowns because of alcohol or gets in an accident or dies or sues us because of it. Since the house is under construction, Gail and Frank also have another special kind of insurance so no one slips and falls and sues us. We have car insurance and house insurance and work insurance and fire and earthquake insurance. All of it together adds up and costs a lot of money.

I forget about all the money stuff and lose track of time when we are in the water. It is a great feeling to lose track of time. This is what my dad must feel when he works and writes and plays music for so long that he forgets to eat or play with us or worry about money or fight with Gail. My dad never swims like me, just works and works.

When Gail comes to bring us lunch, Dweezil and I climb out of the water. I am shivering and my lungs hurt. Gail wraps me and Dweezil in thin towels the colors of a smoggy California sunset. We have been in the water so long Gail's brow furrows and she says our fingers and toes are "wrinkly prunes." I shake my head to one side and then the other to get the water out of my ears. In the lower yard I can hear the uneven symphony of the construction crew.

"Carl," says Gail like a steaming kettle about to whistle, "Dweezil's lips are blue. Don't you notice when they need a break?" Dweezil shows Gail the tips of his fingers and toes. They have little blood blisters. I check mine. I have them too, and they sting.

"It's from pushing off the sides," says Carl. "We all have them. The pool's surface is too rough." Carl is doing his funny trick where he makes his swim shorts fill up with water like a balloon.

"Oh, I'll just have it replastered for you, Your Royal Highness," Gail snaps.

Carl holds his breath and slowly goes under the water so he can't hear Gail, and his bowl haircut looks like electricity. I laugh, then I cough. I am having trouble breathing. Carl bubbles back up to the surface. I laugh and cough again.

"I can't catch my breath," I say, realizing too late I have given Gail another reason for her to be mad at our uncle. Gail gives her brother-in-law a sideways scowl.

"You're waterlogged," Gail says to me.

"That's from the chlorine and the smog," says Carl, heading for the pool steps.

"And being in the water so long," lobs Gail when Carl climbs out to towel off. "Make sure they take breaks and don't leave food or the tray up here."

When Gail leaves to fight with the construction workers, we all sit in the sun eating our bologna sandwiches. Carl slouches. He looks like a squatty tribesman or an island king. "You look like a chief," I say. "Let's start a club. You can be our leader."

"Momo," says Dweezil.

"Yes!" I shriek. "Momo!"

Carl leaps up and does a funny dance while Dweezil and I chant, "Momo! Momo!"

When we finish lunch, we all take turns being Momo, leading in a straight line around the pool and down the slippery stairs to the lower yard, careful not to step on nails and wire and metal and splintery wood and broken glass. We check by the wavy brick archway to see if the concrete is dry from the day we got to do our initials with a stick. My initials spell MUZ, like the word "muse," which means inspiration for creativity.

Ahmet is up now and happily joins our line as we chant and pass the giant outside mirror Gail had the workers install so our garden looks twice as big. Mirrors outside your house are a decorating trick Gail knows about to capture light and also to bounce evil energy away from us back to "the sender." At two and a half Ahmet is tall and easy to send into fits of giggles as we pause to make crazy faces in the glass.

We march past an old toilet and a discarded tub Gail has turned into planters. Then we take turns pulling the lever of an espresso machine that's been repurposed as a fancy door handle. Gail never throws anything away; she just turns it into something else. She is very good at making spaces beautiful and unlike anywhere else. Gail is also having a wall embedded with blue glass bottles and a turret built with brick and plaster on the outside and resin and colored mosaic tiles on the inside. Next time we have money, Gail wants to get rid of our front lawn and build an underground studio and a vault so my dad stays at home to work and record and rehearse. I also want him to never leave, so I love every idea of hers that can make him stay.

Soon enough it is time for Carl to leave. Later, when he's gone, I overhear Gail in the kitchen fighting with Frank. "Carl is disgusting. I watched him stand in the shallow end and let his swim shorts swell with air and water while he let the tip of his penis bob in the pool. He's a deviant and shouldn't be around."

I am confused. Is it bad to let your bathing suit swell up? Is it bad to like the feeling of wet fabric on your body? My dad loves wet T-shirts and wet T-shirt contests. He pours water on ladies' tits at his shows. Is it only okay if dry clothes hug your body and show outlines? My dad's dry pants show his cock and Gail's dry shirts show her nipples and just about all the women who come to the house have see-through or crocheted or skintight shirts and no bra. Why is it bad if wet clothes show your body but okay if dry clothes do?

"Fine, Gail, fine," he says with controlled anger.

I can never tell if my dad agrees or if he just says yes to whatever Gail wants so she doesn't keep being mad. We are down to only one aunt and two uncles from Gail's siblings, and now she wants to ban all my dad's family, too. I hate that we all have to follow Gail and pick sides—*hers*.

That night I am so mad I cut the hair and black out the eyes of two of my favorite dolls, ruining them on purpose—my hairdresser Barbie head and the doll that eats and poops called Baby Alive. I don't feel any better. What I don't yet know is shunning and estrangement are a part of my family's vocabulary, and anger and self-harm are becoming some of my coping skills when I feel powerless and out of control, never knowing when the last day of something that matters to me is coming or how to stop it.

—

CHAPTER 14

Toil and Trouble

My fifth-grade teacher tells the class we're doing the play *Macbeth* and that I have been cast as the lead. I am excited to realize my dream of being the star even if I have to be a boy to do it. When I get home and tell Gail, she says, "It's unbecoming to brag," and points out it's a lot of lines to memorize, which I take to mean she thinks I can't do it. I begin to panic when I look through my stapled pages of the play and see Gail is right. I begin to worry about being in the spotlight. I feel self-conscious about a constellation of miniature pustules on my forehead and my new, weird chest buds. The only things that relieve the pressure and reassure me I can do it are all my TV and real-life crushes. Gail says I am becoming "boy crazy," which usually happens "right around the time girls have the ability to get pregnant." The corners of my mouth turn down. Ew. She says it's "biological." She says if I lived in Africa I'd be married by now and living with my new family in another village. My eyes well up from horror at the thought.

"Those poor girls!" I shriek, grateful to have the American problems and crushes I have.

One crush is on Derek, the blond drummer from the Bay City Rollers with the cleft in his chin, and one is on my dad's drummer Terry.

I love the drive down Laurel Canyon to pick Frank up from re-hearsal. Now Dweezil and Ahmet and I slosh into each other in the back seat. Ahmet is starting to like Dweezil more than me and I am starting to like other boys as much as or more than them.

When we go to my dad's rehearsals to pick Frank up, sometimes I get to watch Terry play. Drums are my very favorite instrument, and he is so good at drumming. I like how angry he looks when he plays even though he isn't angry. That's called showmanship. He makes funny, mad faces but underneath there is calm, like my dad, which I know because when Terry is not onstage he speaks low and soft and smiles a lot. I also like that he plays drums shirtless. I like that I can see all his muscles and his ribs. He has tiny nipples and a smooth chest. My dad has hair on his chest but Terry has none, just the same as Dweezil and Ahmet.

Even though Frank and Gail tell me and my brothers we can say anything or think anything or do anything, it doesn't feel true. Frank also says, "Never do anything stupid unless you're gonna get paid for it." The problem is I can never tell what he and Gail think is stupid until after I do it, so I definitely don't want anyone to know that I se-cretly draw penises in my journal and wonder about them. Of course I have seen my dad's naked penis a gazillion times since he always sleeps in the nude and walks around the house without any clothes on, and I always see him that way when I bring him coffee or ciga-rettes when he is in the bath. Even my friends have seen him naked on sleepovers if we sleep in the alcove. But I never see his penis or any penises long enough to draw them right. Boys and men also have balls. They are hard to draw because I am not sure where they attach.

IT IS LATE AT NIGHT at our house, and I am petting the cat and watching *Three's Company* when I hear Gail on the telephone. I hear her say "Bring her straight to our house" and "She can sleep in Moon's room so she can keep an eye on her." My ears prick up. I sail into the kitchen.

"Who can sleep in my room? What's wrong?"

"Dale," she says, covering the phone with her hand. "There's been an accident, an emergency, and Terry needs someone to help him out."

I positively swoon at the idea I could help Terry out, then it dawns on me I am missing something. "Who's Dale?"

"Terry's girlfriend," says Gail dismissively. I blink in disbelief. Terry has a girlfriend? A *girlfriend*? How does everyone in the world know this but *me*?

"No!" I blurt out.

Then Gail says, "I'll see you when you get here," into the receiver and hangs up. When I see the look on her face, I know I'm in trouble.

"Gail," I whine, "that's not fair!"

She spins toward me. "Earth to Moon, the world doesn't revolve around you. Terry's girlfriend is coming to stay with us right away because she fell. It's an *emergency*."

I feel knocked over, like when I broke my pinkie playing sock ball at recess last year and Gail and Frank didn't take me to the hospital until the next day when I was sweaty and delirious and my hand was the size of a loaf of bread. I needed a needle as big as a bass string in my elbow and a cast for eight weeks. If that didn't count as an emergency for me, what would? What *is* counting as an emergency for Dale now and why is a stranger with one more important than your kid in pain?

"What happened?" I ask.

"She fell out of a building."

Huh? "Shouldn't she be in a hospital?"

"Moon! Stop!" Gail stomps toward me until her face is very close to mine. "She landed on her head and broke several ribs so she's coming here to recuperate. She's lucky to be alive. She will sleep in your bed and that's all there is to it!"

Out of the corner of my eye I see Mr. Roper making eyes at Chrissy on the TV. Jack bites his knuckle.

I cross my arms and march back into my room one last time before it's ruined. I don't even turn the TV off. I feel like Gail when she hears about my dad's extra girlfriends. It's not fair when people you love love someone else.

It's not fair Terry loves Dale and not me.

A SHORT WHILE LATER, GAIL is helping Dale up our stairs. Then I am following them into my room. I am shocked because she is not wearing a bra or underwear under her loose-fitting hospital gown. I am mesmerized by her and her beauty and size. Dale's hair is short and white-blond. She has large brown eyes, and I am almost as tall as she is, which means she is very small for an adult. She is like a tiny bird. Even with scratches and bruises, Dale is so, so pretty. Gail fluffs my pillows for her head and tucks her in. Then she turns off the overhead lights in my room and turns on a little lamp instead. Gail tells me to run and bring her water.

When I return, Dale is alone. I hold the cup up to her lips and she takes two tiny sips. Her skin, where it isn't bruised or bleeding, is so white and smooth. She is like a doll, which makes me want to take care of her without being asked.

"Can you take me to the bathroom?" she asks weakly. She has a deep, smooth voice and a thick, weird accent that sounds like a stuffy nose. Later I'll find out she's from Boston and makes her own outfits. I stand up quickly and let her put her weight on me. She moves slowly and winces. She needs help bending her legs and letting them dangle off the side of the bed. She has to take a lot of breaks. When we get to the bathroom, she pulls her gown up. I see her vagina hair. It looks like a little hummingbird's nest or a fawn's tail. I hand her toilet paper and help her slide forward. I lift her legs to get her feet onto the floor again. Each leg feels almost as heavy as one of my brothers. Then I help her wash and dry her hands. I am still jealous, but I can see why Terry loves her. I think I might even love her a little, too. It's hard and weird to hold two opposing feelings. I wonder if Gail can like the other ladies Frank loves. Could I?

No, I think, *impossible*.

The rest of Dale's time with us is a blur. What I do remember is going to school and asking my teacher to let me play one of the three witches in *Macbeth* instead because they have very few lines. Now I wonder why I did this. At the time I felt overwhelmed and didn't know the difference between self-sabotage and self-care. Was is it easier to play a satellite role to keep the peace—Gail's peace—and thereby choose my father's art and happiness over my own?

CHAPTER 15

Witchcraft

I hate being eleven and I hate sixth grade. I have feathered bangs, weird boobs, and a blitzkrieg of blackheads and white-heads that Noxzema, Sea Breeze, and Stridex medicated pads alone or combined cannot battle. To add to my discomfort, I have to change schools because of something called "busing." A few parents from my public school band together and work fast to open a new, private elementary school a short drive away from us. I hate change because I already have so much of it at home, but Gail pays the tu-ition for River Willow Academy so I don't have to be sent to a place called "Compton" and ride a bus with no bathroom three extra hours each day.

The new school is small with a depressing concrete play yard flanked by two sets of ugly buildings. I know no one there and imme-diately dislike a mean girl in my class who makes me wish I got bused. She is pushy, says rude things, taunts me and many other kids, and always hogs the monkey bars when we all want to have a turn to try a cherry drop at recess or lunch. She's not the boss of the dumb play structure, but the teachers seem hesitant to stop her because she is a "burn victim." The rumor is she was set on fire. If that's true, she has it way harder than me and maybe we should be friends.

Instead of talking to her and trying to understand her, I do what I see Gail do with my dad's contracts and with the women my dad fucks—witchcraft. Gail told me, "The firstborn daughter of the firstborn daughter of the firstborn daughter is a witch," same as her mother and her grandmother and so on, and that we all just *know* how to cast spells. So I sneak into my bedroom after school and write the name of the girl I hate in cursive many times on a piece of my lined notebook paper. I repeat her name in a hypnotic, droning voice. Gail calls that the "incantation." You have to visualize the person and the outcome you want in as much detail as possible when you say the words. I see her in a denim skirt, which is the stupidest thing to wear when you hang upside down on monkey bars because the boys can see your underwear, but I suppose it is also somewhat good, because if your pants are too slippery, then you can't get a decent grip on the bar with the back of your knees. I say my black-magic spell and melt wax on her name as I picture her swinging, then falling flat on her stupid, selfish face. When I am sure the spell has been set and feel certain her doom will come true, I yawn and get into my pajamas.

The next day she falls off the monkey bars *exactly* the way I pictured it. I am terrified. She is crying so hard my heart is ripped open with shame and self-hatred. My sudden clarity of compassion is obscured by feeling so bad about what I have caused, I can't even say sorry. I can't tell anyone. They will find out I am a monster. On the spot I promise myself I will *never* use my powers for evil ever again no matter how much or how bad someone hurts me. I know I am a real witch, and with special powers comes real responsibility.

A week later, my promise to myself gets tested. I have on a ruffly pink halter top and pink shorts. The gray-haired headmaster calls me into his office and says I am in trouble. At first I think he somehow found out about what I did to that girl, which is impossible. Instead he says, "You have to go home and change your clothes because the boys are staring at your navel."

"Huh?" I say. "What do you mean?"

"They can't concentrate."

"Why?" I ask. The headmaster is staring at my belly button. I look down at my innie and the hair on my navel my dad calls a "treasure trail." I look up at him, totally confused.

"You need to wear clothes that do not show your skin."

I am furious and embarrassed but don't know why. I want to cast a spell and burn him alive. But I don't. Instead I do what he says—call Gail and wait in the hall until she arrives. At first she is mad at me for breaking up her busy day. When she hears him explain the problem, she tells him those are his thoughts, not my classmates', and calls him a creep to his face.

On the drive home, Gail explains I am getting a woman's body and I get to stay at the house and do nothing the whole rest of the day. I let myself have a few mean thoughts, but I cast zero spells. I keep my word to myself and never cast another evil spell for the rest of my life. Some things I only have to learn once.

. . . But I do wonder if good spells are still okay.

FRANK IS LEAVING FOR TOUR in a few days and I have overheard conversations about more legal problems with Warner Bros., so my mother is giving my father a massage. Gail is barefoot but dressed in jeans and a blouse and straddling my naked father on their bed. The only time I see physical care between Gail and Frank is when she massages my father for hours at a time—Gail gives and Frank receives. Come to think of it, I never see any adults kiss or hug one another or show warmth and affection except on TV and in movies, and usually only when people first meet. Or in real life on Oahu when airport people give strangers welcome leis when they land. I am becoming obsessed with love. I watch with rapt attention the disparity and lack of it as my depleted but devoted mother gives Frank everything, even after ten years and three kids together.

I watch how Gail moves her hands up and down his long torso

along either side of his spine with thumb presses and flat-palm fanning strokes and pulls. Sometimes she will squeeze cream into her hands and make fast circular motions or lift sections of his skin and knead him, similar to what she does when she gets an urge to bake bread. I watch how he winces with enjoyment as she rubs his back, hips, shoulders, and buttocks with force that briefly leaves his olive skin red. I move in closer and watch how nimbly and attentively she works from the top of his head—rubbing his scalp, temples, ears, skinny neck—all the way to his thighs, calves, arms, and hands, and ending with the soles of his feet.

"Can I try?" I ask. Gail shrugs and scooches over so I can grab his other foot.

"You always start at the head and end with the feet so you don't get dirt on his face," she says.

"Stinkfoot," my father says into his pillow.

I watch Gail and try to mirror her movements and intensity. Sometimes Gail asks me to rub her hands and feet, but this is my first time helping her rub my dad. Sometimes, if me and my brothers are lucky, Gail will give us fast bedtime foot massages, and if we are sick, we get mini ones when she spreads a smear of Vicks VapoRub on our feet, so I sort of know what it's like to have a massage. I have also been memorizing which acupressure points match which organs from the giant double-sided pillow of both feet Gail bought for the TV room.

After a few minutes of feeling around for "crunchies" and rubbing them until my father's skin has pliability, I feel a kind of excitement at learning a skill I think I have a natural aptitude for. "Can you tell who is who?" I ask my father.

On some level maybe I want to learn so I can help keep him around and coming back to us. So I sneak in some white magic through his feet for his safe return.

When my father comes back from tour, I help my mother unpack my dad's suitcases. He has been gone a long time. "No one is to be trusted. Especially fans. Especially female fans," she tells me. I watch her examine trinkets my dad has accumulated that she's never seen before. I am learning from her reactions to the objects how to feel about him and the world and everything he does and everyone he does it with. She holds up things like pens, beads, pins, scarves, socks, T-shirts, calling them "witchy forget-me-not items." Even when fans give him seemingly innocuous items like handkerchiefs or books, it is just so obvious and transparent to Gail, and now to me, that everything is a hook, a trick to get my dad to ditch Gail and our family and try life with them instead.

I overhear Frank say that the other ladies don't mean anything. "It's just fucking." If it doesn't mean anything to him but it does mean something to Gail and me, then why does he make himself and the other ladies happy and not us?

All I know is lately my mother is extra sad a lot and sleeps a lot and cries a lot and yells a lot. I try to make her laugh. I want her to get up and drive us to school in the morning or make our meals at dinnertime. I hate having to be the one who constantly reminds her. Most of the time when she's sad like that she just lets us skip and stay home and eat Nutter Butters and watch as much TV as we want.

As mad as Gail seems, she is happier having him back than when he's gone. I don't understand why Gail keeps forgiving him. Or why I still love him even though I am so mad at him, too. One of my biggest fears is that my daddy hurts us on purpose and doesn't care. That would make him evil. And I don't want my daddy to be evil. If he is with other women by accident or because he is selfish, that is also bad.

ANOTHER THING HAPPENS WHEN I take my dad his coffee.

"Here you go, Daddy," I say, and place his espresso cup on the side of the tub. I'm looking at him and at his penis in the water and his naked body like usual, but his face looks different, as though he is noticing he is naked in front of me for the first time. He can't move to hide himself or walk away quickly like he does when I have sleepovers and he marches through the living room with nothing on. I think maybe this is the first time he feels embarrassed to be seen naked by me, and the first time he realizes he has embarrassed me, and that he has been embarrassing me for a while. Maybe it's okay to be naked in front of your kids when they are little, but not in front of your kid if the kid is becoming a woman.

I feel something invisible being taken away from me, and in its place is a new distance on top of the existing disconnection.

This is all too much for a kid to manage. I might be a witch, but I'm not a wizard.

Dear Frank HOW
are you?
I wish I could see
your concert but
I cannot come see
it because you
are someplace else
you are in Atlanta
and I love you!

FROM
moon   To Frank

CHAPTER 16

—

Cause and Effect

M iss Scarlet in the conservatory with a candlestick," I say over Frank and Gail's fighting. Dweezil opens the small envelope. Ahmet briefly glances up, then continues studying the tiny weapons from the board game.

"Nope," says Dweezil.

Even from the living room, where Dweezil, Ahmet, and I are playing, we can hear Gail screaming at Frank in their bedroom. Since I am two years older than Dweezil and seven years older than Ahmet, I always feel it is my duty to keep some semblance of calm and happy distraction. I hold my tiny pencil and double-check my answers as I listen to them argue.

Gail is a flamethrower today, screaming, "Whatever amount you spend on *her*, I will spend on myself and the kids, and I promise you

I will spend down our money four times as fast!" She means the one who lives in Germany.

Selfishly, I am listening and trying to gauge whether this fight will result in Gail's lashing out at me later or spoiling us to punish Frank or both. This one sounds trickier than usual.

"It can't be Colonel Mustard . . ."

"Is that your answer?" asks Dweezil. Ahmet can't read yet, but he peeks in the envelope anyway. I try to get a hint from his sneaky look. Hopeless.

Gail fires off a few more rounds of fury, then I hear Frank's feet as he heads out of their bedroom, down the hall, and past us, with Gail following closely behind. Frank's body is stiff, like a member of a bomb squad securing the immediate area, as he strides past us in silence. Gail advances with glass-shattering expletives and movements that are fast and jerky. My brothers and I freeze and hold our breaths. Their storm passes us like a close-call tornado and lands them in the kitchen.

"Calm down, Gail," I hear Frank say with a bit of gravel in his voice.

Gail doesn't listen. Her mouth is a runaway train. From what I can gather, Frank's latest "home-wrecker" is named Gerda and my father is calmly explaining he's giving her serious consideration. I don't quite understand what he means, but I don't like the sound of it, either.

Frank intercepts every fireball of anger and escalation like he always does, with an equally formidable nonplussed, take-me-as-I-am, I'll-wait-until-you're-done demeanor.

"But we already have a May fifteenth in our life!" Gail plead-shrieks. She means Ahmet. "*His* birthday is May fifteenth!" I can hear their familiar dance—Gail using her emotional, spiritual-destiny, family-first logic on my father's you-knew-what-you-were-getting-when-you-signed-up iciness. It's psychological warfare. "Right birthday, wrong person, Frank."

My ears and heart burn as I listen to Gail trying her hardest to make my dad feel guilty and only associate that date with my brother, his son, not his temptress. I can hear her making sure my dad understands there are correct and incorrect astrological choices—Ahmet is the correct choice and Gerda is the wrong one. Now I want to go in the kitchen and help Gail scream at my dad. I look at Ahmet and Dweezil. My little brothers seem to have a shutoff valve I am missing where they can tune this agony out. I look at the Clue board with all its little murder weapons. Why can't I be calm? Why can't Gail? Why don't *our* feelings count? Why can't my dad be happy with just us? Why can't that lady leave us all alone? Why can't we be a happy family?

I reassure myself that screaming is just louder talking, and I dread it ending with me losing sleep to their other kind of bellowing, without their clothes on.

I look at my sweet-faced allies and my eyes say "I wish this wasn't our life, but it is." Then I say, "Professor Plum in the library with a rope." And the three of us burst into spontaneous, hysterical laughter for absolutely no reason whatsoever.

WHEN MY FATHER LEAVES FOR his latest tour, Gail takes us to Buddy Brown's toy store. Ahmet is learning what Dweezil and I already know—sometimes the madder Gail is at Frank, the better your chances of getting a good toy for no reason, or, even better, more than one toy. Buddy Brown's has everything you could ever want—sketchbooks, art supplies, stickers, skateboards, walkie-talkies, Slip 'N Slides—as well as stuff none of us care about, like Breyer horses, doctor kits, model planes, collectible porcelain figurines, Hula Hoops, train stuff, puzzles, and dollhouses.

Dweezil and Ahmet head for the Star Wars section and the Godzilla figurines from Japan. I look in the Easy Bake Oven aisle, then peruse the Madame Alexanders and the Sasha dolls that come all the way from Europe. I love their outfits and how foreign their clothes look—ball gowns and crowns and kilts and pom-pom hats. Stuff we'd never wear in sunny California. I really want to go to Europe. That's where my dad goes a lot. I really want to go everywhere he's ever been, like London, and other places he hasn't, too, like Cairo.

Even though we all live in California, Gail calls England home because she went to school and modeled over there. That's where she learned about tea and that's why I love tea now, too. So I decide to look at the tiny porcelain tea sets stacked near the Baby Alives.

When my mother goes to pay, Gail sees us eyeing the Yes & Know books with the invisible pens and the Mad Libs and throws some of those on the counter. Buddy smiles and keeps on tallying up the total.

Dweezil, Ahmet, and I skip around with excitement. The most depressing thing at the toy store is the miniature license plates. This is the easiest way for us to know we are different from other families, since there are no Ahmets or Dweezils or Moon Units. Dweezil and I try to look for the weirdest or ugliest names they have. Ahmet laughs when we say the names out loud—Bruce, Lon, Debbie, Wanda . . . Even Gail looks over and smiles when Dweezil ups the ante and makes up even uglier names, like "Borch" and "Prakkus."

Gail's real-life car license plate says RDNZL, which is our dad's nickname for Gail. I think it's a mixture of the word "redundant" and "Rapunzel" because Gail has crazy hair. I don't think it's a compliment or that she likes the nickname, but she made it her license plate anyway. I think maybe to show my dad she can take whatever he dishes out and then some.

I admit I feel dirty for getting a toy knowing how mad my dad would be, and yet I want the tempting items desperately. Especially if Ahmet and Dweezil don't see it as an issue that when Gail is sad or mad at my dad she spoils us with over-the-top Easter, birthday, Christmas, and no-reason splurges.

WHEN FRANK COMES BACK FROM tour this time, he brings Gail a present, a small bundle wrapped in tinfoil in the breast pocket of his jacket. It is a buckwheat pancake. "This is the best pancake I have ever tasted in my life!" he announces. We gather around this half-eaten five-star-hotel room service carb like cavemen discovering fire. "I want you to taste this and re-create it," Frank says to Gail, who looks up at him with both disbelief and readiness to reverse-engineer the breakfast for her beloved. Gail nibbles first, then me. Dweezil and Ahmet give it a look and decide resuming play with their new lightsabers holds more appeal. I marvel at my jealousy of a day-old flapjack that's traveled farther than I have and received twice the praise.

To add to the insult to my mother, Frank has brought two *actual* gifts home, and they are both for only me—a set of expensive-looking enameled rose gold charms with the Union Jack flag of the United Kingdom on them, and a brown-haired doll that says "Mama." This is extremely unusual. I am dumbfounded.

"Thank you!" I say, completely stunned. I cannot help but feel they were last-minute airport purchases, or maybe someone gave them to him and he passed them on to me, because I can't picture him going to a store somewhere on purpose to buy me anything. "Thank you," I say again. "I love them!" Then I notice my dad is wearing jewelry. Then I notice Gail noticing Frank is wearing jewelry. A necklace. I can see Gail eyeing it and I know exactly what she's thinking because I am thinking it, too: Frank's been marked. That talisman is clearly from *her* and therefore *evil*.

Game recognizes game, and like my mother I am furious that bitch gave Frank some keepsake with a force field connection to her and we have to all endure its pull.

To my amazement, Gail full-stop surprises us both and breaks the bedevilment with a two-word sentence: "I'm pregnant."

CHAPTER 17

Diva

Late July in California. I'm almost twelve, with hair everywhere and curving hips crammed into pink shorts that used to fit me just fine. It's too hot outside, so I'm inside, skipping, listening to my bare feet slapping on the cool wood floor of the living room. When I stop, I notice the house is quiet. "Gail?" I call out to no reply, so I go look for her.

I step in something wet. I look down. Red spots, splotchy and uneven. Some are the size of quarters, some as small as puka shells. It looks like blood.

I look at the underside of my foot. A small smear is drying. I notice a trail of red leading down the hallway. My stomach balls into a knot. Fear shoots through me. Wide-eyed, I follow the droplets to my parents' room. Gail is in bed, ghost white. The blood is her blood.

It's on the bedspread and between her legs. I think the baby must be coming, but something is wrong with Gail or the baby or both. My heart is suddenly beating very fast. I take her limp hand. "Gail?" Her breathing is strange.

"Get your dad," she manages to say.

"Okay," I say, and start running. My mind is racing faster than my legs as I rush down to the basement. My dad is shirtless at his console. "Something is wrong with Gail," I say. "There's blood in the living room all the way to the bedroom." My dad is up, lightning-bolt fast. "Call Alice," he says. I don't understand why we need to call the neighbor.

But I must have called, because Alice is soon at our house. Then there is commotion. More phone calls. Fast decisions, and the maid and the secretary moving quickly but trying to seem calm. Someone says, "An ambulance is on the way." Another says, "Alice can stay with them," meaning me, Dweezil, and Ahmet. Then the paramedics arrive. White uniforms and black equipment. My teeth are chattering.

"She's lost a lot of blood," says someone. "Rh negative," says someone else. When they say we aren't allowed in the room with Gail, only my dad is, I am suddenly very scared my mother is going to die. My dad and the men standing over Gail are the last thing I see before being led away to another room. I can't catch my breath. My ears start to ring. I feel like I might faint.

"I can't see," I blurt. Someone tells me to sit down. That's good, because I am trembling uncontrollably, and my legs are buckling and going numb. Now I am sitting in the living room on a long, narrow bench with my back against the wall. "I can't see," I repeat, panic rising.

Fast feet, then someone hands me a brown paper bag. "Breathe into the bag." I feel the paper lunch sack in my hand, find the opening. I do as I am instructed and put the opening around my mouth. I make a seal with my hands. I smell the familiar brown-bag-lunch smell. "Lean forward and take a deep breath." The bag inflates and deflates like our fireplace bellows. "Long and slow." Air squeaks into my lungs in small shallow sips. A hand is on my back. The calmer I become, the more my vision returns.

Then Gail is on the gurney with her giant belly under a white sheet being wheeled to the front door, accompanied by my dad. Then sirens. Then we are at the neighbor's house waiting.

ALICE IS CATHOLIC AND FUNNY, has moles on her face, is an art teacher, and cooks salty Lebanese food for us. Dweezil, Ahmet, and I stay in a huddle as she shows us the rooms we are allowed to enter and the ones we are not. She points out her husband's record collection and a turntable we can't touch, with albums from Yes, ELO, Jethro Tull, Boston, and Foghat. She says we are allowed to touch their game of Othello, but it's in their living room and it's too dark in there to play, even with the lights on. I can't concentrate anyway because the longer we wait, the more I worry. If it's a girl and she is okay, Gail said Ahmet can name her—he picked Rainy May. I am sending good white magic as hard as I can.

When Alice's husband, Barry, comes home, he makes me nervous because he is so grumpy. Barry looks young compared to Alice, which makes me think he's a cheater like my dad. He is a proctologist, has a tan, wears yellow nylon shorts, and belongs to a gym miles away in an area called "downtown." Alice laughs when she explains their differences—he likes air-conditioning and she likes open screen doors, she likes dogs and he likes no pets. I am surprised and glad when he makes an exception and lets us watch TV the whole time even though the sound annoys him. He also says we can stay over if we have to. I am so worried that all I can do is pace, eat sourdough bread, pet Alice's Pekinese, and draw. It's a long day of waiting. And then it's bedtime.

I'm desperately wondering what is happening. Ahmet and Dweezil hog the brass daybed, so Alice makes a spot for me on a little sofa. We are watching Lenny and Squiggy do dumb stuff on *Laverne and Shirley* when the phone rings. My skin prickles. I sit up. "It's your dad. You have a sister," says Alice with her hand over the receiver. Soon she is laughing and relief washes over me. "When they heard her scream in the hallway, they knew what to name her. She was the loudest baby in the ward. A little opera singer," she says, laughing. "Her name is Diva." Ahmet and Dweezil smile, too.

"Diva," I repeat to myself. I look over at Ahmet and wonder if he's mad they changed her name. "Diva," I repeat to myself. My wishes came true: I have a sister and Gail is okay.

THE NEXT DAY I HAVE to dress up in Gail's high-heeled shoes and makeup to make me look older for the visiting requirements. I clomp down the hallway to my mother's room. Gail is pale but smiling. Frank is holding Gail's hand. A male doctor and a nurse are there, too.

"Gail had an emergency C-section and hysterectomy," says my dad.

"That's correct," says the doctor pointedly. "She lost a lot of blood and has severe anemia and will need to eat a lot of liver." The doctor turns to me. "Your mother will need to have a round-the-clock nurse for a while, so your parents are going to need you to do your part to help out." I stiffen from worry about even more responsibility and nod. But when I see my new sister, I melt. All I can do is stare. She's wrapped in a hospital blanket, on a little bed on wheels beside Gail's bigger bed on wheels. She is so pretty and tiny with so much black hair. She looks like a baby werewolf with shining black eyes. I silently swear I would do *anything* for her.

Something feels new and complete in me. Two girls and two boys. We are, as far as I am concerned, *finally* a whole family. Balanced. Perfect.

I loop my finger around her tiny hand and say, "I've been waiting for you."

CHAPTER 18

Big Sister

My baby sister sleeps in my room and seems to want me to hold her more than Gail. I love it, but I wonder if it makes Gail mad because Diva is the last baby Gail can have, so she gets extra special attention from everyone.

But I am glad Gail is finally better. No more anemia and no more round-the-clock baby nurses. Better enough to cook again and drive us all around. Better enough to sometimes sit in the kitchen again and deal herself cards, then lay them on top of each other in several rows.

Frank parted ways with his manager, so he and Gail are sorting out a lot of complicated things. It is my job to help Gail help my dad.

One night I wake up to fighting. Again. I hear Frank one room over saying, "Calm down," in a voice that isn't loud but feels like strong arms pushing you into a chair. I check to see if Diva is still sleeping in her crib beside me in my bedroom—she is—so I put a pillow over my head to drown out the sound and drift back to sleep.

A short while later my dad is shaking me awake. "Gail is on a rampage. I need you to hide the gun." I sit up. My warm-blanket grogginess turns to icy alertness.

"Okay," I say. I didn't even know we had a gun. My stomach clenches.

My father runs toward the sounds of Gail's frantic feet. My legs feel like jelly. My heart is pounding in my ears. I am scared . . . But, thinking hard, I remember seeing Gail's brother show her *his* gun once. Or maybe I just thought it was his? It was small and black and he was showing Gail "the barrel" and where the bullets go. They were in the kitchen . . .

I stand up. I feel the carpeting on my bare feet. I tell myself, *This is important, Moon.* I try using my remote viewing to "see" it. A place high up where us kids wouldn't look? In my mind's eye I "see" the alcohol cupboard, with Tutu's bottles of Kahlúa, Bailey's, and Irish cream that she drinks when she visits. Whether because of logic, intuition, a memory, or imagination, I rush to the kitchen.

I grab a stool and climb up.

I try to calm myself—Gail usually just drives away when the fights are this bad. Maybe she will just do that now. But maybe this time she'll never come back. No, I tell myself, Gail always comes back because she wants Frank to stay and the only way to get him to stay is to monitor his every move. And manage his business and control the money.

Up on the stool, I stand on my tiptoes. I open the cupboard.

I am so scared my dad wants to leave us to be with Gerda all the time. But I also kind of hope he does, because the fighting and screaming and fucking are too much. But if they split up and I had to choose between Gail and Frank, I would pick him, because he never yells, but Gail wouldn't let me and he might not want me. So, the next best wish is wishing for things to stay the same.

I fish around behind the bottles. The gun's not there.

New fears grip me. Does that mean Gail got to it first? Should I get my brothers and sister and hide? I feel like I've done something wrong by coming up empty-handed.

I climb down off the stool knowing I have to tell my father, but I will have to wait until he leaves their room. I head back to their fighting, but it has stopped. Gail is moaning now, but I still feel worried, so I check on my baby sister. She is small and round and sleeping soundly, so I climb back in my bed. I lie still, but tremors shoot through my body. I pull my blankets up to my chin to try to get warm and stop my teeth from chattering. I feel the future rush in like a flash flood. Soon I will get my period. Next year I will start seventh grade. Frank will leave again.

I want to stay little and not have grown-up problems. But if I have to get older, I tell myself, like a mantra, *Never forget, Moon, always remember what it feels like to be a kid.*

Blast Off

1980-1989

CHAPTER 19

Like, Omigod

The year *The Blue Lagoon*, *9 to 5*, *Airplane!*, and *The Empire Strikes Back* secure their top-grossing spots at the box office, I start junior high. I'm twelve going on thirteen going on put-a-bag-on-my-face. In fact, bag my whole body. If my new school were *Charlie's Angels*, every girl here would be a Farrah. I am a Sabrina, but with gruesome cystic acne and thick, hairy tree stumps for legs. Cystic acne is the kind of acne everyone can see but no one ever mentions. I am wearing the elephant in the room and it's everywhere—on my forehead, cheeks, chin, neck, chest, and back, like an invasive ground cover. To appear somewhat normal and acceptable, I awake early each morning and apply some of my dad's old "pancake" makeup, which he sometimes still uses for TV appearances and photo shoots. Though it is not a color match and blending eludes me, ever the optimist, I simply hope for the best.

Whether Frank and Gail realize it or not, I am desperately craving stability, structure, socialization, purpose, and a school uniform. One out of five isn't bad; it could have been zero. Since Gail is "the only one driving everyone around all over town," she does the deciding and chooses a private school for me to attend that is close to where she drops my brothers off. Oakwood is a tiny, elite "college preparatory" school in the San Fernando Valley. It's slightly bigger than my last school but extremely puny for a high school.

Oakwood's rigorous academic approach is counterbalanced with a shoes-optional policy and a call-your-teachers-by-their-first-names vibe, which is new for others but familiar to me. What *is* different for me is being with kids my own age and listening in on *their* debates about music, TV, movies, books, sex, politics, food, spirituality, and family complications. Even though I come from a family that apparently shocks other people, I am the one getting shocked here when I overhear "normal" kids discussing stuff like circle jerks, finding lubes on their parents' nightstands, or divorce as a result of late-bloomer adult gayness or cheating or both. *Wait*, I think, *people split up and stay split up? Because of cheating?* I am finding out I am sheltered in strange ways and that normal kids have different crazy problems.

Some of my peers have dads who have started whole new families with stepmoms barely older than we are. Some people have moms who date other moms, change their names, begin to meditate, or start doing pottery out of nowhere. I get flattered *and* mad when I meet a kid in my English class whose mom changed her name—to *Moon*, after *me*, because she is a fan of my dad's! I don't want to share my name! I feel sorry for kids who have the same name as other people or who have to keep their stuff in different houses, but I think I would die if I ended up with extra siblings from a teenage stepmom.

My favorite things about my new school that I have never seen before are the Spanish tile roof, the open-air courtyard, and the vending machine with only organic pippins and Red Delicious apples for twenty-five cents. The best people-watching is by the lockers or at lunch when the whole school mingles by the picnic tables or by the food truck where you can buy Cup-a-Soup, Gatorade, and Mountain Dew if you forget your bagged lunch. The bands the boys talk about by their lockers are Pink Floyd; Queen; Styx; Cheap Trick; Foreigner; Van Halen; Rush; Blondie, because "Debbie Harry is so hot"; Aerosmith; and AC/DC. I already know about Van Halen from Dweezil, and Blondie because my dad showed me the album and played it on our record player. From what I gather, if they worry at all, the boys my age seem to be apprehensive about peach fuzz, cracking voices, and surprise boners, while the girls make sure they have the right accessories, they don't have tan lines, and their stomachs are flat.

What is also new to me here is a hunger for attention through academic achievement.

At Oakwood I am not friends with the popular girls with license plate names, but I finally make friends who seem to like me back in spite of what I look like. Maybe because they are oddballs, like me. There's tomboy Karen, a.k.a. "Monkey," an undersized blonde who climbs chain-link fences like she has suction cups for hands; "Weirdfoodgirl," a bug-eyed brunette who eats peanut butter, mayonnaise, and sprout sandwiches on whole-wheat hot dog buns; "Supercrayon," an obese boy who draws cartoon action heroes 24/7; and "Whirlybird," a skinny double-jointed boy who can wind up his bony elbows and spin his forearms like airplane propellers.

And then there's Sam. Sam Harris is my favorite male friend at school. He has ice-blue eyes and beautiful hands and a deep voice. He speaks slowly, like he thinks before he says something, like my dad, only his mom is the famous earner in his house—she is a successful TV writer with shows "on air." Sam is my crush, but his crush has blond hair and perfect skin and is skinny with medium-sized boobs. Kim's legs don't touch at the top, and what little hair she has on her arms and legs grows in blond. She has no hair at all on her lower legs, but that's because she uses something called Nair. Sam is the smartest boy in my class, maybe the whole school, so he must have good taste. I feel doomed to be the wrong thing to be in my family *and* at school since I am starting to notice it is popular to be blond and skinny. Blond and fat is okay. Brunette and skinny is okay. But you can't be brunette and fat. Worse than that is to have dark hair on your body. Dark, wiry hair runs on both sides of my family. Some of the women even have beards. Add in a big nose and acne too, and I'm at the absolute bottom.

Everyone says I look just like my dad. My dad is always saying he's ugly. If I look like him, I guess that means I am ugly, too. He is not ugly to me, but I know I am ugly because no boys like me. Well, they *like* me okay, but only as a friend. I hate being considered just a friend. I want to be special to someone. I want to matter to someone who matters to me.

Even though all the kids here speak English, many of them speak with an enchanting, lazy, lyrical Valley accent I can't get enough of. Especially the hair-flipping girls who use the word "like" all the time. When I do the accent for my dad at home, I actually make him laugh!

I love to listen in on the popular girls discussing diets I have heard Gail mention—the Pritikin diet; the Carnation canned shake and cereal bars diet; the Beverly Hills diet, with only fruit for lunch; Weight Watchers, where you get points and weigh yourself every day; and the craziest of them all, a diet where you only eat cookies! "If cookies are two hundred calories apiece, and you can only eat a thousand calories a day, then you will still lose weight if you only eat five cookies every day," says the highlighter queen who is currently on the Beverly Hills diet, sucking down pineapple spears. "That's just basic math."

Of course, I'd like to chime in on some of the conversations to keep listening to their lilts, but I am way too insecure about my hideous 3-D zits. I wish I could wear something backless or sleeveless or strapless like they all do. I wish I had a "hot beach bod" like they all do.

I get so jealous when I hear them talk about eating dinner at the table or getting taken to restaurants or having their parents' help with homework or getting an allowance. I am jealous of their family vacations and second homes in Aspen or Vail or Jackson Hole, their predictable schedules and screening rooms and floor tickets to athletic events and reliable live-in help and two sets of grandparents who also love and help them like on TV or in the movies. It makes me wonder what it's like to feel wanted by everybody, like Sam and Kim. And my dad.

THANKFULLY MY DAD IS HOME right now for a little while, so there is a small buffer to Gail's anger. This time he's returned with cool new music for me to listen to—Lene Lovich, the Mo-Dettes, Gang of Four, Nina Hagen, Yello, and a band he absolutely loves and thinks I will, too—the B-52's. The cover of their album has two silly boys like my brothers and two cool girls with beehive hairdos. They sing hilarious songs seriously with completely unusual but beautiful harmonies, including one called "Rock Lobster." Listening to the music he brought for me makes me feel special and happy and gives me a feeling of closeness to him even though we don't listen to it together. He also gives me some super-embarrassing stickers that say "Stiff Records—if it ain't Stiff it ain't worth a fuck," which I put in a drawer.

The albums are a lifesaver. At school, the new music has given me a bit of cachet with a couple of artsy seniors, who perform a "ballet" in a baby pool full of oatmeal in the school courtyard to a B-52's song. At home, I listen to the songs over and over again, memorize and sing along to the lyrics, and dance-bounce on my mini trampoline. I love to lip-synch and look at myself in the mirror, daydreaming about Christopher Atkins, Billy Idol, Matt Dillon, and Adam Ant.

Then another miracle: I am seated at the kitchen table admiring several fancy invitations with my name and home address in luscious cursive on thick paper in envelopes lined in blue and silver and gold. Gail is taking a break and playing solitaire across from me. Even though I am ugly and not popular, somehow I'm invited to a bunch of the Bar and Bat Mitzvahs of both the popular kids and the not-sos.

The Bar Mitzvahs have two parts to them, the service at a temple and the party after. The service always concludes with bread and wine for everyone, even kids, and the evening party always has a band or DJ, portable dance floor, heat lamps, flowers, and catered food with separate tables for adults and kids, at their house or in the ballroom of a hotel. This is where I really see firsthand what kids my age are into—the girls reapply lip gloss in the hotel bathroom and gossip about the boys, who drink as much alcohol as they can poach before sneaking off to chuck egg bread at the heads of the swans swimming in the man-made "lake." I love all the dancing, though. Especially when the DJ plays "New Wave" and all the KROQ bands I like. KROQ is THE radio station in LA, the one that makes or breaks artists. Especially Jed the Fish and his morning show. We all go crazy for Oingo Boingo's "Only a Lad," the Knack's "My Sharona," "Whip It" by Devo, and a popular single from Europe I adore called "Ça Plane Pour Moi."

At one boy's house deep in the heart of Encino, his post-service celebration turns into a huge block party where kids who did not get invited to his Bar Mitzvah swarm his cul-de-sac and commingle with us, bringing kegs and pot, both of which I have no interest in, just like my father. It is there, in the spontaneous Mardi Gras by the light of a streetlamp, under a light-polluted but starry San Fernando Valley sky, that I very briefly meet a bubbly extrovert with the craziest Valley accent I have ever heard. The talkative blonde is wearing a white blouse, matching white miniskirt, and gold headband like a halo, and speaking so fast and so strangely about so many unrelated things, she might as well be hiccupping feathers. I am mesmerized.

This girl sonically and comically stands out to me in a sea of visual noise and then, like a comet, is gone.

I have no idea this is a glass-slipper moment.

I leave the Bar Mitzvah party that night having no clue that I, too, have celebrated the holy transition and become a thirteen-year-old adult.

CHAPTER 20

A Plan

When I think back to the dad void and the endless deserts of time that stretched in every direction in my luminous father's absence, I touch the old pain I imagine the five of us all felt. Without Frank around, I saw Gail, Dweezil, Diva, Ahmet, and myself as insects suspended in amber or stuck like statues in a cruel game of freeze tag, waiting for him to return and say "unfreeze." That way, we could come back to life again. Or maybe I was alone in this. No one ever said.

For now it's 1981, and I am so happy Frank is still home, even though we all fall into our familiar routine with military precision— the pharaoh lifestyle where my father is at the top of the pyramid. I don't question it aloud or push back yet; it's just how things are done. Even Diva, who is only two, gets that we all have to be quiet all day so Frank can sleep until 5 p.m., then we are allowed to see him while he eats his breakfast in bed that I've helped prepare—usually scrambled eggs covered in cayenne, buttered toast, a side of pancakes with real maple syrup, fresh pressed orange juice, and an espresso. After his breakfast he gets up and goes to work all night in the basement as Dweezil, Ahmet, Diva, and I eat our dinner in front of the TV or out of sync with one another. Gail eats standing up or in motion, or snacks on what everyone else doesn't eat as she and I load the dishwasher. I wish we ate meals together as a family. Frank and Gail never sit at the table or in front of the TV with us. I especially wish we could go to Benihana and Lawry's like other kids talk about doing with their families, so I could see an onion volcano or try scampi and pasta primavera or whatever it is they serve.

Monday through Friday, leaving Frank alone is sort of easy because my brothers and I miss most of his day by being at school. During school holidays or on the weekends it's a lot harder, because we want to play and laugh and invite friends over during daylight and see Frank. Sometimes it feels like we have all been sent to our rooms 24/7/365. I am starting to wonder if you can die from nonstop working. I overheard someone on a TV show say, "No one looks back on their life and wishes they spent more time at the office." But whoever said that hadn't met my father.

To offset the isolation, I sometimes get dropped off at a mall called the Galleria, and I ride the escalator and people-watch and window-shop at Judy's and eat corn dogs or see movies with my friends. At home I hide out in my room and listen to records, read books, watch a ton of movies on Z Channel, watch "videos" on a new music channel called MTV, or pick through Gail's vast magazine collection. She has everything from *Interior Design* to *Seventeen*, *National Geographic* to *Kerrang!*, *Mad* to *Vogue*, and everything in between. Gail calls it "research" and "a tax write-off." Frank calls it "getting trapped in print material." Dweezil and I even write a song called "My Mother Is a Space Cadet" because Gail is so unreachable with something glossy folded in her lap.

I love it when my dad surprises us by coming upstairs to grab a hunk of frozen Sara Lee pound cake or cook something for himself. Even though he does not offer me any or sit at the table with me, I watch everything he does whenever I see him. Here is what I know about my dad so far:

My dad is shy and depressed. Shy because he is not good at talking about his feelings and he always makes jokes or cuts conversations short if anyone gets emotional. Depressed because he sleeps a lot, never

smiles, never plays with us, and always complains about people not taking him seriously, respecting him, playing his music on the radio, or
paying him enough money. He is also quiet and impatient and always
wants you to stop crying and feel better right away or just not bother
him with it. It is hard to tell which one, because in both cases the result
is the same—him in his room alone ASAP, and you alone in yours.

I also know Frank loves to make fun of people. He hates people who say "nucular" instead of "nuclear" or "supposably" instead
of "supposedly." Gail and Frank are both sticklers about this kind
of stuff. Frank drinks a minimum of twelve cups of espresso a day.
Frank points out most people say "expresso" instead of "espresso."

What I know about me is I want to do stuff with him and he
doesn't want to do stuff with me. He really likes it when I do my
surfer voice or impersonate the girls from my school or the ultra-
spacey one from that Bar Mitzvah in Encino. He lives to work. So . . .
I get an idea.

I grab a blue Bic and write the following on white, lined school
paper:

Dear Daddy,
Hi I'm 13 years old. My name is Moon. Up until now I
have been trying to stay out of your way while you record.
However, I have come to the conclusion that I would love
to sing on your album, if you would like to put up with me.
I have a rather nice voice. For further information, contact
my agent Gail Zappa at 6504947. I'm available day or night,
generally speaking. I would love to do my "Encino Accent"
or "Surfer Dood Talk" for you. Later Days Dood!!
Love, Moon, xxxooo.

Then I run down the stairs, slip it under his studio door, and race
back to my room to do my homework and help Gail with absolutely
everything.

CHAPTER 21

Valley Girl

Moon," says my father, shaking me awake on a school night. I have a brief *What now?* reaction, then see he is in a good mood. "Come downstairs," he says. "We're gonna record a song."

🌐

I AM STILL GROGGY, WITH unbrushed teeth, as I follow my father to the studio and the soundproof vocal booth. I slip on the headphones and he adjusts the mic to my height. It's starting to dawn on me—he read my letter, we are doing my idea, it's actually happening.

"You're just going to talk and improvise as that funny voice," he says.

"Okay," I say, like we do this all the time.

Then he exits the booth and heads for his state-of-the-art control room. From there he makes sure I can hear him in both ears, that I can hear myself and the track, that the levels are right, and that I can see him from where I am standing when he gives me his hand signals. "Listen first so you can hear where you'll come in, between the choruses." Then my ears are flooded with the instantly catchy bass line. I "hear/see" the talking section as a bracketed space I am supposed to stay inside of before and after the shorter sections where the band sings, "Valley girl, she's a Valley girl . . ."

I smile and I feel a swell of happy energy. He really *did* listen to me.

I easily jump into the character I do that he likes. I exaggerate the way girls at my school speak and just imagine what they would talk about, blended with riffing on my own experiences in my house. My dad snort-laughs from the control room after the first take, then asks me to extrapolate on the stuff he remembers me saying that he thinks is funny. "Say more about the cat box."

"Okay," I say, laughing too.

"Talk about bagging your face," he says. "Try to work in 'gag me with a spoon.'"

"Got it." I find it fun and easy to pretend I am this other person and just make up something silly on the spot. I also enjoy the fun challenge of trying to include his requests in a natural way. It is a form of acting. I feel playful and professional, seen and heard. I let myself say anything that comes to mind.

"Throw in a 'tubular,'" he says. I do. And so it goes, me blabbing on and on in a stream-of-consciousness way and my father laughing and urging me on with his little prompts. Bass line, bracket, chorus, bracket, chorus, bracket, outro, pause, prompt, repeat . . .

Then he makes a hand motion that lets me know it's done, we got it. Then I hear his voice in my ears asking me to come into the control room to hear a rough version from start to finish. Then a hug. It all goes by in a blink. Then I am back upstairs in my bed wishing we could keep recording and that the hug lasted forever.

CHAPTER 22

Alliance vs. Acne

O ur house is under construction. We are building a new kitchen for Gail where our front yard used to be, Diva's room is my old room, and my new room is my parents' old bedroom. I love my parents' old bathroom because it has a heat lamp, a skylight, wood paneling, and a Jacuzzi bathtub. It also has two mirrors that when angled just so allow me to see my profile, which is convenient for seeing the acne on the sides of my face and on my back. I am standing at the mirror when Gail enters my room without knocking.

"Here," says Gail angrily, placing an already opened box on the bathroom counter.

The box is addressed to me from Europe. No name, no return address, and full of yummy-smelling German organic skin products designed to treat acne. "I don't know anyone in Europe," I say, and I certainly don't know anyone there who knows about me and how bad my skin is.

"*Gerda* sent this to you."

My skin sizzles and my ears turn hot. I stare at Gail, telepathically screaming: *Germany Gerda? The problematic Eurocunt my dad keeps going back to?*

"You can keep it if you want," says Gail, which means I definitely can't keep it. If I keep it, it means I am betraying my mother and choosing my father and his shitty cheating choices over her. But if I choose Gail, I unchoose myself. Doesn't Gail understand I really need for my skin to clear up if I am ever going to like myself?

I am very confused and conflicted.

But then I remember my place and that my allegiance to Gail is more important than my concern for myself. I look into Gail's eyes. They are reptilian half slits. "I would never keep anything from *her*," I say, and I pick the box up and drop it into the garbage can under the sink. Then I hug her. Her arms remain stiff at her sides, her body as rigid as the concrete foundation pillars in our front yard.

When Gail leaves I feel weird, because my dad must have told Gerda how bad my skin is. Which is mortifying. Is he embarrassed by me, or does he care about me? Why has he never talked to me about my skin or tried to help me himself? Why does my own mother, who lives with me, who sees me every day, not try to help me? Why is a lady Gail hates, a lady I have never met, who lives far away, trying to help? Does the lady care because she's nice or because she wants me to like her and hate Gail? Is she trying to send a message to my dad? I can't help myself. I pull the box out of the garbage.

There is a cool crystal deodorant in the box. I have never seen anything like it before. The cleansers and creams are all natural and smell fresh and floral and herby and foreign. Everything in the box from Gerda smells so good. I desperately want to try everything, but of course I know I can't. I give everything a final smell, then throw it all in the trash a second time, in honest solidarity with my mother.

CHAPTER 23

Tampons Require Instructions

I follow Gail toward a building. The scent of big yellow flowers overhead pulls my attention to tall magnolia trees planted in a row.

She swings a glass door open. I love the clack of her platform shoes on the sidewalk and the different sounds they make on the marble of the air-conditioned lobby.

"It would help if you washed your hands and hair more," she says without looking back at me. She presses the up button next to a fern in a yellow pot painted with two Chinese dogs. "The oil and dirt from your scalp and hands sit on your skin."

"Sorry," I say.

I stare down at the ground.

❂

"YOUR SKIN IS AN ORGAN," says the ancient little man my mother brought me to see. He makes slow movements with his hands, like he is scooping air and pushing it around him. He makes shoving gestures at me. His fingers are bent like mannequin hands. "The organ of your skin is spread out across the land of your body. Like your inside organs, the lungs or liver or heart, the skin is always taking in what is around it."

My skin is an organ? I try to grasp this idea.

His office has a paper screen with bamboo designs, and I can hear the sound of running water and the street sounds outside. There are paper scrolls on the wall with red edging and black writing, framed certificates of his education, wind chimes, and shelves holding clear jars of herbs and roots and leaves. I am sitting on a massage table. My feet don't touch the floor. Gail is sitting in a chair in the corner next to a rubber tree. No lamps are on, just natural light.

His accent is thick and hard to understand, but his eyes twinkle with steely intelligence, willing me to comprehend. "Pollution goes in your skin and into your nose and lungs," he adds, "and your skin filters it out. If you eat junk food, your skin filters it out. Your body makes anger. Too much fire element. Do you understand?"

I nod, hoping that's what Gail wants me to do.

"Take off your shirt," he says.

I look at Gail with wide eyes. I have never had my shirt off around a boy or a man I don't know, just my dad and brothers, and only by accident or if I am changing into or out of my bathing suit. My heartbeat speeds up and my breathing stops. But this man is old and Gail is here, so I guess it is all right.

I turn my back to him and pull my shirt up. He pulls it up higher and secures it over the back of my head. I cover my boobs and hunch my back. I feel his old, dry hands on my oily lumps and bony back. He presses into my skin with little strokes and firm little shoves. "No, no masturbation," he says.

What? I think. *I have* never *and would never! How* dare *he think that about me. Screw this guy.* I pull my shirt back on, furious and embarrassed.

"Drink water," he says. "And I will give you a tea to drink here and at home." He scurries to a little cupboard, blends some of this and a little of that, then comes back with a plastic bag full of what looks and smells like twigs and dirt and rotting leaves. Then he scurries over to a tall thermos, pumps a bit of steaming brown liquid into a little cup, and returns to hand it to me. "Drink. Drink," he says. "Special tea."

I smell it and recoil, then look at Gail's disapproving face, which signals: "Drink it, Moon, we have come all this way. For *you*." I swallow it down and gag, but I do not barf. I am very good at not wasting anyone's time.

ON THE DRIVE HOME I rest my head on the car windowsill, feeling the air on my face, until the nausea and humiliation pass. As we turn onto our street I excitedly say, "I forgot to tell you, Judy's boyfriend came to school."

"Who is Judy?" she asks, turning into our driveway. She clicks the remote. The white metal garage door squeaks and lifts. Gail drives in.

Huh, I think, *how does she not know? Doesn't she ever listen to me?* "Judy is my jazz dance teacher. He's a dancer, too. They met doing dance together. He's very well hung."

"What?" says Gail, erupting in laughter. I don't know what is so funny. "What do you mean?" She puts the car in park.

I've done something wrong, but I don't know what. "I mean he was, you know . . . nice, friendly, well hung, polite . . . ," I say, frowning. "He had good manners."

"Oh," she says, turning off the ignition. "That's not what 'well hung' means. Moon," Gail says in a voice I don't recognize. My stomach seizes. "I spoke to your dad, and we think maybe it's time to get you a diaphragm and your own apartment."

"What?" I say. "Ew!" Why does she want me to move out? Why does *he*?

"Now that you've started high school, you're going to start to want to . . ."

Because of *sex*? SEX? That disgusting thing *they* do? I would *never ever*. "EW!" I shriek, undoing my seat belt.

"It's not *ew*. I found your underwear." My face burns. She means my period underwear. I have been hiding them under my desk. "Why didn't you tell me?"

I start crying. "Because you're *mean*!" I scream. Then I open the car door.

Gail grabs my arm and squeezes. "Do *not* get hysterical with me, young lady, just because you don't like the information I am imparting. These things must be said."

"Not if they're *mean* they don't!"

"That's your warped perception," she hisses.

I glare daggers at her. "Can I get out of the car now?" I yank my arm away. I'm on my feet now where she can't touch me.

"Do you not know how to use a tampon?"

"I *have* been using tampons! They don't even work."

She looks confused. "*How* have you been using them? Do you insert them?"

"What do you mean?" I say angrily. I sneak three out of every full box, so Gail can't tell they've gone missing, and use them sparingly. Afterward, when I am done, I wrap them in toilet paper and shove them deep into the garbage so Gail and our maid Conchita can't find them, but I sure as hell am not telling *her* that.

"Yes. I take them out of the package and lay them in sideways. But . . . then the string gets all bloody."

She looks at me with disbelief. "Why didn't you read the directions?"

"The directions weren't in the box! You take them out and throw them away when you tear the top off because you already know how to do it!"

She chews the inside of her lower lip. Her look says she knows

I'm right but won't admit it. She snorts like a bull instead. "The end *without* the string goes inside you."

I stare her down. My face is frozen with hatred and confusion. All I can think as I look at her face is *I wish you were dead.* I slam the car door and run up all our stairs, thinking, *Fuck you, Gail! Fuck you fuck you fuck you infinity fuck you until the end of time.*

"Stop being histrionic!" screams Gail.

"FUCK YOU!" I scream back.

Back in the safety of my bedroom, I head for the bathroom and pick my skin into a bloody frenzy. *Why do they want to get rid of me? If I never have thoughts about boys, can I stay?* I go to town on my face and back and chest. Finally, bloody from self-mutilation and vibrating with fury and anxiety, I flop down on my bed, exhausted. All I can do is cry. No one comes to check on me. After a while I roll onto my back. As my breathing settles, I picture a tampon in my head, focus on the components. The paper barrel applicators that slip inside one another, the small cotton lump with a tail, the dark opening between my legs.

The next time I am in the bathroom I see a new box of tampons by the toilet, with the box top torn off. I notice a slip of white paper inside, alongside all the individually wrapped tampons lined up like soldiers. Gail has left the instructions inside.

"Ohhhhhhh," I say out loud as I read. I was wondering why it had a string.

But what does my period have to do with a diaphragm, an apartment, and sex?

🌐

NOT LONG AFTER, I NOTICE my skin has gotten worse. So much so, my posture has begun to change from all the contortion I do to squeeze the hard-to-reach pustules. My shoulders roll inward, my back rounds. I slouch, which affects my breathing pattern and makes my lower belly protrude. My tears burn my eyes and my open wounds. I cannot hear or say "zits" or "pimples" without my entire being seizing up.

"The nasty tea isn't working," I say to Gail. She's playing solitaire in the kitchen, next to a plate of old spaghetti.

"It isn't working because you aren't drinking it," says Gail, not looking up from her card stacks. She's right. I only had it for a few days, then gave up. I hate that she's right.

"But I don't think that stuff works anyway and it tastes awful. There has to be another way," I say.

She doesn't say anything. The cat makes some retching noises, dry heaves a few times, then hocks up hot, yellow bile. Gail looks back at her cards and keeps playing against herself, so I get a paper towel and watch the liquid spread as I wipe it up. Then I keep standing there, waiting for her to say something or do something.

Silence.

I give up.

CHAPTER 24

Two Besties, One Punk

I'm nearly fourteen. I am so excited because I get to see both of my best friends in the same week. The funny thing is they are both named Karen, but I call the new tomboy one by her nickname so Gail doesn't get confused when I ask for a ride. Old Karen lives in Studio City, Monkey lives very far away, in Encino. Since Gail can't drive me to old Karen's today, she is letting me walk all the way down Laurel Canyon Boulevard by myself even though there are no sidewalks on some parts of the road. It is my first time walking a mile alone; in fact, it's my first time doing anything outside of my house all by myself. I'm scared but excited. I do my hair in a side braid to go with my Val Surf half shirt, yellow dolphin shorts with built-in underwear, purple Vans, and felted pig purse.

Gail says, "Watch out for flashers and perverts."

"I know," I say.

Karen and her family are all "gingers" from England, and like me she is the oldest of her siblings. When she lived on my street, we'd ride the school bus together, then watch after-school specials about bulimia, PCP, and bed-wetting. Or we'd overdose on *Little House on the Prairie* since we both loved Matthew Labyorteaux. Now we both love Adam Ant. It is good to have things in common, even if we don't go to the same school or live on the same street anymore.

Sundays are the best days to visit Karen's new house. That's when her mother does a traditional sit-down dinner at 2 p.m., and even better, she cooks the same meal every time—prime rib roast with mint jelly, Yorkshire pudding, peas, potatoes with Bisto gravy, and hot Bird's custard over spongy cake for dessert.

After we eat dinner for lunch, we wait until her mom can drive us to the record store, and we look through her parents' *Playboy*, trying to make sense of why the centerfold women say their weight. I try to picture how much 122 pounds is—four large dog food bags?

Then Karen suggests, "Let's spy on the neighbor boys. If they come out, we should skinny-dip so they can spy on us."

"No way," I laugh. She might be even more boy crazy than me.

Soon her mom calls out, "Girls, get in the car. I can drop you off at Music Plus on my way to Nautilus."

AS WE MOVE ALPHABETICALLY FROM one section of records and cassettes to another, we discuss the whispers at our schools about cherry popping. My old bestie might be ready; no way for Monkey. I think I am somewhere in the middle. I'd like to try kissing first.

During lunch at school, people joke and kiss their closed hands to practice. Kissing with tongues is called "frenching." I have seen it on *General Hospital* with Luke and Laura, and in the best movie in the world, *Little Darlings*. Gail and Frank never french.

I pause at a section dedicated to honky-tonk. I try to make Karen laugh by holding up an album I know she'll hate and loudly saying, "I found the Eddie Rabbitt album you were looking for." She squeals, then grabs one, shouting, "Here's the Falco you want over here." This goes on until we are giddy. Then, a miracle: we spy a boy in the corner who looks just like Adam Ant, only more punk and fifteen.

"Go say hi," says Karen. "You know you want to."

"I don't know . . ."

"Go on," she says, nudging me. "How cool would it be if you frenched someone, and from another school!" I consider her confidence-building idea and stare at the skinny boy in all black with teased-up hair. "And he looks older, too, more mature."

"How does my skin look?" I ask.

"Fine," she says.

I double-check in my compact mirror—my face spackle is holding. Electricity shoots through me. "He is sooooo cute."

"Go on, I dare you. Now is your chance. What if he leaves?"

She's right. I don't want this moment to slip away.

"If you don't say hi, I will."

That does it. Bolstered by competition and my best friend's encouragement, I boldly walk over.

"Hi," I say, staring into the older boy's midnight-colored eyes. "You're really cute."

"Get the fuck away from me, you're so fucking ugly," he snaps back, lightning quick, and resumes his album hunting.

My face burns. My ears turn red. I feel like I might faint, only my feet stay planted to my spot. The punk pirate glares at me. I blink a few times, then pivot as my paralysis wears off. I make my way back to my waiting friend as if walking the plank.

"Well?" she says enthusiastically, all smiles. "What happened?"

"I said he was cute."

"You *did*? Eeeeeee," she squeals. "What did he say?"

"He said . . . thank you."

"That's it?" she says, both of us knowing the timeline doesn't add up.

"Yup." I nod with a knot in my guts. Then we wait for him to leave and walk past Pioneer Chicken to our meeting spot, where Karen's mom is honking for us to get in, and she drives me home.

🌐

THE FOLLOWING SATURDAY I AM sporting black eyeliner and a new, longer-in-the-front, shorter-in-the-back, asymmetrical Vidal Sassoon–adjacent bob courtesy of Supercuts. Gail and I are in a fight because she says I am "too social," so she is taking her time to drive me the thirty-five minutes west to Encino and making me late for a sleepover with my brand-new Karen, a.k.a. Monkey.

In frustration I pop into the studio to say bye to Frank, who's having a photo shoot at the house. "Jump in here, Moon," he says. I don't want to because my skin is bad, but it's my dad and I have not had my photo taken with him since I was nine. I loop my arm around my dad's neck. A few quick snaps of me wearing a plastic bangle and holding my magenta ripper wallet that closes with Velcro, and I am out the door. Little do I know this image will become immortalized as album cover art within the year.

EVERYTHING IN MONKEY'S HOUSE IS the color of lightly toasted bread. It smells like vacuumed carpet and honeysuckle. The lights are off in the rooms they aren't using, and the house feels quiet even though music is on. Monkey's mother has a soft voice that sounds like the padding in a jewelry box even when she sweetly tells us the bad news: "I'm so sorry, girls, but your friend Greg has died in a traffic accident."

This is the first death of someone I know who is my age. I picture him making "okay" fingers and flipping them upside down and covering his eyes like they're weird sunglasses and chanting "Oy-ty oyt!" on the 88 bus line from the Galleria to the beach. Our friend being dead makes no sense. He is a popular, comedic boy. "Was" is hard to wrap my mind around. My brain is a swirling snow globe, searching for meaning where there is none. If he could die, any kid could, including me. I feel a tidal wave of anxiety, like strangling, too-thick seaweed I have to swim through.

Monkey's mom gives us both hugs *and* asks us if there's anything we need. I am astounded by her concern. She makes us a snack plate. Then "Tainted Love" by Soft Cell comes on the radio! I can't believe how terrible things and lucky things are happening at the same time, and I can't believe how much I love this song.

As the music plays, Monkey and I take turns climbing into a sleeping bag and sliding down her family's carpeted indoor stairs and giving each other Indian burns, and soon we're jumping and dancing around like everything is fine and no one in the world ever dies.

Later that night, her dad and older sister come home, and we all sit in the hot tub. I can't imagine spending this much time with my family. Then they talk to each other about school and camping and things they read or think about and look at the stars in the sky. Everything here in Encino feels safe. I kind of want to cry because I'm so jealous. But I don't. I just try to enjoy the feeling.

In the morning I can smell food coming from the kitchen. Monkey's mom has baked a puffy, homemade apple pancake in a cast-iron pan. It is ready and waiting for us in the oven when we come downstairs. The table is set. Her family eats with place mats and forks and knives and spoons in the right place. And no one is yelling. Then, after breakfast, "Mad World" by Tears for Fears, which I like even better than "Tainted Love," comes on the radio, and we laugh and dance some more. Then we ride bikes to the Thinnery for a slushy chocolate-ice milkshake that only has ten calories. I can't believe how lucky Monkey is all the time, and I can't believe how lucky I am to know her.

Afterward, Gail picks me up with big sunglasses and unbrushed hair and no makeup, and I go back to my family's world, where everything is a mess, I feel unlucky, and nothing makes sense.

IT'S DUSK WHEN I FIND Gail in my parents' room on her back, crying. I am scared. Gail never cries. She screams but never cries. "Gail," I say, "what's wrong?"

"Nothing," she says, but the tears keep coming. The anguish is clear.

"Something's definitely wrong," I say.

"Your dad doesn't love me."

What a thought! You can't unlove a person you know you love! "Yes, he does love you," I pronounce with certainty.

"No," she snaps, "he doesn't, he *told* me." She rolls away from me, onto her side. I am flooded with anger at my dad for hurting Gail. I put my hand on her back to soothe her. Her body is hot and the bed is wet.

"Well, *I* love you," I say. Gail wails and shudders and burbles on, smothering her cries in a pillow. "Did you hear me, Gail? I love you." She continues convulsing. I don't understand. Why isn't this working? Why isn't she feeling better from what I am saying? "I love you and I always will," I reassure her. Gail's body shakes and tightens. I am terrified and furious with Frank for putting her in this state. "I love you," I say again. I wrap my arms around her, curl my body into a C to match her shape, but nothing shifts. Isn't my love enough? Why isn't my love filling her up? Why isn't my love enough? Isn't love a fire or a sun that never burns out? How can mean words about love destroy her but kind ones do nothing?

I kiss her and hug her with all my might. I summon everything I am. "I love you, Gail," I say again. I say it like an incantation, a prayer, a white-magic spell that breaks all black-magic ones for good.

Nothing.

Gail is inconsolable and can only limply pat my hand.

"If Frank doesn't love you, then I don't love him," I say. "It's as simple as that."

—

CHAPTER 25

Leave No Trace

It's 1982. Frank is away again, I'm fourteen, and my heart is a closed fist. The house feels as isolated as Alcatraz. Maybe that's because Gail has installed cameras, an alarm system, and actual salvaged jail bars for our front gate. In spite of the fact that we now have trip wire beams and cameras to see whoever wants to be buzzed in, there is no safety, rest, or refuge for me at home or in the outer world, except for the occasional feral fun with my inmate siblings or a jailbreak sleepover.

Gail and Frank have started a new record label and mail-order company called Barking Pumpkin Records, so she's busier, more scattered, more stressed out, and angrier than ever. I hate that our house is a place of business as well as a house. The workday never ends and the barrage of work clutter is mixed with the clutter of daily life, and all of it is littered on every table, chair, stool, desk, staircase, and sofa. Everywhere you look is a teetering pile of something with a logo, potential album artwork, previous releases, vinyl, cassettes, videos, boxes, packing tape, bubble wrap, stickers, T-shirts, bumper stickers, posters, postcards, fan mail, inquiries, and legal letters, next to dirty dishes, cat food, coffee cups, ashtrays, open containers of food, spices, oil, cooking utensils, laundry, toys, books, and homework. All is tangled, claustrophobic, and all-consuming.

With the construction going on, I am sleeping on a single bed in the room where we keep the freezer. Since the freezer is where we keep the ice cream and Popsicles, it's Grand Central—I have no privacy or rest, just arctic blasts of cold when someone tries to combat the California heat or fill the void of loneliness with a sweet, frozen mouth hug. I don't have the words or skill to express the panic swirling inside of me. No one does. Instead we all lean on silence and excessive consumption of all things greasy, fatty, sugary, processed, and caffeinated.

THE CLEANEST ROOM IN THE house is my father's studio—it's only packed full with instruments. But they stand in orderly rows. Sometimes I sneak into the vocal booth when Frank is away, or after school when he's home and still asleep. There I scream as long and as loud as I can until I am hoarse and overheated.

To complicate matters, I am really missing my father. I don't want to, but I do. We never go visit him on tour; he seems to be away longer than he's here with us and he never calls home. Or if he does call, I never get to say hello. Even though this is how it is in my family, I don't like it. I can never tell if my dad is sad about it, too. My guess is no, because this is what keeps on happening.

I come to understand that going "independent" is very risky because you are responsible for every artistic and practical choice, employee, and unexpected problem, and all of the debt. Now that Gail is managing my dad and running Barking Pumpkin Records, I feel the constant pull of her unspoken expectations even more.

I am angry about the burdens that fall on me just because I was born first and born a girl, but also incredibly worried about Gail, so I ignore my feelings and instead think of ways to help. I watch her trying to feel better by controlling everything. I hate when I see Frank take her for granted and I hate that she allows it.

The truth is, as angry as I am at Frank, I miss how he makes us all laugh by making fun of whatever is happening in the world. Right now he hates televangelists, so I do, too. He says they are charlatans who swindle idiots by saying they are the only ones who can interpret the Bible. I don't tell him I feel sorry for people who get fooled, or that in spite of her weird look, Tammy Faye seems genuinely nice.

The stuff my dad likes on TV is the news, Elvira, all Godzilla and monster movies, and a woman on public access who is obsessed with Rick James and only reviews ambrosia salad and other vegetarian dishes. When my dad is home, I still help Gail with the day-to-day stuff—answering the phone and taking messages; washing and putting away dishes; separating the mountains of wash into colors, loading the machines, then folding the laundry; feeding the pets and cleaning the litter box; taking out the trash; cleaning out the fridge; making school lunches for me and my brothers; wiping down countertops; staying on top of what's getting low in stock; and ordering from Chalet Gourmet or Greenblatt's, then carrying endless bags of groceries up our crazy flights of stairs, then putting it all away. All this on top of watching my siblings and doing my schoolwork.

Sometimes the fun I have with my brothers and sister is swimming, and sometimes it's making prank calls and getting Diva, who is now three, to ask, "Do you have Prince Albert in a can? Well, let him out!" Dweezil and Ahmet don't know I secretly push the switch hook down and only pretend to be rude to strangers when it's my turn. I never want anyone to feel hurt or bad since I absolutely hate how that feels.

I love when Diva sings songs wrong, like "Dirty deeds dunderchief," instead of AC/DC's "Dirty Deeds Done Dirt Cheap." I also love to give her a bath and sing the songs we learned from Gail, like the bouncing pony ride carnival song, and, of course, I love drawing with her and looking at the art she makes, and reading our favorite books to her and Dweezil and Ahmet.

If I am honest, it's hard for me to keep my promise to myself and to Gail to hate my father and only love my mother, especially on the days

Gail takes everything out on me. Instead of blaming her, I learn to blame myself. After all, I am the one who swore total allegiance to her.

Then, a miracle occurs: I get the chance to go on a school field trip to briefly get away from everything. Five whole days observing marine life up close in the Marin Headlands. My first time in nature, and for this long. My first time away from my family, my first time away from everything familiar. My first time away all by myself.

"CRATERS ON THE MOON!" SOME of the mean boys shout as we board the chartered bus. I just ignore them. Our stinky bus spits black smoke into the already smoggy air and heads north on the 5 freeway. Six hours later, the boys and girls are divided among two beige rectangular buildings that smell like seaweed, mildew, and almond-scented soap. I take a lower bunk in the squelchy girls' dormitory and settle in.

I un-Velcro my magenta ripper wallet to remove a men's magazine tear-out. I unfold the glossy image for the four hundredth time. The dark-haired boy with the crew cut, shirtless and lithe from water sports, has appeared in *Seventeen* magazine alongside my favorite female models, tomboyish, fresh-faced Tara Fitzpatrick and blond, vaguely androgynous Bonnie Berman with a cleft in her chin. The all-American brunet hunk is more handsome than the popular, dreamy Perry Ellis model, maybe even as handsome as my other impossible megacrush, Matt Dillon. I tape my aspirational stranger near the knots and whorls of the wooden ceiling of my bunk bed. My friends are jealous and impressed by my forethought in bringing something from home to decorate my bed. I kiss my finger and plant it on his tiny, shining face. "Michael Schoeffling," I whisper to myself with a longing sigh.

During the day, I carry the male model around in a waterproof plastic pencil bag as we hike along coastal ridges, watch whales migrate, and study tide pools teeming with life. A sign on the trail reads "Leave No Trace."

By day three with my dreamboat in my pocket and no contact home, I feel an unexpected, totally foreign freedom and upliftment I have never had before, which completely decimates all my troubles. I get a small, intoxicating taste of happiness.

By days four and five of strenuous, long-distance walking, even the model can't compete with the clean air and my headful of inspirational discussions about early life-forms, topography, anatomy, and the difference between fast-twitch and slow-twitch muscles. I am years away from realizing this feeling is pleasure and that relief and peace come from being immersed in nature.

The last night, we watch slideshows about pollution and its impact on the environment, and marvel at how protozoan-inhabited ocean water lights up Day-Glo green when stirred and viewed in the dark. When we rally around a campfire to make s'mores and stargaze, and the popular girls sneak off to kiss the popular boys, I feel thoroughly immune to jealousy.

When I get home, the high from my trip is subsumed by my father's return. Life immediately rushes in and takes the solidity of my happy experience with it. Then, when I do the wash, I forget to take my ripper wallet out of my pants and my prize photo takes a beating. I am oddly devastated, unaware it is a placeholder for a different grief. I keep my disproportionate wallowing to myself, rush to my room, close the door, and cry into my pillow until it is soaked. I am puffy faced and red eyed when there's a knock on my door. It's my dad. "I'm gonna put the song on the record," says Frank with an expression I clock as mild excitement. He means the one we recorded in the basement a while back. "The album title is *Ship Arriving Too Late to Save a Drowning Witch*."

"Cool," I say. It hadn't occurred to me to hope the recording would go any farther than the fun time I spent with him. He doesn't notice I have been crying. Or if he does, he has no reaction.

—

CHAPTER 26

The Plan Has a Plan of Its Own

That was Moon Unit Zappa doing 'Valley Girl' with her father, Frank Zappa." My favorite radio personality, Jed the Fish on KROQ, just said my name, and now everything in the carpool lane is in slow motion—I can see other kids in their parents' cars hearing it, too. Some that I know look back at me and smile or give me the "hang loose" or heavy metal "righteous" fingers. Others on the sidewalk stare at me when I get out of the car. They see me and look away, but I can tell from their body language I am now on their radar. Gail pulls into position to let us out. Dweezil and I gather our books and lunches.

At my locker I am suddenly ambushed by the most popular brunette in my grade and her two blond shadows, all in matching home-cropped, off-the-shoulder *Flashdance* sweatshirts and legs-for-days shorty shorts. "I didn't know your family was rich!" she says, beaming. "I was at Tower Records and they were playing your song in the store and I went to the Z section. Your dad has a lot of albums so you must have a lot of money!" It is the first time she's talked to me on purpose. I have no idea how to respond, so I stare at her mole. I am pretty sure we are not rich. I think I would know if we were. How does she not realize having a song get played on the radio is totally different from having money? More importantly, how is she so popular with a mole that big?

Nothing in this world makes sense.

Before I can graciously exit this awkward conversation, she continues. "What kind of car does your dad drive?"

"Uh . . . he doesn't drive," I say.

"Wow!" she says. "That is the richest you can be." Her chesty followers nod in collective awe. First bell rings. "See ya," she says with chirpy San Fernando warmth, then they all pop Hubba Bubba in their mouths, wave, and move on.

WITHIN DAYS GAIL EXPLAINS TO me that "Valley Girl" has gotten so much surprise radio airplay that my father and I have to divide and conquer the promotional opportunities. Since Frank is away touring overseas, I have to do the bulk of the US press by myself. I feel the panic rising. I am a shy teen with terrible acne and I am expected to talk to adults *and* appear on camera. I feel frozen with dread.

My real, regular friends are excited for me, but the song is no big deal. They are used to me making them laugh, so it makes sense to them that I have the ability to make other people around the world laugh, too. Me? I'm freaked out. I didn't realize that this fun, personal thing would become so public. I do not like having strangers' attention on me. I do not want a spotlight. No one checks to see if I am okay with all of this. No one lays out any clear picture for me. No time frame or strategy is discussed. I am just told when my next interview is and thrown onto a one-person luge.

To complicate matters, I am still mad at Frank for hurting Gail, but Gail hasn't left him, so what *exactly* is my responsibility to her, Frank, and the family here? Now, whenever Gail speaks about her feelings about Frank these days, she reframes their married life as a "cottage industry," in essence a business arrangement, to keep us all together as a family. She makes it sound like she's become Zen about his cheating and *prefers* her new role. "He always comes home to me," she says with a mixture of pride and power.

Throughout the "Valley Girl" promotion I learn to compartmentalize my interactions with my father as part of "the family business" of keeping his career going, of keeping the family together. I try not to have too much fun, lest I show a lack of loyalty to Gail. Secretly I love every second with Frank, but sometimes I want to scream *I just want to be a kid!* But that ship had sailed and I know I have no choice but to defer to the adults and the publicist.

As my TV appearances and newspaper and magazine interviews are scheduled, I'm inundated with spots with morning radio DJs around the country that always end with me speaking like a Valley girl for their station IDs. I hate it. From big-shot stations to tiny college outlets I have never heard of and everything in between, the song starts getting even more attention. I start to get fan mail! Most of it is from girls my age from suburbs everywhere, letting me know about their local versions of vapid airheads in their hometowns. Then letters start coming in from as far away as the Soviet Union, Australia, and Japan. Long, handwritten letters also come from prison inmates, which scare me.

I really feel the strangeness when my father flies home to travel to New York with me to do *Late Night with David Letterman*. I have never heard of the guy, so I do not know about his reputation for one-upmanship, snubbing lame guests, and cracking wise, and I am not intimidated in the least. David Letterman lobs his direct questions couched in humorous potential–put-down territory while my dad looks on, and I simply answer back, unaware I am toggling among precocious, clueless, and performing monkey.

On the flight home from JFK to LA with my dad, our plane is tossed about in my first taste of rough turbulence during a lightning storm. I am terrified. When I turn to my father and tell him I am scared, he says, "Don't think about it," and puts a blanket over his head and goes to sleep. This is a distinct moment when I realize this is who my dad really is. He will turn his attention outward, but only when required.

⊕

AFTER MY LETTERMAN APPEARANCE, I am somehow lauded by adults and strangers for being funny and holding my own opposite the handsome comic with the gap in his teeth. When I watch the clip as an adult, I see a frightened girl parroting her father, people-pleasing like a motherfucker, and trying not to let anyone down. All I remember thinking at the time is *Why does everyone keep asking me how much money I am making?*

People begin to tell Gail that I could parlay my exposure into achieving my dream of acting. Suggestions are made regarding the best West Coast acting teachers—Peggy Feury and her husband, Bill, or maybe Lynette Katselas. We are also told improv class with Helaine Lembeck is a must because I am naturally funny.

I am thrilled.

But there is a strange shift, rift, and divide happening between my mother and me. In between interviews or when Gail is overwhelmed by organizing a calendar for people to have their chance to adore me, I notice Gail getting more impatient with me instead of more and more proud. On several occasions she is quick to remind me, "I am the only reason your father gave you credit on the album and the only reason you are getting any money."

"You mean you filled out the paperwork?" I naively ask the first time.

"No," she hisses, "Frank didn't want to give you any writing or performing credit, period. Earth to Moon, improvisation isn't writing." This on the way to an improv class. Or a talk show or a photo shoot where I'll be fussed over and she won't.

I am devastated, of course, and bewildered. Does Frank really think so little of my efforts? What are all my efforts for, then? When my dad makes things up, isn't that writing? And improvisation? How is mine not? Is that *really* what he said or what Gail wants me to *think* he said so I stay aligned with her? Is it normal to have to wonder all these things about your parents?

The song gets nominated for a Grammy. I attend the awards ceremony without my father and we lose to Survivor's "Eye of the Tiger," but I am the only one there to feel disappointed and humiliated.

I try to hold the paradox of being told at home by the nearest and dearest to my heart that my contribution means nothing while the world sees me as clever and funny and talented.

This will take many steady years of therapy to untangle.

Upon reflection, what seems far more honest and likely is I had raw skill in my own right with no support or nurturance at home, and maybe both of my parents were mad and jealous for different reasons. My father for being forty-three years of age with thirty-five albums to his name and here, with me, having his first mega hit. And, worse, with a lighthearted ditty that in no way reflected the full depth and breadth of his work. Did this make him question his relationship to his music, to aging, to the world, to his money, to his fans, to me? He never said.

For Gail, I think she must have seen me as the one who would always be linked with my father forever. Publicly declared by my father, and the planet, as his partner. Another breadwinner. His blood. And this pushed her into the shadows. Again. She had to make sure I knew my place. The *other* other woman. The one who loved him without exception. The one who wanted nothing from him and took nothing from him. The woman he didn't fuck or fuck over. His daughter. The real one my father would always come back to and never leave.

CHAPTER 27

Household Name

"Earth to Moon, it's for you," says Gail, holding out the phone for me to grab even though the cord stretches to where I am seated at the kitchen table. I stop doing my algebra homework, stand up, eye-roll without her seeing, and think, *If I were Frank or Dweezil she'd walk the phone over to me.* I take another bite of some high-fat, high-sugar, high-carb after-school snack, then grab my plastic egg full of Silly Putty and head for her outstretched hand and impatient face. If I have to be bored on the phone, I can at least make fake, pinkish-beige rubbery fingernails.

In only a few short months, I am already a "household name" and an "old hat" at radio and print interviews as well as the talk show pre-interview, after having appeared on Letterman, Merv Griffin, *Real People*, *Solid Gold*, David Brenner, Rick Dees, Casey Kasem, Dick Clark, and a bunch of local daytime shows from one coast to the other. The pre-interview is designed to create a little day-of-show safety for the host and the guest. No matter who interviews me, they all seem to think they are the first to ask the dumbest shit, or they forget I have probably been asked this stuff a thousand times already or don't care. Still, I do my best to be polite and answer with some friendliness. My father can be very rude, as he is more annoyed and impatient than I am because he has work he'd rather be doing.

As predicted, the stranger rattles off the usual: What was it like growing up with Frank Zappa for a dad? What's your brother's name, Star? How did "Valley Girl" come about? Do you have any fun stories about growing up Zappa? I tell him and anyone else the same thing but try to make it sound fresh or funny or different or like I just thought it up. Like dialogue from a play where they keep recasting the journalist opposite me. Even though I am underwhelmed by the tedious, unoriginal, but perfunctory questions and the lame personalities of whoever I interface with, I remain "professional."

The print interviews and the intros on talk shows link me and my father with words like "nonconformist," "free spirit," "bizarre," "counterculture," "unorthodox," "unique," "offbeat," "eccentric," "close-knit," and "far out." I know some of my stale stories still get a big reaction—like the one about the Kiwi groupie moving in, or the me-missing-my-dad-and-sliding-the-note-under-his-door story, or the "unconventional" parenting story about the time Gail handcuffed me and Dweezil together by the ankles, recorded our fight, and played it back for us. Each time I retell my repertoire of "shocking crowd-pleasers" or I "do the voice" on command, I just feel gross.

After I hang up, I admire my rubbery nail extensions and sigh, knowing I must do it all again for the real show, only funnier and less robotic. Then I squish my fake nails back into a ball and back into the plastic egg.

Day of show, the stage is always cold, the sets are always ugly, and the lights are always hot. The makeup "base" is always thick, and almost every makeup "artist" paints two dark lines down the sides of my nose to make it look "less ethnic." After that, every zit and red splotch is spackled with yellow concealer, then powdered to take away the shine. Next my hazel eyes get the "natural look," with my lids and creases brushed and blended with smoky browns, golds, and rusts, followed by black liner on my inner lids that makes my eyes tear. My "Clara Bow lips" are lined, then filled with colors chosen to match my pants; my hair is piled high and set in place with aerosol hair spray. I never look like me and am never sure if I look better or worse.

⊕

`SELLING REAL ESTATE` IS WHAT Frank calls it. Sometimes I try delivering the "parcels" with a straight face. That's called "deadpanning." Or I try to make myself laugh or laugh along with the audience. That's called "endearing yourself to the public." Or I try making it look like even I am surprised by what I say. That's called acting. I remind myself I cannot embarrass Gail or Frank and that as much as I hate this unpaid job of mine that is causing me to be unable to keep up with my classwork, I am helping my dad sell records. If he sells records, then he makes money so we can live.

The host will sit behind a desk or beside me on some steps or across from me in a better chair. When he launches into his canned vaudevillian setup lines, like "What was it like growing up with Frank Zappa for a dad?," I politely answer with my rehearsed punch lines, saying things like "We can stay up as late as we want, curse, watch TV, and eat any kind of dinner we want, alone, on the waterbed, and we have to shower with our friends to save water."

Laughter.

"Did you like your name growing up or did kids tease you?"

"They teased Dweezil and teased me about the Unit part of my name, but my little brother had it the worst being called Ahmet Vomit, so he changed his name to Rick."

"Then what happened?"

"They started calling him Rick the Dick."

Laughter.

I look at the men with headsets behind the giant cameras. Or the audience being cued by the flashing red "APPLAUSE" sign. Or the guy eating a bagel in the corner. Or the feet of the next guest under the curtains waiting in the wings. Or anything honest behind the scenes.

Through it all, the biggest and best and briefest thrill is spending any moment with my dad. When he is around, it is easier for me to reinforce the pretend story of our "kooky" family closeness. In these moments in the spotlight, I try even harder to believe it all myself.

In my adulthood I will come to realize I was pinballing between the outer, public fake me; the under-my-roof, family fake me; and the real me, who desperately wanted to feel safe. Gail and showbiz and the pressure to keep my dad happy trained me to hypnotize myself and the audience. And it always came at a price when I was alone again: a crashing, dark low of numb nothingness.

I am only fourteen. And overwhelmed. I am also loyal to a fault.

Eventually I learn about hard work and self-discipline in my acting classes. I begin acting professionally and meet some of my heroes as peers. Luck and grace shower me with connections to humans who still amaze me, like Andy Warhol. His magazine, *Interview*, fascinates me. I am taken with the interviewing style, which is often a clean, transcribed, peer-to-peer conversation. It is the first time I think it might be fun to be on the other side of the tape recorder or camera. To be the one who understands how annoying the process is and how to facilitate an artful showcasing of the subject being spotlighted.

Warhol will plant a journalism seed in me. He will also defend me in his diary, which will be published posthumously a few years from now and point out a thing no one currently acknowledges but that I feel acutely—Warhol will describe his experience of my father and privately criticize Frank for viewing me as something he alone invented, a tool at my dad's disposal. When this icon's journal entries are made public, they will become concrete validation and confirmation of my own unarticulated experience, a tiny light in the dark that lets me start to see my way out.

Always, my secret fuel is my commitment to *also* getting my siblings safe passage. One thing I was born intrinsically knowing that has never left me: life is not worth living if those I love suffer, suffer alone, or get left behind.

CHAPTER 28

Outsider

There is a drive-on for me at the studio's guard gate. I have booked a role on a TV show called *CHiPs*. "If I didn't bring you here, you wouldn't be able to do this. Your father certainly wouldn't," says Gail, following the guard's instruction about where to park.

"Well, he doesn't drive, so he couldn't even if he wanted to," I say, undoing my seat belt.

"Well, he wouldn't even if he could," she says, setting the emergency brake.

I tell myself Gail is already in a bad mood for two reasons: (1) she has to drive me somewhere she has never been that's far away, and (2) I will get more attention than her, which isn't my fault. I don't want to fight with her, so I let her have the last word like I usually do, because I am too nervous about my first professional acting job, and I want to make sure I know my lines.

My scenes are with Ponch and Jon. The pages were delivered by messenger to our house last night and I stayed up late learning what I have to say, who to say it to, and when to say it at the shoot today. That's all acting is.

I feel fancy having a full script and a call sheet delivered to me, even if it is only for a dumb part with no name on a TV show I don't even like or watch. "Hitchhiking Val" may be a stupid character with stupid dialogue a Val would never say, but this acting job will help me get my full SAG card so I can work professionally and legally in film and television. Also, a Valley girl would never hitchhike, but who cares because right now my friends are probably just waking up to go to school and here I am already heading to WORK! People my age stress about grades in high school so they can go to a good college, figure out what they will do for a living, and get a good job, but here I am already doing what I want to do!

I am greeted by a man with a walkie-talkie when I arrive. I am told I still have to attend school, even on set. "The state of California requires a three-hour minimum and doesn't let kid actors work as long as adult actors." First, though, I am to go to a little trailer on wheels that houses the hair-and-makeup people. Gail is told to wait in my "honeywagon," which is another trailer on wheels with little rooms and an even littler bathroom.

"Come here, you little heifer," says a large hair guy as he runs his plump, dry fingers through my hair. I have recently had it cut in the style of Brian Setzer from the Stray Cats. To my father's dismay I absolutely adore ducktails, or DAs, and mods and ska now. Since I am not a lead, I find out quick that peon day players get peon hair-and-makeup people. I will learn a lot of things today about being a working actor. For example, the real actors can cut in the food line, and "Time is money" is a real thing, and peon actors cannot afford to be the reason budgets balloon, so you have to hop to it when they call you.

My hair is back-brushed, then shellacked with hairspray until it is an unmovable helmet. Then comes the makeup. I smell his hot onion breath.

"What are you doing?" I ask, concerned his eyesight is failing.

"My job," he says as though he is exhausted by me. "Certain skin colors and facial characteristics need certain things based on conditions like outdoor or indoor lighting," he explains. "Ethnicity and type of complexion, scars, blemishes, if noses are too big, eyes are too small, and so on. Usually I mix the yellow-toned bases for olive complexions; purple or green takes out certain kinds of redness, whereas oranges and pinks and browns are reserved for people with blue in their skin tone."

Then the man with the walkie-talkie is back to take me to my honeywagon, so I can change into my costume and he can escort me to "location" to "block."

When I exit my dressing room, Erik Estrada is there in his highway patrol costume. I am introduced to him and I extend my hand to shake his, but he impulsively embraces me, dips me, and kisses me instead. On the mouth. I suppose he means it in a fun, chivalrous way, but I have never had a boyfriend or kissed a stranger before. Even though my first kiss has been stolen in an instant, no one reacts, so I write this moment off as an annoyance, as par for the course I am learning to navigate in showbiz and working with actors with bravado.

We block at the location, which means doing a rehearsal of the scene for the director, actors, and camera people in the exact spot where the scene will take place and mapping the exact way we plan to do it. I am learning about knowing where your "key light" is, not looking into the camera, hitting your "mark" so the camera can stay in focus if you are moving around, getting used to your costume or props so you seem like a real person who always wore those clothes or had those things, and trying to look natural while moving and speaking and wearing and using that stuff. The director has final say on everything and is the one who tells you how to say a line if you don't naturally know how to. After we block it, it's time for me to go to school on set.

I am led to yet another honeywagon, where I meet a kid actress who will become my lifelong friend. Elle is one year younger than me, looks just like a miniature Brooke Shields, and has been a working actor since she was a baby. In spite of our many differences both physically and professionally, in between shooting our scenes or racing through homework we discover we share a sense of humor, mean moms, and boy-crazy crushes on all the actors in *The Outsiders*. She looks out for me and gives me showbiz advice, saying, "Always make sure any production company you work for doesn't lie and put down the wrong end and start times in any paperwork you are asked to sign, in case they have to work you past your designated kid hours and try to avoid paying you for overtime."

And then the job is over and Elle and I become inseparable. She has a muscle car her mom got her that she lets her drive illegally all around their Bel Air neighborhood off Mulholland because it has so many dead ends and cul-de-sacs. Inside her house she shows me her mom and working sister's extensive collections of makeup, jewelry, clothes, shoes, skin care products, watches, lingerie, and furs. I am in heaven. I feel like Cinderella getting a crash course in how to be a real princess when I grow up.

One night her sister comes home from a date and her mother insists we watch her sister bait the wealthy suitor for another date. This feels wrong to me, but her tan, coiffed, larger-than-life mother insists this is a necessary tutorial, the proof being she already married off her eldest daughter to one of the wealthiest families in the country. Rich. There it is again. So, the three of us crouch down at the top of the stairs and watch her middle daughter kiss and roll around on the couch with Lucille Ball's son. Then Elle's sister tells the young man she's tired and has to get up early for work. They kiss at the door, and she comes running up the stairs saying, "Mommy! I did just what you told me to do, drop him and end the date the second he got a boner."

And I think *my* family is weird.

If we aren't sunbathing our skin to a crisp slicked in baby oil or Bain de Soleil or lightening our hair, mustaches, and bikini lines with lemon juice and experimental amounts of hydrogen peroxide, and planning our weddings to Matt Dillon for me and Rob Lowe for her, her mom drives us around Beverly Hills. That way we can dine, be seen, or dance at all the right places and be photographed there, including a club called Touch where we are underage but recognizable, therefore VIPs, so they make an exception. Elle's mom teaches us other things too, like to always look at a man's shoes and his watch to see if he is truly wealthy or just posing. Or she'll pull alongside a very expensive car and explain with disdain and a flick of her beautifully manicured hand that even if it's a fancy brand, like the powder-blue Mercedes idling at the light beside us, "if it's a diesel, it's Pass-adena," which is her way of saying the owner is a worthless cheapskate and likely lives in an undesirable location. Beverly Hills or bust for her girls.

Then, miraculously, I audition and book an acting job working with one of the cast members of *The Outsiders*! The next time I stay at Elle's, she and I leap around her bedroom, ecstatic! I feel like she is a lucky rabbit's foot and it's only a matter of time before we meet all our favorites. In person, Emilio Estevez is a dreamy hunk and I develop an instant crush. Unbelievably, he likes me back and asks me on a date. It will be my first date ever and my first *car* date, *and* it's with an Outsider! I think I have died and gone to heaven.

He takes me to a screening of the movie *The Toy*. As soon as he sees the red carpet and all the flashing paparazzi bulbs and press, he starts acting weird. As we walk toward the theater, a handsome friend of his I recognize as another greaser approaches and joins us as Emilio explains to us both that he can't walk in with me or his girlfriend will find out. I feel knocked sideways. He already has a girlfriend? I am devastated. He negotiates with me to salvage the date: "I'll walk the red carpet first and you'll walk in after, then we will meet inside and sit together."

Tom Cruise pipes up, "*I'll* just walk her in."

CHAPTER 29

—

Cheeky

Thanks to "Valley Girl" and Frank and Gail's decision to do everything in-house with Barking Pumpkin, I think we have some money and maybe even a cushion of it, because Gail is insisting on taking the whole family to Europe while my father does shows in the UK, Germany, Switzerland, and Vienna—something we have never done.

Maybe it's also to make sure he doesn't try to leave her for Gerda.

On the flight over, my dad sits in first class and we ride in coach with Gail. I am disgusted and angry he won't sit with us or let us sit with him, but Gail explains he needs to rest in order to work. Eye roll: What. Ever.

When we land, Frank heads for a fancy hotel, and we are taken to the home of a woman my parents know named Pamela Mayall. She is tall and skinny and striking, with straight brown hair and rings of real gold on every finger. She is very intimidating, probably from raising seven kids by herself. She peers at us with skeptical glances, but I absolutely *adore* her and her London house, or "flat." The flat is four narrow stories, old, cozy, and loved, with tall ceilings, carpeted stairs, and a history of collectibles from exotic travels to places like Greece, India, Japan, Malta, and Italy. In the front she has a little garden and views and sounds of the city, with its fun double-decker buses, its swanky taxis, and the gorgeous, expansive Hyde Park nearby. Couches and window seats become my siblings' beds, and I am installed in Pamela's closet on a little bedroll. I love the close-family-quarters, sardine quality of this adventure, plus her home is right near Vivienne Westwood's punk rock clothing store, which I am currently obsessed with. Before Gail heads off, she takes us all shopping on the "high street."

I have no problem being left behind at Pamela's with Ahmet, Diva, and Dweezil while Gail has some alone time with Frank for the first time in years. Plus Pamela's kids and their motley friends swarm the house. Each day we are taken to experience some new, amazing sight—a walk past the guards with the tall fuzzy hats at Buckingham Palace, past the carriage houses and horses to eat greasy fish and chips served with malt vinegar. Or we take "the underground" and see the Sherlock Holmes tiles at a tube stop, or walk by the canals and houseboats to see the locals' version of a swap meet. In Trafalgar Square we laugh hysterically when Diva is briefly engulfed by rowdy pigeons until she drops her paper cups full of birdseed. Then we head to Gaz's, a cool club Pamela's eldest son runs that plays rockabilly, reggae, ska, and everything in between.

At "home," drinking tea is a daily occurrence, which I love. We each choose a mug from Pamela's vast collection in the basement kitchen, put the kettle on, and retire to the sitting room. Once we go to Fortnum & Mason to have a proper "high tea" with scones and clotted cream. Then I meet a funny guy from Yugoslavia with a cool black pompadour. He looks just like a greaser from *The Outsiders* but with a cool accent. He charms me by challenging me to a footrace, then tripping me and rolling on top of me as I come to a stop on a sprinkler head. I develop bruises and an insta crush but can do nothing about it because Gail is coming back to collect us and take us all to the lands of schnitzel, Mozart, the Alps, and the autobahn to see my father and his shows. In Germany, Frank informs me I will perform "Valley Girl," no rehearsal, just me winging it. "Throw in a few observations about your time in Europe," he says. I am stricken but obey and perform it live as instructed, in front of a crowd who stare back at me with blank faces. If this is being a musician, I want no part of it. I look at Frank, who is laughing, not at what I am doing but at the buffoonery of the circumstance. I feel like a court jester here solely for the king's amusement, not the peasants'. No one explains to me that the audience is unresponsive because they don't speak English and that the song is not as popular here as it is back home. Then Frank cues the band to go into their next song and I know that's my signal to head for the wings. I make my way off the stage, careful not to trip.

In the dark behind the curtains, I feel nauseous. I am furious with my father for setting me up for failure. The experience scars me. Maybe I could do better if I could practice or try it in front of people who like the song or understand it, but I never get a second chance.

Backstage, Gail says, "Now we can write your trip and purchases off as a business expense." Then it's back to England we go, without Frank.

This time Gail installs us all in the Hyde Park Hotel with her, but we visit Pamela's again, where I am reunited with the dreamy, hilarious Yugoslavian mod with the pale skin and ducktail hairdo slicked with pomade. It is nice to feel flirted with and wanted. I make my decision. On my last night in Europe, on July fourth, the day America celebrates its independence, at the ripe old age of fourteen and three quarters, I embrace my independence by losing my virginity to the boy who calls my zits spots, smells like Aqua Velva, and teaches me to say "Help me, help me, my hands are cut off" in his native language.

I tell no one. I don't need to; I do not plan to see this son of a boat builder ever again. I want to call my best friend back home, but I am not even sure it counts because I kept my dress and panties on, and it happened as fast as you can say "Harrods."

But fate is tricky, or Gail Zappa is, because when we head to Pamela's for a last goodbye, he's there to see me off, she meets him, and she offers to hire him on the spot and move him to California with us, to be our male nanny back in the States. Gail even talks about adopting him. Like, omigod, *for real.*

Back at the hotel, as we pack up, I hope this is all a joke, a dead-end daydream. I notice Gail has filled her suitcases with silverware from the room service trays and must have been taking it from every hotel she's visited because she has amassed quite a pile. Gail has taught us to never steal, yet here she is! She catches me seeing her booty and gives me a dismissive wave. "If they notice it's missing after we're gone, they'll just put it on the bill," she says.

I feel completely off-kilter.

"I can marry you and get my green card," the Yugoslavian boy whispers in my family's kitchen a week to the day after I said goodbye to him in London.

"Absolutely not," I whisper back, frozen with terror. Instead, I ignore him and lock my door each night until my iciness breaks him and he slides a note under my door telling me I am a cheeky monster and, within weeks, slips out in the night and back to his home in the UK. This turn of events is a complete mystery to Gail, who somehow senses I am responsible for his departure and therefore her lack of help. I channel my guilt and responsibility into picking up the household slack with renewed vim. I polish Gail's new silverware and feel a bit of relief, excited to be starting tenth grade soon.

CHAPTER 30

New York City Sounds

Frank gets us our own room to share at the Mayfair Regent Hotel, which is very fancy. Gail told him to take Dweezil and me with him to New York, and so he did. I can't believe he agreed to this idea, but here we are. This is a another first—just us and Frank—and I want to savor every moment.

Today we get to go shopping with a bodyguard he's hired for us while he has meetings and interviews, and later on Frank is taking us to see the musical *Cats*.

Gail told Frank to get a connecting suite with his room. Even though there is a door that could be opened to make the rooms connect so we can all be together, my dad doesn't ask the hotel to do this, so neither do we. I guess if we really need him, we could always call him, but since we never bother him at home, I'm pretty sure we are not going to do that here either.

I check to see where the fire exits are, and I look out our window to see if we have a fire escape. I want to know that we could safely jump to the ground below if we had to. Hypervigilance and safety are on my mind, since Gail warned us there are so many murders and mob hits in New York. Gail also told us to never make eye contact with anyone and to know exactly where we are going and to just keep walking when we are on the sidewalk and never look like a tourist.

Our room is mostly blue and cream with powder-blue curtains. My dad's room is almost exactly like ours but much bigger and in pale pink. He also has a big living room. His also came with fruit and cheese and crackers and flowers and fancy bottled water. There are two beds in our room. My father's hotel bed is a king and is bigger than the one he shares with Gail. It could easily fit all three of us if he wanted that, which he doesn't. I have no idea what that would be like, to snuggle with my dad for a whole night, or even an hour, and probably never will, but if Gail were here and he weren't, my guess is she'd order too much dessert from room service and let us eat it in bed with her.

In New York, even when it's the middle of the day, the tall buildings block out the sunshine, making everything look and feel colder. Even if you are being driven around in a town car. Which we are. My dad's usual driver is Al Malkin, a bug-eyed guy with a loud voice and a lot of long stories about crazy stuff he's seen or tried with funny results. I don't exactly think his stories are funny, but he tells them funny, and I think it's funny he thinks he's funny. Today Al is driving my dad to all his meetings and interviews, so Dweezil and I get a barrel-chested stranger as our bodyguard, driver, and babysitter. He wears a suit and has a Three Musketeers mustache. His name is Jimmy Dennedy. He used to be a cop. Now he raises dogs upstate and takes occasional gigs like this. He's been instructed to take us to Smitty's—Frank's friend Phyllis's vintage store. I like Phyllis's thick New York accent. She's nice to us. I don't know if she has had sex with my dad or not, so I'm only a little nice back to her just in case. I say, "My dad gave me and Dweezil spending money for our trip, a hundred dollars each." She helps me pick out a coat. It has flecks of cornflower blue mixed in with mostly gray wool woven in a herringbone pattern.

"The coat is forty dollars," Phyllis says. "It's a good price." It's my first real coat that I pick out myself and that I know I like. We don't need coats in LA because it never really gets cold there—not see-your-breath and need-a-winter-coat cold. But we definitely need one here in New York. Dweezil buys one, too. We think about getting one for our dad since we both have money left over, but we aren't exactly sure we know what our dad would like.

On the way back to the hotel to meet our dad, Jimmy the body-guard makes good on his promise to give us a tour of all the locations where mob murders have taken place and to fingerprint and take mugshots of us like we are criminals. Before we go inside our hotel, Jimmy says he wants to give me the standard test that police give drunk people when they are pulled over.

"Yes please!" I say eagerly.

I set my shopping bag down and Jimmy firmly says, "Stand straight. Close your eyes. Touch your left finger to your nose. Touch your right finger to your nose. Open your eyes."

"It's pretty hard to do when you're not drunk," I say, even though I am not sure what being drunk would be like in the first place.

"Now put one hand on your hip and the other one out to the side parallel to the ground. Now walk straight ahead with one foot in front of the other like you are walking a tightrope." I do what he says but wobble, and he begins to sing, "Here she comes, Miss America . . ."

Dweezil erupts into laughter. They both do. The doormen of our hotel, too. My body tenses up. My face goes hot and red. I try to laugh it off, but my feelings are hurt. I hate being tricked.

When we see Frank, he tells us we are allowed to order as much room service as we want and watch as much TV as we want. He's going to eat dinner in a restaurant downstairs, his favorite. It's called Le Cirque. You have to wear a tie so Dweezil can't go, even though my dad didn't invite him. He didn't even ask me, so I guess he wants to eat alone.

After Frank eats his dinner, we head off to see our first Broadway show. Dweezil has never seen anything like this. I sort of have, because one time Gail and Frank took me to see Lily Tomlin, but this will be different because it's a musical. When our dad says he has already seen it, I feel bummed out that it isn't a first for him, too, but he must really like it and want us to see it if he's willing to see it twice. He says he especially wants us to see the set and how the theater is transformed into a junkyard world. Plus, "it's a show about mangy old cats" and we have a bunch of cats like that at home.

The show is good but long, and the songs are tearjerkers. I am surprised my dad can sit through this show again or tolerate this music. It's nothing like his.

Afterward we go backstage, which I always hate. People act extra weird around my dad, especially women and male superfans—women get shiny eyes and are flustery and want to hug or touch him, and my dad makes sounds at them or leans in and says funny things. The women always laugh and twitter and bat their eyelashes. Shy, skinny men talk too long and don't get the hint; business guys puff up their chests and talk too loud. And there's never anywhere for us to sit while we are ignored.

The dancers are way smaller than they seemed onstage, and you can really see the shapes of their bodies; the costumes are so tight they almost seem see-through. I watch my dad's eyes. I watch what he watches. The girls. I notice the girls move with lightness and grace and gaiety. Anyone can see the dancers are very attractive and athletic, electric and feminine, the opposite of Gail, the opposite of me.

When we finally get back to the hotel to go to sleep, my dad says we can order hot chocolate. He lets us ride up in the elevator alone. He has a meeting with someone in the lobby. I recognize her from backstage at the show—pretty with big blue eyes.

In the middle of the night, I wake up to the sound of banging. I realize it's my dad's headboard banging against our wall. It sounds similar to the fucking I hear back home, but the lady is a little quieter. "Dweezil," I whisper, "Dweezil."

"Huh?" he answers groggily, but doesn't wake up.

I feel like crying. I cross my arms and stare at the ceiling. I try to listen to the other New York sounds—traffic, garbage trucks, police sirens, honking. I put a pillow over my head and turn onto my side. My lips quiver. At home I get mad when this happens, but now I feel sad because I know something my mom doesn't know, and I know it would make her furious. I'm guessing it's the backstage lady. I suddenly hate my father for taking us to see *Cats*, because now I am wondering if he truly wanted us to see the show or if he wanted to see this woman. I have no idea if he knew her from before or if she's just the flavor of the night who robs us of our time and peace.

IN THE MORNING I ASK Dweezil, "Do you remember when I tried to wake you up?"

"No."

When I tell him what I heard, he just shrugs. I can't tell if he doesn't care, doesn't understand, or doesn't want to think about it.

—

CHAPTER 31

Omertà

My budding "career" alternately taxis on a never-ending runway or gets a promising liftoff. When I book jobs, then my confidence to keep trying is reignited and Gail's Hollywood parenting pride kicks in, and my mother and I form a temporary truce from our usual fighting. Elle has told me about getting "emancipated," which is where a court legally makes you an adult so you can have a career without relying on your parents. My secret plan is to get my driver's license as soon as I am old enough, then get emancipated, book jobs, make my own money, and move out. Once I am on my own, I can help my siblings get out, too.

I manage to book a small role on *The Facts of Life* as "Bully," and then I get a small role as "American Girl" in a big film called *National Lampoon's European Vacation* that will shoot in Rome, for a month!

I am beyond excited because my acting wish is coming true. Two of the weeks will be us waiting on my work visa. Gail almost ruins my chance to go when she negotiates an extra plane ticket so Dweezil can travel with us for my exciting job.

On the flight over I find out from Gail that my dad wants a divorce. I study her face and take her cues on how she needs me to feel about the news—Gail is refusing to accept Frank's childishness and describes his behavior as yet another passing phase to get through, so I casually dismiss his antics, too. But I can tell she and I know this one is different. I scribble my seething anger into my journal. When we land, Gail lets Dweezil have my hotel room all to himself even though he's thirteen and isn't here working. Instead she insists it would be weird for her to share a room with him because he's a boy, so she makes me share a room with her even though I am here for an important job in a real movie-studio movie and I have to rest and relax and learn my lines. Because she's so upset about Frank, I give in. How come Gail doesn't make sure I have what I need so I can do my job, the way she does for Frank, even when she is so hurt by him? Does that mean she is angrier at me than at him? If so, what did I do to deserve her wrath?

Soon we meet the actors from the film. The ones who play the kids are sweet and fun. Gail's mood picks up when we meet Chevy Chase, Beverly D'Angelo, and a British guy named Eric Idle, someone Gail says is one of the Monty Python guys. They are all amped and funny in different ways, talking and laughing and one-upping each other, but the director, Amy Heckerling, is my favorite person. She's so pretty and smiley and encouraging, but also tough and fit. It's inspiring to see a strong and soft woman in charge of everything.

I am told I still have to wait for my work visa to come through while the cast and crew shoot in other places. That will give me a chance to get used to this new time zone. Gail, Dweezil, and I eat a meal in the lobby of our hotel. I am astonished when I watch our waiter make our salad dressing table-side with equal parts lemon juice and olive oil in a large silver spoon with a pinch of salt. I vow to never eat fake, store-bought, processed bottled dressing again.

In "our" room, Gail throws her clothes and toiletries everywhere and argues with my dad over many lengthy, stressful, loud, crying phone calls. I get no sleep, and then she organizes a dinner she drags us to with a local I can tell lies and covers up for my father to help him cheat on Gail, so I don't even know why she is meeting with him. Maybe to get his help to change my father's mind.

Over coffee and dessert, here in my father's ancestral homeland, I have my second major panic attack. I start hyperventilating and crying in that restaurant and cannot stop. Back at our hotel it eventually passes, but I can't shake the dread and it affects my ability to concentrate over my shooting days. I am underwhelmed by my performance and long for a second chance. I feel I've let Amy and myself down. I have a few more scenes to go, but they are just reaction shots to a car chase with no lines. When Gail asks one of the producers, Stewart, to put Dweezil in the film and give him speaking lines and Stewart says yes, I feel a strange mixture of happiness for him and utter fury and betrayal.

I leave Rome defeated and aware that our American family staples of Chef Boyardee and Ragú do NOT taste like real Italian food at all.

🌎

BACK HOME IN LOS ANGELES, I do what Gail does when she's stressed—I go shopping. Over-the-top shopping. At Betsey Johnson on Melrose. When it comes time to pay for my giant pile of floral dresses, ruffly shirts, crinoline skirts, and striped leggings, I throw down my parents' credit card. As usual, we go through the boring process of the salesperson speaking to the bank and the bank asking her to ask me more information to make sure the card isn't stolen so the funds can be released—I spell my mother's maiden name and the purchase is rung up and finalized. But today it's taking way longer than usual and the lady behind me with just one item is growing impatient. "That's what you get for being a flash in the pan!" she loudly announces to me and the rest of the shoppers. I feel a strange kind of embarrassed and humiliated but I don't know what I have done wrong. I never wear one item of clothing the salesgirl puts in the brightly patterned plastic bags I bring home that day.

Now words like "novelty song" and "fluke" and "one-hit wonder" are being thrown around when people refer to "Valley Girl." What little pride I have left starts to disintegrate. Then I start getting hate mail from girls who say I ruined their lives because people now make fun of the way they talk, walk, and dress. Once some mean girls spit at me at the mall. From now on I avoid the Galleria and I cross the street if I see girls in pumps and miniskirts or teased-up hair. I feel unlovable inside my home, and now it seems to be spreading unpredictably out in the world. I begin to dread waking up since each day is a repeat of never being able to tell if I am going to be welcomed or bullied, or when, where, and by whom. If my mother and strangers can be mad at me and mean to me out of nowhere, either they are right about my being deficient in some way or they are wrong—either way I feel a sense of shame I can't shake and an acute sorrow that cement the feeling I should not exist.

Even though I have been told by Gail I have nothing to do with the song's success, I feel linked to and responsible for its downturn. How have I peaked and crashed before I've even gotten my driver's license?

WHEN FALL RE-ENROLLMENT CONTRACTS COME from Oakwood, I receive an "invitation" to return, but Dweezil, who is supposed to start eighth grade, does not. Loyal as I am, I know staying enrolled in the Ivy League feeder isn't an option for me anymore since the school has insulted my family. Publicly we are seen as close, Italian, with a last name synonymous with integrity. When I ask Gail why they don't want my shy, polite, and funny brother back at school, Gail tells me it's because Dweezil made an anti-pollution poster with a silhouette of a cartoon guy pissing in a river littered with tin cans, plastic bags, old tires, fishbones, and other debris. "What?" I say, flummoxed. My principal seems like a total oddball to me now. "Who cares about an art poster with a penis in silhouette? No one wants urine in their fishing hole or drinking water, do they? That's nothing to kick someone out of school for! Dweezil is a genius like Frank, don't they see that?"

Gail tells me Frank wrote a scathing letter defending Dweezil and condemning the school for having the nerve to only offer me a spot and insisting I stay! I am devastated because school and seeing my friends are my sanctuary, but going against my family is not an option.

WHEN THE HEADMASTER FINDS OUT I will also not be returning, the soft-spoken man asks to have a meeting.

"Is there trouble at home?" he asks.

"Huh?" I say. "What do you mean?"

"Is there some child abuse in the family?" he asks. "Because if you want to still try to come to school here, we can help. We can intervene on your behalf."

I sit there red faced and blinking, my face contorted in confusion. *Child abuse?* What the hell is he talking about? No one punches me. I have no hidden bruises. Is that what he means? Is that what he thinks? Why on earth does he think this? Anger rises in me. First he kicks Dweezil out and now he calls Gail and Frank *abusers*?

"I really have no idea what you mean," I say. I stand. He can only nod and look at me with helplessness in his eyes, and something else equally disturbing: pity. Another blank stare back from me, then I turn and leave. I feel confused and embarrassed, ashamed and particularly protective of my mother and brother.

"Child abuse," I repeat to myself on the way to the parking lot, where Gail is waiting for me. "As if."

I hop in the car and immediately tell Gail everything. A silence grips her. Her jaw tightens. This comes as a shock to Gail, too. Someone questioning her, someone outside of her sphere seeing something and labeling it as abuse. On the drive home I see she is a shark with dead eyes, with the wheels of retaliation and revenge spinning.

And like that, it is decided. The end of my education. I will take the GED and get my high school diploma three years early and just keep working. No saying goodbye to my friends. No graduation ceremony. No college.

I shore myself up with this: I want to be an actress, so who needs school or a degree when you already sometimes work, and you know what you want to do, and you are already doing it?

I push aside the "one-hit wonder" talk and the feelings of being washed up before I've even really started. I have to keep trying to win. Besides, our family sticks together—at least against the outside world. We are Zappas, united until the end.

YEARS FROM NOW, I WILL think, *WOW*. What did my school headmaster see that he was willing to take a chance and intervene on my behalf?

How brave, how kind.

CHAPTER 32

My Complicated Face

G ail picks Valley Professional, a school devoted to working children getting their required learning out of the way so they can get back to their day jobs. And they have spaces for both my brother *and* me.

The "school," if you can call it that, is more or less three shitty mobile rooms that were clearly wheeled onto a flatbed truck and dumped on a wide and treeless street next to a gas station deep in the bowels of the San Fernando Valley. It screams meth lab rather than educational mecca. Enrolled here to do the bare minimum are rambunctious working actors of various ages, Olympic ice-skating hopefuls, rando locals, and Janet Jackson. My "required" books don't even fit in the lockers we're assigned.

Jason Bateman is the kingpin prankster here, and he and Dweezil are the same age, so they hit it off right away. Through Jason I meet his sister, Justine, who goes to a normal public high school a few miles away, and she and I become fast friends, too. Most days kids make paper airplanes or origami or get hyper and rowdy and just crinkle paper up into a ball and lob it across the room at our main teacher, who looks like a human Muppet. I am horrified by the level of mutual disrespect. Students feel emboldened to move bookshelves in front of entrances to block teachers from entering. Exasperated teachers fight to find another way into their classrooms, only to hand us simplistic xeroxed multiple-choice worksheets to fill out in silence. Mostly Jason, Dweezil, Janet, and I walk over to the gas station to buy vegetarian burritos to microwave. This is where I wait out my GED results, and the second I succeed in graduating early, we never go back. Instead, I start going to more auditions between nine and three, and Gail hires a teacher to homeschool Dweezil. She goes to the trouble of creating an actual "school" in our house, called Beigemont Academy, just for him, which, according to Gail, simply involves "filing some paperwork and making sure there is a fire extinguisher by the back door" until he can take the GED, too.

I book a few more acting jobs, but nothing consistent. Given how many actors there are in this town, I am a success story if you believe the paparazzi photos of my professional socializing. My agent tells me "schmoozing" is part of the hiring game—being seen at cool clubs and movie premieres and having your photo taken helps casting people "keep you in mind." The problem is I still need Gail to drive me and pick me up everywhere I go, sometimes after midnight.

"Earth to Moon!" Gail screams. "The world doesn't revolve around you." We are nose to nose, and she is shrieking in my face.

"I know that!" I scream into hers.

"Fuck you!" she screams.

"Fuck you!" I scream back.

"Go to your room!" she screams.

"With pleasure!" I scream back. Gail has it out for me. I don't get it. I do everything she asks of me and then some. If anyone else gets screamed at, it's usually Ahmet, then Gail yells, "You're just like your sister Moon!" As if I am a poor role model and the worst thing a person can be.

Lying on my bed and staring at the ceiling at age fifteen, I take personal and professional stock. I consider other factors surrounding Gail's anger—I know she hates Tutu, and since I look like her mother, maybe Gail takes stuff out on me because I remind her of her? Gail is also mad at Frank all the time, and I look like him, too. Maybe all she sees is Tutu and my dad in my face, and I can't do anything about that.

Or *am* I truly just some awful piece of shit?

Maybe things will be different when I can drive.

Professionally speaking, I am not fat or ugly enough to be cast as "the friend," not skinny or pretty enough to be cast as the lead. My humor seems to be too specific, offbeat, skewed, unrelatable, or weird to make everyone normal laugh. My acting range is limited due to my sheltered and rather unique life. My lack of training rules out Shakespeare and theater work. I am not athletic, don't have a hot bod, and am a prude who has never had a boyfriend, so I won't be asked to do stunts or appear in a bathing suit or do nude scenes— things required to book a lead. I know I am not exceptional, but I don't work enough to improve enough even for lesser roles. And I have a mean mom who is known for making contract negotiations a hellscape, so even if I get a job, I could lose it in negotiations.

Or maybe I am not booking jobs because I am simply not talented enough.

Anyway, I tell myself, *I want to be a character actor.* It sounds too stressful to carry a whole film, to always have to stay underweight, to never grow old, to always lead with your sex appeal. And being beautiful isn't a guarantee anyway—plenty of beautiful working actresses and models get cheated on and discarded just as often as anyone else.

I wouldn't want to be in the tabloids and get caught eating in line at a supermarket or have my jiggling skin photographed when jogging at the beach. Out of the limelight but working steadily would be fine by me.

What would be super unfair is to be under the radar and still under someone's thumb in the entertainment business, just like here at home. Another problem I see is no one has bad skin in the movie industry, except James Woods and Edward James Olmos, and they usually play drug lords or bad guys. Both would be a stretch for me since I don't do drugs and am a people-pleasing doormat, but work is work. Of course, none of this is my current problem. I'd have to book enough acting work to even be considered for such roles before I'd suffer the next tier of problems.

Then I try to calculate the pittance I have made so far and its distance from my dream salary when it suddenly occurs to me that Gail never tells me when I can come out of my room after being sent there. It also occurs to me that if I pay taxes and commissions, even occasionally, maybe I am too old to be sent to my room in the first place.

Soon enough I receive a copy of my high school diploma, and when the state allows, I get my driver's license. Then Gail and Frank do something big—they buy me a car, a navy blue Subaru four-door sedan, Gail's choice for me because it's cheap but also safe enough for me to drive my siblings. Things improve slightly—I can now drive *myself* to auditions and to acting class and to see my friends—but, of course, there are strings attached. My responsibilities around the house increase, too. Since I don't go to school anymore, I am expected to do more. Like drive my siblings everywhere and grocery shop on my own and run whatever errands Gail needs done.

I love seeing my working-actor friends and I am so happy for them as they continue raising their profiles, landing steady jobs on sitcoms or in big movies, but I also feel jealousy and self-pity. I want my own money and my own life and my own independence, but I have no idea how to get those things. Do they want me to suffer and be broke and homeless? Do a different job? I have no other skills that I know of. No one has real conversations around here. There is no real support or help, just judgment and attacks on me for what I don't know, or for what I don't know that I don't know.

The bum-out is that whenever my dad *does* pay me any attention, Gail gets mad at me for getting more than she does, instead of fighting for all of us to have more of him. I am almost seventeen now and I feel demoralized and depressed. I wonder if maybe I am not cut out for acting at all. I wonder if I am cut out for living under my parents' roof and Gail's thumb forever.

I feel certain no one I love would notice, or care, if I simply vanished.

BUT LUCK AND FATE HAVE more hands to deal me. World-famous fashion photographer Bruce Weber wants to do a portrait of me for his book. They didn't even *ask* my dad. Just me. I am thrilled. Great images with a photographic giant help raise a profile. But I am worried about my skin, and my self-esteem is in the toilet, so even on my best days I feel like a fraud—which I'd happily settle for, honestly.

"Can you call back and ask them about the makeup?" I plead with Gail.

"I am sure it will all be provided," she says dismissively.

"But can you call back and ask, just ask? Can you just double-check and make sure?"

Gail moves with deliberate slowness, like I am ruining her life by asking her to help me. When Gail gets someone from Bruce Weber's team on the phone, Diva, five, runs into the kitchen in her underpants and covered in blue paint like a Smurf. Gail twists her fingers around the curly black cord. Her barely perceptible anger is my cue to get started cleaning Diva off. Gail turns her body away from me and my sister as I begin wiping her down with wet paper towels. "Eeeee," she shrieks, and tries to get away. It's a chasing game now, which I promptly stop as soon as I hear Gail say "Thank you" and hang up.

"Hair, makeup, and clothes will be provided," says Gail flatly.

"Are you absolutely sure?" I ask again. I am so nervous about my cystic acne.

Gail turns to face me whip fast. "Yes!" she says with revving anger. "They said you are to just show up with freshly washed clean skin and hair and no makeup. They will do the rest."

I am relieved, if only for a moment.

🌐

I ARRIVE AT A MODERN-LOOKING home in the Hollywood Hills. This house with a view has been rented for the day. Bruce Weber is pleasing and plump in a handsome way, with a beard and a do-rag on his head. I am promptly shown a metal rolling rack with black clothes that have been selected and labeled with my name. Based on the sizes my mother gave them, these items have been chosen just for me. I notice right away that Julia Roberts and Laura Dern and Diane Lane and a few other more well-known actresses have far prettier selections set aside with their names on them. I immediately feel disappointed and insecure. I am told to slide behind a screen that constitutes a makeshift dressing room, remove my clothes, and try on a loose black slip dress. I step out to show Bruce and his assistants. They all shake their heads. I am instructed to squeeze into a sleeveless, form-fitting leotard with a boatneck. Smiles of agreement.

I am shown to the hair-and-makeup chair. A skinny man squirts moisturizer with a hint of sunblock in his hands to warm the cream, then pats my face as a skinnier woman brushes my hair back and flat against my scalp and wets it down with a spray bottle full of tap water. "Okay," they say. "You are good to go."

There is no hair and makeup, just that cream and that spray bottle.

I want to die.

I almost wish someone would paint stripes down the sides of my enormous nose.

I want to leave or scream or say no. But I can't.

I am told to stand on a spot marked with a piece of paper tape in front of a giant roll of white paper. "What do you want to listen to while you shoot?" asks yet another thin assistant in all black. I am not sure if they are asking me or Bruce.

"I want you to sing something, Moon. Sing it a cappella," says Bruce.

"What?" I say. Panic washes over me. I want to say I am not a singer and explain "Valley Girl" was acting, that I was doing a character voice. "Uh . . . like what?" I dutifully ask instead.

"Anything you want. Just sing and be natural."

"Okay," I say. As if I am a singer. As if it's the most natural thing in the world for me to be center stage, singing, for adults. Ever the good girl, ever compliant, I follow the orders and struggle to eke out a song I listen to on repeat—Paul Young's cover of the Marvin Gaye song "Wherever I Lay My Hat (That's My Home)." I decide I will treat this like an acting exercise. I am playing the role of "singer." The words catch in my throat. I can't look at anyone. I close my eyes and hide deep inside myself. I am furious at my mother, furious at the photographer. I just want to get this experience over with, so I sing and I keep singing. I sing the words like a mantra, like a lullaby to soothe myself.

WHEN I LOOK AT THE photo now, I feel deep tenderness for the girl who wrongly felt ugly and insecure, and unending gratitude for the photographer's visual embrace of my skin, my nose, and my raw, un-edited, uncredited vulnerability. And for capturing the moment I felt anything but beautiful.

CHAPTER 33

Art and Artists

I am eighteen and still recovering from seeing *Sixteen Candles* and finding out that dads can say sorry to their daughters. It's 1985, and my father decides to go after the Parents Music Resource Center, or PMRC, a group of Washington wives hell-bent on music censorship. The story going around our great nation was that children were vandalizing property and committing suicide because of heavy metal music, so these women began to insist that record companies affix labels to albums to warn people of what they consider objectionable content. I overhear Frank explaining the danger of their proposal to Gail, his attorney, and the press. From what I gather, the problem is multipronged: Who has the right to say what constitutes a danger? Wouldn't this kind of labeling directly impact sales, not just his but any artist's? Additionally, I hear him discuss something called "the HR 2911 tape tax," hidden within the PMRC's proposal, that would create "handshake profit" and control between the government and record companies, another blow to any artist because they wouldn't receive any of the piggyback revenue and the label would be allowing artist censorship. Not yet a voter myself, I am struggling to grasp all the potential outcomes my civic-minded father foresees so easily, that he fears and feels he must prevent.

He invites Dweezil and me to go with him when he speaks in Congress. Frank wants us to see how our country is run, but also to show the politicians proof that children raised in a First Amendment-loving home exposed to all things do not become degenerate. It is scary and thrilling, but also a bit sad, watching my father get hammered by the self-righteous religious robots. A wave of press follows. Frank does *Crossfire* and does so well his wheels start turning about a future in politics. I can tell he feels good in this new role, and he likes wearing suits. I feel so proud of him but also powerless about what I can do to make a difference.

The invisible external and internal pressure to follow in my father's footsteps intensifies. I want Frank's depth and breadth and intelligence and work ethic, but I also want his mutual respect and love. I have chosen acting instead of music to entertain and educate the world and win my father's respect, but it's not choosing me back. Do I have to become political too?

We return to LA, and my father sends Washington a message by crafting his own hilarious, scathing warning labels for his albums, announcing "This album contains material which a truly free society would neither fear nor suppress" and satirizing their "God-fearing concerns" to an extreme, stating his albums feature music and lyrics that "are GUARANTEED NOT TO CAUSE ETERNAL TORMENT IN THE PLACE WHERE THE GUY WITH THE HORNS AND POINTED STICK CONDUCTS HIS BUSINESS." Even his classical music gets this over-the-top warning sticker. Me? I am still so angry that heavy metal music is being blamed for inspiring kids to take their own lives, instead of the blame going where it should—being exposed to a cycle of terrible, neglectful parenting, living in shitty, chaotic homes with no education, no affection, and therefore no chance at a successful future—that I write and perform a monologue in my acting class where my character commits suicide while listening to the national anthem. It's the best I can do in my attempt to be like my father and satirize what I see around me, to turn my worldview into art. Maybe it's good, maybe it isn't, no one says, so I only perform it once, but it's my first solo stab at translating the free-floating powerlessness I feel into a tangible something. Even though my piece doesn't offer a solution, I hope it will inspire the sixteen other people in my class to possibly rally to action of some kind. Ever the optimist, I crave think tanks of creativity, feeling certain if just one problem could be solved all the way to the end, there'd be a universal map and template for how to solve every last problem down to the tiniest detail, no matter how tangled, unjust, or complex.

Soon enough we find out the record companies have decided to put parental advisory warning notices on everything with "explicit content." My father seems disappointed but not surprised no one fought back except him, John Denver, and Dee Snider from Twisted Sister. Another wave of press follows, this time including me. I appear on a talk show to say listening to speed metal, bad words, disturbing sexual content, and violent fantasies, or seeing music videos with that content, does not inspire violence and suicide in teens. I tell my old chestnut "unconventional parenting" story about the time Gail handcuffed Dweezil's and my ankles together and locked us in an echoey bathroom with a tape recorder so we could hear for ourselves how "annoying we were" and how "fruitless our arguing was." This is meant to illustrate how fun and freethinking a First Amendment family we are and prove exposure to everything has no impact on mental health. The smiling blond host looks aghast.

When they go to commercial, she turns to me and says, "That's child abuse." She has warmth in her voice and soft, pitying eyes. Her straightforward words and resounding clarity make me feel slapped, exposed, outed, like she knows something about me and my whole life that I don't.

My mic is removed and then I am quietly led back to the green-room with a shrieking all-hands-on-deck siren blaring inside me.

THEN I FIND OUT VAN Halen replaced David Lee Roth. I sink. The world feels positively upside down. If this amazing band can't stay together, how can anything ever work out?

CHAPTER 34

It's Fun Being Me

I t's 1986. I am nineteen and Dweezil is seventeen and he gets a job working as a VJ for MTV. Gail can't take that much time away from raising our younger siblings—Ahmet, who is now eleven, and Diva, who is now six—so she sends me to New York to be Dweezil's legal guardian. This way, his career can get some traction, since mine appears to have stalled. Boyfriendless, jobless, and desperately needing a break from my mother, I am thrilled to share a fancy hotel room in my favorite city, order mashed potatoes and hot chocolate by night, and stand around watching my brother have fun by day.

His job consists of reading music "news" from a teleprompter and "throwing" to a video. Soon enough the higher-ups decide that since I am already there, they may as well put me on camera, too. Wherever we go, girls swoon and dudes bro out asking for Dweezil's autograph or for me to take a photo of them. I am never included in these photos, even though I now have equal airtime. One time we are standing in front of a wall of TVs, and we are both onscreen, and people *still* don't notice me. Dweezil and I joke that I have the power of invisibility and we laugh about a career of petty crime pickpocketing. Goody Two-shoes that I am, my idea is to surprise people and *fill* their pockets with hilarious stuff. Of course, the job includes a bunch of fun stuff too—I adore the interviews with cool musicians and actors. We meet everyone from the Beastie Boys to my current crush

Spalding Gray. On one occasion Mia Sara, fresh from *Ferris Bueller's Day Off* and the film *Labyrinth* with David Bowie, and her boyfriend Justin, who plays guitar for Julian Lennon's band and who looks a *lot* like Dweezil, come on the show. We all improvise a dumb comedy bit where no one can tell anyone apart. Mia and Justin seem like a perfect couple to me. They look like they weather all storms together and rely on each other as their chosen family. I am so happy for them, so happy to see a good example of a polite and loving man and a strong but vulnerable woman and the reciprocity between them. I am also a little jealous. Then the subject of pants comes up, and Mia mentions something bonkers—that she always knows what clothes to buy and buys very little because her sizes are predictable and never change. I am gobsmacked. Reliably wearing the same favorite things? Confidently trusting your body and always being skinny? I tell them my weight fluctuates based on what's happening in my life, my resulting mood, and the overeating of carbs and sugar to cope when things are going wrong. Justin and Mia's heads tilt askew in unison.

I look at everyone differently after this conversation. Can *everyone* always fit in their pants? How do others manage their emotions if not through overdosing on muffins and cheesecake?

On a day off, instead of a mousse or blackout Bundt, I buy a human-baby-size teddy bear that's heavier than an actual newborn. I buy baby clothes for the bear and start to bring it with me wherever I go. Jacket, purse, keys, lipstick, journal, bear. My family and friends don't say anything about it to me, and strangers likely just think I am being eccentric considering who my father is, but I don't do it to get attention. This is before therapy animals, service pets, and the understanding of complex PTSD we have today. I myself do not realize this is my subconscious's primal attempt to soothe myself and pacify my free-floating anxiety. I am replacing cannoli and croissants with something I can hug.

In New York, three other extraordinary things happen:

1. Dweezil and I get a fan letter and befriend a Jessica who is our age and the straightest, most normal, kind, and fun non-showbiz per-

son I have ever encountered. We all hit it off right away even though she has a crush on Dweezil and would probably ditch me in a second given the chance. She's tall, slim, and from Connecticut and wears ballerina flats and a big wool coat. She and I share common interests in authors, movies, caffeine, and journaling. She accepts my teddy-bear-and-baby-clothes obsession and reframes the behavior as stemming from my desire to be a mother and my longing to have something meaning-ful in my life outside of a job. This feels true. I adore her for her insight, which she sees clearly because she also hopes to be a mom someday. She sees the bear and baby clothes as keepsakes to give my future baby. Jessica and I begin sending each other vintage postcards of babies, and soon I have amassed a pile of goal-setting reminders about who I could become. Phew. I can have a life outside of work. My beady-eyed inanimate companion with a nose I've rubbed off from excessive wear and tear is just a 3D vision board I can dress up.

2. Walking around the Upper West Side, I run smack into a baby clothes store called Moon Unit Baby Clothes. Seeing my name con-nected to baby clothes drives the point home. I am me and I need to have my own career and life. Jessica is right and the universe con-firms it.

I go inside and buy a black-and-white-striped prison inmate new-born onesie, a pair of blue bloomers, and a pink baby tee with the store logo for my future daughter. When they ring everything up on my credit card, the look on their faces is one I can't quite understand. It will turn out to be horror and fear of a lawsuit, because the store closes within the month without my saying or doing anything.

3. I'm standing around on the floor of the air-conditioned MTV soundstage waiting to read my lines from the teleprompter. Dweez-il's nearby, likely in his dressing room, or talking to Beth, our floor director, or maybe Martha Quinn. On a TV screen I see an interview clip of a newly famous singer dressed like a Valley girl in a minidress and headband. Is that why she catches my eye? She is promoting her radio hit and video, called "I Wanna Dance with Somebody."

Her name is Whitney Houston and she is clearly already a seasoned pro, with confidence born of years of beauty, charisma, poise, and songbird talent. The young woman keeps answering the interviewer's questions with a giant smile, repeating, "It's fun being me."

I feel a tidal wave of anger and jealousy at this response. *Who says that? What the hell does she even mean? It's fun being her? Who thinks it's fun to be who you are?*

I briefly try to inhabit her shoes and see the world that way. I try to imagine what it would be like to be her, to be her liking being her, to be her liking herself and liking her lot in life. I can't do it. Then I try to imagine what it would take for me to feel that way about myself, about my own life. I can't even begin to locate how that could happen. Do *other* people, besides Whitney, *like* being themselves? I look around at the cameramen, the producers, the interns. Do they like being themselves?

Walking back to our hotel along crowded streets, I search the faces of the people I pass and wonder about them. Then I write Whitney off and decide this rail-thin rising star is either an anomaly or bloated with arrogance. I could never be friends with someone with such an overdeveloped sense of self. That's what Gail would call it. "Like people who throw birthday parties for themselves. Or the people who put themselves at the center of everything and make everything about them, putting the emphasis on 'I' and 'me' and 'mine.'"

. . . But Whitney's words haunt me. For the next forty years.

"Self-love" is what I heard her describe that day. *Here's a spark of it. Here's what it looks like. Here's what it feels like. It feels good.*

GIVEN WHITNEY'S EVENTUAL FATE, I now have to wonder if I saw something else that day, a cautionary tale of a shining light of a girl being pushed, a girl being used, a girl wanting her words to be and stay true, a girl like me.

CHAPTER 35

Sex, Awkwardness, and Rock and Roll

MTV, the big city, and time away from Gail and Frank's upsetting marriage has given me a little more confidence. So has getting hired as a "language consultant" for Cameron Crowe and Amy Heckerling's television version of *Fast Times at Ridgemont High*. I am brought on to keep the teen dialogue authentic. I parlay this job into a small role they write just for me. I just love getting a taste of life on both sides of a production.

I am in our family kitchen in a slip dress and thick socks, my long hair piled high, hands covered in flour, making "rotten" banana bread, a family recipe. The recipe is pretty standard but includes two secret ingredients—sour cream and overripe, almost entirely black bananas. I am mixing the batter when I hear Dweezil beckoning, "Moon! It's on!" I take off running, a Pavlovian response to his familiar call.

Everyone in the family knows that if Jon Bon Jovi's "Runaway" video comes on MTV, they have to call me ASAP and I will stop whatever I am doing and race full speed to the screen. I sail past the library, living room, and alcove, down the hall to the back room, like I'm running for my life. I adore Jon Bon Jovi. It is pretty much love at first sight. He does me in. I just KNOW we are meant to be together.

How do I know? Uh, *duh*, in the video he's wearing a little crescent MOON necklace around his perfect, pale, New Jersey–scented neck.

By the time I slide in front of the TV set, Dweezil is doubled over laughing. It's Tom Keifer from Cinderella on the screen, NOT my soulmate Jon Bon Jovi. I punch Dweezil in the arm. "Asshole." I never considered he'd lie about the Jove.

Deflated, I trudge back to the kitchen to finish making the bread. My younger siblings don't yet realize that when your parents conduct a whole sexual revolution in your childhood home, you have to choose your launching pad wisely. And they shouldn't! They are far too young to consider such things.

Then again, maybe it's different for guys. I am pretty sure Dweezil's already done *it* a bunch and he only wants to date models and actresses since there aren't any rocker-girl musicians who are his type. My dumb brother cannot possibly understand my needs. Anyway, I wouldn't want him to. It would be embarrassing if he knew that I love how, in the video, Jon walks like he is buckling under the weight of his cock, or how much that sparks my imagination and sets my virgin groin aflame. Okay, virgin adjacent. Yes, technically I *sort of* already did the deed in London, but I don't really think it counts because:

A. *It was four years ago, when I was fourteen.*
B. *We only did it once.*
C. *I kept my clothes on.*
D. *I haven't done it since.*
E. *I've never done a blow job.*
F. *We weren't in love.*

Now I know better. I am doing a redo and saving myself for my soulmate. I simply MUST lose my *real*, naked virginity to a keeper. I choose Jon Bon Jovi.

I knock the cat off the counter with my elbow and preheat the oven to 375 degrees. As I pour batter into two loaf pans, I assure myself that even though I have had tons of other crushes—Sam Donaldson, the news anchor; Sam Kinison, the comedian; Sam Harris, my spiritual schoolmate; and John Taylor from Duran Duran—this one's gonna stick. Why? None of them turned me into a hunter stalking its prey. None of them made me lose all reason. None of them turned me into a cowgirl lassoing her cowboy. Steel horse or not, I want him. I want to marry him.

I know Jon Bon Jovi isn't just marriage material, he is my first-choice baby maker, someone I could grow old with, someone I will never tire of listening to or looking at, someone I can share makeup and headbands with. I know he is mine. I also realize it is time to do a bit of research about this man. If I'm serious, I have to be informed.

I start reading every rock and roll magazine I can get my hands on and try to find out who I know that knows him, who his agent and manager are, who he hangs out with and where—the Rainbow? The Whisky? We have family contacts in those places. This feels like the right time and use of my last-name break-glass-in-case-of-emergency perk. I listen to KLOS for when his tour might be coming to town, and I try to guess which hotel he might choose. Maybe there's a club owner we know or photographer we've worked with who can help introduce me.

Within weeks of developing my super-ultra-megacrush, I track down a publicist and Dweezil and I get on a guest list for a charity event that Jon Bon Jovi is expected to attend. I think, *All I have to do is show up. He'll see me and ask me to move out of my parents' house, and we'll live happily ever after.*

It's night and way past my normal bedtime, and I'm driving to a bowling alley in Orange County. Dweezil, my wingman, is in the passenger seat. We both look and smell great. I'm wearing a half shirt and a tuxedo jacket, a miniskirt, wrestling shoes, and Fidji by Guy Laroche. Dweezil is wearing a lime-green jacket and pants with playing cards on them, and Drakkar Noir, the male counterpart to my fragrance. I keep checking the rearview to see if I've spackled enough concealer onto my raised zits. Dweezil fidgets with the radio dial, barely speaking to me. I can tell I'm going to owe him big-time for this. I don't care.

We arrive at a bowling alley lit by fluorescent lights. We smile for paparazzi, sign a few autographs, then enter the large, one-story, loud adult fun zone. Crashing pins, metal blaring on the sound system, swells of competing party laughter, big hair and bright clothes, BO, beer, and hard liquor assault our senses. Dweezil immediately gives me the Look.

"Thirty minutes max," I say with pleading eyes. "You look that way and I'll look this way." With our backs to each other, we stand, as the only non-drinkers. Like father, like kids.

I scan the crowd of hair-sprayed rockers, lingerie models, porn stars, and posers. We see the drunk guys from Dokken, the drunk guys from Poison, the drunk guys from Rough Cutt, and a host of other Jack Daniel's–from–the–bottle types . . . but no Jon. "Maybe he's not gonna show," says Dweezil.

"He'll show." But . . . will he? Until this moment it hadn't occurred to me that he might not show. I mean, who gets invited to an awesome party with their peers and doesn't show? I look at the clock. I admit to myself I'm starting to panic but say nothing. Dweezil is getting restless. "We'll give it until eleven oh seven," I say.

"Eleven," he says.

"Fine," I say. "Wanna play Ms. Pac-Man?" I think this may buy us a little more time.

"No," he says, leaning against the wall closest to the exit.

Nine excruciating minutes pass, but the wait pays off. Dweezil spots him before I do. He looks just like he does in the video—maybe a little shorter and a little skinnier, but even from where we are standing, I can see *it*, the moon necklace. I can't believe he's wearing it. I take it as a sign. We beeline over.

"Hi," I blurt, interrupting his conversation with some dude I don't recognize, who therefore doesn't matter. I'm on a mission. "I'm Moon," I gush, pointing at his milky clavicle, "and this is my brother Dweezil." He has on skintight light-colored jeans, pointy boots, and a vest over a shirt with the sleeves cut off. Tufts of chest hair glisten and protrude from the crew neck and artful slashes of his tee.

"Hey," Jon says, sipping his beer and looking past us. I look where he's looking, at a sea of scantily dressed, very stacked young ladies I didn't notice before. There's an army of them. I see them now. They all look like centerfolds.

"I like your necklace," I say, taking the most direct line between two points. "Yunno, because my name is Moon."

"Oh yeah?" he says. He's polite but disinterested. Dweezil is shaking his head, giving me the "Come on, this isn't happening, Moon, so give up" vibe. "What sign are you, Jon?" I say suddenly as a last effort to snap my fiancé awake.

"Pisces," he says, signaling to a cocktail waitress.

"Pisces?" I say, my face contorting like I'm neck-deep in raw sewage. "But . . . But . . . I'm a Libra." Right then and there I decide it will never work between us. "Bye," I say, now equally disinterested. "Come on, Dweezil, let's go."

🌐

I DRIVE HOME CRYING. *HOW? HOW?* is on repeat in my head as we careen home on the 405 North. What an amateur move on my part. I easily could have found out his sign and avoided this completely. The sting of never having had a boyfriend feels like acid burning my skin.

"What is the big deal?" asks Dweezil. "Just pick someone else to obsess over."

"You don't get it," I say. I grip the steering wheel tighter, step on the gas. Even though I had a hit single on the radio a few years back and it still gets played, and even though I have done some television and have a couple of parts in some movies under my belt, I feel like a freak because no one wants to get close to me. Really love me, the forever way. Or at the very least deflower me the right way.

Outwardly I blame everything on the fact that guys are afraid of my rock-icon dad. Inwardly I fear it's because all guys are like my dad. No one loves honesty, directness, earnestness, vulnerability.

No one loves a reader.

I AM IN NEW YORK taking meetings with casting directors and hanging with some friends in the lobby of the Royalton when I meet a heavy metal drummer in a band with more double consonants than vowels. He's a grown-up. He even dresses like a grown-up—spiked wrist cuffs, shredded jean shorts, blond highlights, and eyeliner. He asks for my number, also like a grown-up. Back in LA he actually calls me, as he promised, from various hotels on the road, and we talk for hours. Well, he does most of the talking. And mostly about the Beatles. Yawn.

He's a Libra, like me, which is good, but married with kids, which is bad, but ultimately fine because we are just friends—just two friends talking until we both fall asleep on the phone several nights a week.

One summer night I'm lying on my bed in my bedroom, which Justine Bateman and I just splatter-painted pink, aqua, and yellow. I am staring at my ceiling, twirling the phone cord around my finger, when the dreamy drummer I'm now regularly talking to says, "You should come to Florida." I freeze.

Laughing, I try to play his flirty invitation off. "Oh, should I?"

"Yeah, you should," he repeats with no irony in his husky, married voice. "I'll get you your own room. It'll be fun. You can just visit as my friend." I sit up, but my heartbeat is thunder in my ears—he means it.

"As your *friend* . . . ," I say back, stressing the word "friend."

"Yeah. I think of you as a friend. Aren't we friends?"

"Yes . . . well . . ." I assess his question. I don't think this suggestion is in any way a good idea, but I can't say that. What if he stops liking me or stops calling me? If I am honest, I think of him as an older friend I'm attracted to. Then again, a lot of my friends are attractive. I reason, *Beauty is important to me. Does he think I'm attractive? Can guys actually be friends with girls they think are attractive? Can older guys be friends with girls under twenty?* I decide to ask Dweezil and some of my other guy friends what they think about this, after I get off the phone.

"Well?" he says. "How about this weekend? You can hop on the bus and stay for a few days. C'mon."

"What would your wife think?" I say, warming to his invitation but still a little wary. "Shouldn't she visit you if you are lonely?" I blurt out. I feel a surge of pride, being protective of his wife and protective of myself. I wonder how many of the women my dad approached had the courage to be so direct and respectful of my mother.

"She just visited, and anyway she's home with the kids. You and I are . . . friends," he coos. "Look, I'll even buy your plane ticket."

No one has ever bought me a plane ticket before, besides my parents. He must really like me.

"Let me ask Gail and Frank," I say, stalling. I mean, I do have to ask them. I do still live at home. "I'll ask them and let you know what they say." I feel another swell of self-protection pride. "Hold on."

I set the phone down on my flowery Laura Ashley duvet, take a deep breath, and head for my parents' room. The door is open. I knock loudly anyway.

"Hello?" I call out. "Can I come in?"

"Yes," comes my dad's voice.

I walk past their bathroom, which is festooned with discarded clothes and towels on the tile floor. I glance at the big window showcasing the little courtyard. When I enter their sleeping area, I see

Gail and Frank sitting in their California king bed together, topless. Which means they are also bottomless. Anxious to exit quickly, I speak fast. "Can I go on tour with a married heavy metal drummer? He's paying. And I'd only be going as his friend."

I recoil when they say in unison, "Go! It'll be fun!"

I must not have been clear. I repeat myself, this time more slowly, enunciating the words I need them to focus on. "I have been invited to go *on tour* with a *married* man, but we are *just friends*, so . . . go?" This time I pantomime airplane wings.

"Yes! Go!" they say again.

My posture screams disbelief, outrage even. I want them to say no, to protect me, so I can say no and protect me, so I can blame them for not being able to go, so the very cute married drummer will still like me and be my friend without being mad at me. "Go?" I ask again in a small, tight voice.

"He's paying, right?" says my dad.

"Yes," I say.

They stare at me.

I stare back.

My dad slides a Winston out of an open pack, lights it.

A few minutes later I am back in my room staring at my phone. I pick it up. I can hear Sade's "Smooth Operator" playing in the background. "You still there?"

WHEN I LAND IN FLORIDA, I am driven straight to the show. I am given an all-access pass and ushered into the venue past a chain-link fence of screaming girls with visible underboob.

In the middle of the concert, the married drummer pulls out all the stops. He makes sure I'm seated by the soundboard, where the acoustics are the best and he can find me in the crowd, because he's doing that twirly-finger drummer thing and pointing directly at me and mouthing the word "YOU!" I have to admit, it's pretty intoxicating. And flattering. And sexy.

After the show, we can't stop smiling at each other. He hugs me all sweaty with a towel wrapped around his neck. Pheromone overload. He keeps the obligatory postshow backstage band hellos to a bare minimum and we head for the hotel bar, even though I'm too young to be in there. He's drinking champagne and I'm sipping a Shirley Temple. After I hurl a fawning multitude of post-concert compliments his way, we don't have that much to talk about. I start yawning. "Good night," I say, "thanks again for such a fun show. It really was so great and so, so cool how you singled me out."

He polishes off the last gulp of his drink, sets the flute down a little too firmly. "Wait a minute," he says. "I flew you all the way out here. You can't just go to your room." He stands up and grabs the open champagne bottle out of the ice bucket. "We can go to mine."

"Um," I say, "okay . . ."

I follow him, staring at my feet. Then we are standing at his door and he's unlocking it.

I want to run back to my room and call an actress friend and ask her what to do. Her cherry was claimed by a *Tiger Beat* pinup and now they are a real couple with real problems. A few weeks back I even drove her to get a secret abortion. She'd taken some of her acting money out of the ATM two days in a row because there's a three-hundred-dollar limit and the abortion was four hundred in cash. We pinkie-swore to never tell her boyfriend or her family. After her procedure I felt bad for judging her, so I took her to get her favorite turkey sandwich on Italian sesame bread, with shredded lettuce and extra mayo, and made it like a girly spa day with a special treat.

Heavy metal drummer opens his door and turns on the light. "Well, don't just stand there, come on in." He holds the door with his foot until I'm inside.

His room looks just like mine except his clothes are everywhere and he has a VCR and a boom box. He puts on the Madonna *Like a*

Virgin video concert tour with the sound down for the visuals and plays INXS's album *Listen Like Thieves* for the music and mood. He offers me some quaaludes and I pass. He eats my portion and drowns it with more champagne from the bottle, then strips down to nothing and hops on the bed. I want to ask him about a condom but feel frozen. He pats the mattress. I obey and robotically take a seat beside him and begin to undress. Everything above my waist. Then I lie down next to him and awkwardly remove the rest of my clothes. I do not mention I am new to all of this, despite the one "romantic" attempt in the UK.

He lies on top of me and grinds his hipbones into mine until our stomachs are sweaty. I feel a soft, thick dampness making circles in the space between my legs. It isn't pleasurable. Is this what Frank and Gail feel? If so, why be so noisy about something so . . . nothing? Then he fast-pumps a few times and it's over. He rolls off, spent, leaving me to sleep on the wet spot. Even though he is out cold within minutes, I am wide awake. I just lie there feeling . . . confused.

A tidal wave of remorse hits me. How could I do that to another woman, knowing how mad it makes my mother when my father cheats like the drummer and I just did? Does my dad ever feel regret like I do now? Does this drummer? Do my dad's slutty side dishes? If not, how do any of these people live with themselves? I am feeling a permanent kind of dirty I can't wash off.

As soon as the sun is up, I make arrangements to leave two days early. The drummer is miffed but doesn't say anything, just flicks his long golden hair and waves goodbye as my taxi heads for the airport. When I get home, my parents ask me how the trip was. I say, "Fine," and leave it at that.

Back in the safety of my bedroom, in my own bed, I let myself feel some small amount of relief about having tried naked sex and finally at least heading in the direction of normal, like all my friends. Maybe now I can find a real, steady boyfriend. Sting seems like a good option.

❀

I'M HAVING TROUBLE SLEEPING, THOUGH. Every day I still feel like a shit and worry the drummer's wife will find out and confront me, not that I know who she is, where they live, or what she looks like. I am drowning in self-hatred and fear of running into her. Even if I apologize, I know the drummer's wife will still hate me and feel as shitty as my mom feels. The hate Gail feels never goes away.

Thankfully I don't hear from him or his wife. But I do throw up at Disneyland.

A group of us are there doing a photo shoot for *Life* magazine to go with a piece on my pal Molly Ringwald, who is now Dweezil's girl-friend. I write off the puking to drinking Carnation milk with a hot dog and riding the teacups. But when I puke again a short time later while exiting Tomorrowland, I decide I better take a pregnancy test.

Later that night, I see the two plus signs on the stick. My baby dream is coming true in the exact wrong way, so I call my actress friend, the same one I recently took to get *her* abortion. Now it's my turn to go to the bank two days in a row, to take out four hundred dollars of my "Valley Girl" money. She drives me to her Beverly Hills gyno who takes cash and we pinkie-swear to keep this from the drummer and from my family. On the way home we get girly spa turkey sandwiches again, and when she drops me off at my parents' house, my pupils are the size of pins. No one notices.

That night I lie awake feeling certain I am being punished for having sex, and for having it with a married man. I have a full-blown panic attack and become absolutely convinced I have AIDS, too. AIDS is on the news all the time now. Isn't that the karma I deserve?

Earlier my doctor mentioned I am supposed to stay off my feet so I don't clot or get an infection. I didn't tell him I am pulling dou-ble duty as a language consultant and an actress and have to be up at 5 a.m. and on the *Fast Times* set by 6.

After two days of being on my feet for too long at an abandoned high school in the Valley in the full heat of a California summer, I do start clotting. I'm terrified. I convince myself that I'm gonna die from blood loss, infection, and AIDS. A kind, older red-haired actress named Kit notices I seem "off." Through tears, I confess. "Let's call your doctor and get your legs up. Maybe you can also get tested before you write your will." She is so kind that my self-hatred and panic briefly subside. So does my bleeding, and I decide I don't have to out myself or say goodbye to my parents just yet.

But that night, I still can't sleep. I knock on the wall next to the open door of my parents' bedroom. "Can I come in?" I call out. I tell them everything without taking a breath, like a fire hose extinguishing a hillside blaze. "I slept with the married drummer when I went to Florida but only one time and I got pregnant and I used my 'Valley Girl' money to get an abortion and I'm scared I have AIDS as extra punishment for what I did."

They both stare at me. Finally, my dad says, "Wow, you are a good actress." It's the first compliment he's ever given me. Gail says nothing. Not a single word.

Then they hug me. I don't feel comforted, but I do feel relieved for telling them the truth. The AIDS test comes back negative. I have no proof, but I am pretty certain it's a reward for my confession.

ONE YEAR LATER I RUN into the drummer, rounding a corner in Chicago of all places. With the shock of seeing him again, in person, randomly, everything comes bursting out of me, including the part about me technically having been a virgin. His eyes immediately well up. "Can't you see, Moon, it's a sign! I'm supposed to leave my wife for you."

"No! It's not a sign. I just . . . needed to tell you."

He calls me from the road a few more times after that. Usually, I don't pick up. One time I do, though. It's late at night and he sounds sad and drunk. "Love Me Do" is playing in the background. "I just had to hear your voice," he says. "I'm just so sad about what happened and I'm so sorry."

"That's okay," I say, attempting to make *him* feel better.

"I really think it's a sign," he repeats.

I don't say anything. Then a long silence passes.

We both just listen to each other breathe for a little while, knowing that when we hang up it's really going to be the end. "It's just . . . ," he begins, "you're the only person I can really talk to about this. You . . . and my good friend Jon Bon Jovi."

CHAPTER 36

A Different Loneliness

Gail is alone in the kitchen playing solitaire when I approach her. I am terrified because this could go a million different ways. Up until now I have been able to compartmentalize Frank's treatment of Gail and appreciate his underwhelming but semicool attention when I get it. Now I've hit a point of no return. We've ridden "Valley Girl" as far as it will take us. I have been unable to parlay that opportunity into a steady revenue stream or a steady boyfriend. I do not yet understand I am missing a strong foundation upon which to grow the rest of my life. I do not yet know I am seeking something outside myself to fill the inside of myself.

I decide that I am better off alone.

Step one: Get a self. But how?

Start by getting away from what's hurting you. At home I am a puppet, a parrot, dressed up for show when my parents need me to appear a certain way to the public. It is a veritable loony bin inside my head, a tangle of ways to be in any given situation. I've got to escape, or I'll never know who I am. And can become.

Of course, I can't articulate any of this in a house where no one talks about anything, least of all feelings or each other's needs. I only feel it like a slow strangulation and death by a thousand cuts. It feels bad enough for me to take a new action. Or at least blurt one.

"Gail," I say, "I want to move out."

"Okay," she says without looking up. There is no emotion in her voice. I guess she really meant it when she suggested I get a sex apartment, and it was just a matter of time until I did it her way. "You should buy a house," she continues. "Your father and I have set aside your earnings from 'Valley Girl,' and you could use the forty thousand dollars as a down payment."

"Wait," I say, "I didn't know I had *that* much money." Gail looks up at me like I am an idiot. I am utterly clueless about whether this is a little money or a lot of money. My parents have never had a single discussion about money or budgets or debt or spending or savings with us. No practice runs for me and my siblings with piggy banks and chore rewards like other families. We've repeatedly watched Gail overspend at the same time she said we have no money. The best conclusion I can draw is that this is a leap-and-the-net-appears universe. For me, Frank and Gail are both universe *and* net, and I am on autopilot.

Gail helps me "house hunt." After looking at seven properties Gail vets, including one the Realtor tells us was a getaway cabin for movie stars in the heyday of Hollywood, I make my selection. It has a fireplace; a useless "garden" full of shade, dirt, and ivy; and three fruit-bearing avocado trees. It has a covered back patio with a leaking roof, but a cool sunken tub and steam shower. It has a deck with an ant-covered Chinese elm tree and is too close to the sounds of traffic on Beverly Glen. It's perfect.

Gail handles all the paperwork, including something called "cosigning the loan," and I move into the tiny one-bedroom, one-bathroom house, eight miles away from my childhood home. Sure, I have neighbors who scream all day and often block my car in, but Gustav Mahler's daughter lives up the street; I never meet her but feel a daughter-of-a-composer kinship with her.

With some rest and distance, what I realize that first month is I feel better feeling alone and lonely while actually alone than feeling alone and lonely around other people, as I often did with my family.

Yet, I don't know what to do with myself. In the beginning I read and watch TV and stay up and sleep in as late as I want. Soon I realize I can expand my options. I don't have to share my food or shower every day. Hell, if I choose, I never have to fold someone else's laundry or clean a litter box or answer the phone and take a message or be at someone's beck and call or get yelled at as long as I live. I do know that solitude allows my mind to explode and to go slow enough to examine old feelings, thoughts, and events and make sense of them.

The longer I am away, the more clearly I see that my father and the culture at large have been giving me the steady message that women have feelings that don't matter, that women are fuck toys wrapped in lies about female empowerment and responsibility for our own orgasm.

Gail and Frank continuing to fuck and fight and stay together or not fuck and fight and stay together has warped me. I feel responsible for making sure she is okay, so he is okay, so we kids are okay, but isn't that the adults' job? Gail and Frank don't seem capable of being kind, patient, affectionate, or problem solvers. Frank uses his talents out in the world. Gail adopts a stance of smiling enlightenment and phony Zen acceptance to visitors, but inside she is actively vindictive, putting witchy curses in contracts and on women my dad cheats with. Dweezil and my dad seem particularly fragile to me from my new distance, Gail meaner and more broken. I wish I could rescue Ahmet and Diva. None of us seem built for life.

Without any distractions, I feel weird, numb, bad, lost, confused. I do not realize I am trying to heal. These kinds of scars are invisible. I do not know I am depressed. I do not know I have no coping skills. I only know my name and new address, and neither of those things truly feel like they belong to me.

CHAPTER 37

Matchmaker Frank

In the year I turn twenty, Frank calls me on the telephone for the first time in my life—to tell me he wants to fix me up with someone. "He's here now, come over," he says. I am so shocked my dad has *called* me *and* that he wants to play *matchmaker* that I drop everything, get in my car, and drive straight to the house to meet "an economics major from Carnegie Mellon" whom Frank met while on his political lecture circuit. They are seated in the basement drinking coffee when I arrive. Ali stands to shake my hand. He is tall with a hand that is soft and the size of a catcher's mitt. "She'd make a good Muslim," Frank says to the young man. They smile and nod.

"Ha ha," I say, shaking his hand. I feel like I am on offer at a livestock auction. I take him in, my potential husband. He's wearing expensive preppy attire from head to toe, polite, and doughy, with wavy black hair, dark skin, and intense dark eyes. I can't tell if Frank is serious about this guy or joking, then notice my father is all smiles. He is sincerely getting a kick out of talking money and politics with this warm Middle Eastern brainiac. I settle in and join the conversation, and eventually find him enjoyable enough to exchange phone numbers. There are no sparks, but I am glad to have met him, glad my father is taking an interest in my life in this way.

Unbelievably, I book a decent-size role in a crappy vampire movie that is filming in Ali's town of Pittsburgh. Out of deference to my father, Ali and I meet for a meal. The second meeting confirms our differences and total lack of chemistry—it's mutual—but he's a good ear and sweet to let me vent about the low-budget film I am shooting. The movie is a flop. So is our potential love match.

Back in LA I get a job doing an ad-free radio gig showcasing new music. I love the freedom of making eclectic playlists, discovering new artists' music, and working with the kind engineer. I am trying out all sorts of gigs to see if something will stick. I am getting more and more used to living in the shadow of my dad and trying to accept that's just something I have to overcome.

Then I discover the comedy scene and start seeing live shows. Laughter relieves my stress. Newcomers Chris Rock and Janeane Garofalo are my favorites. I wonder if I could ever perform comedy. I wonder if I would enjoy the safety of admission to a darkened, faceless audience but with the immediate feedback of laughter, or of none. I meet Janeane and gush. She says, "Try comedy a hundred times before you decide." I tuck her advice away.

While I am visiting my family one afternoon, to my great surprise my father sings my praises *again*, this time to a visitor named David Carson, who tells me he is starting an innovative magazine with experimental typography called *Ray Gun*. Frank tells the skateboarding entrepreneur he should put my art in his cool new magazine and maybe hire me as a journalist. Because of my father's introduction,

I get a foot in the door. This is how I try writing for a living. The shadow feels useful, if still weighty.

After David leaves, my dad tells me and Gail and my siblings that he's looking into running for president. *Oh great*, I think, *more people wanting his time.* Then I put two and two together. Maybe my dad is suddenly investing in my life because mine currently reflects poorly on him. Maybe he needs me to get my shit in order, and fast, in case we move into the White House.

—

CHAPTER 38

Like, Om-migod

I am still on the family payroll even though I have moved out. I feel like a twenty-year-old twelve-year-old with an allowance who was sent to her room, only her room is a tiny house eight miles away. With each downturn in my career I feel like a hot mess served on a garbage can lid. I'd rather die than get a normal job, so I feel inferior to anyone who bucks up and tolerates fluorescent lighting. I have no humility and no self-worth, which seem diametrically opposed, but it's who I am. Not a great combo, especially if we are going to be a First Family for the next four years.

To make things weirder, I've met almost all my entertainment heroes and they seem not an iota happier, just less financially insecure and more party prone. I know that my exposure to art and entertainment is rare and I should feel lucky. Or at least cool. But without strong family love, what is the point of achieving? What is the point of anything?

It is when I am in this vulnerable, isolated, and highly susceptible state that a new path comes into focus.

I read a piece in the *New York Times* about an acting teacher who has turned Mickey Rourke's and Jessica Lange's careers around—with her help, Jessica got nominated for not one but *two* Academy Awards in the same year. It occurs to me that maybe I have been doing the wrong things in the wrong order. Instead of trying to build my career and life from the ground up, maybe I need to skip ahead. I need to find mega-success first, out of the gate, like with "Valley Girl." With mega-success in my own right, I will naturally walk toward a life full of love and joy. And maybe be friends with my hero peers Jodie Foster, Jennifer Jason Leigh, and Juliette Lewis.

I read on.

Then I contact the teacher.

This mysterious woman with a voice like soft, padded cat paws informs me she will "meditate" on me and on my name and I will be contacted if and only if her meditation reveals I am "ready." She also warns me that people's careers either flourish or stall out completely when they work with her. As in *forever*.

Raised by atheists, for the first time in my life I pray. To *her* God. To anyone and everyone's God—I HAVE TO GET IN THAT CLASS. I HAVE TO FLOURISH. And fast. I may have a country to help lead. Or at least not embarrass.

It works. I get the call. I'm in. The Berkshires in Massachusetts, here I come. I am a chosen one.

APPARENTLY THIS TEACHER HAS ALSO meditated on my accommodations and much older roommates, who seem a little less carefully chosen in my estimation. I have never shared a living space with anyone I wasn't related to before, and now I am with four strangers with two bathrooms in a split-level home in the snowy Bay State.

The space where we will be transformed by our "shadow work" and "dream work" is a large room with a wall of windows providing natural light and a view of a snowy bank, a mill, and an icy river rushing past. There are several mats on the floor arranged like napping spots. In another section of the room is a cozy, warm carpeted zone with a single photo of a skinny woman, the teacher's "guru," who has a red dot on her forehead. She looks like an Indian version of

Edie Sedgwick, emaciated and beautiful with intense eyes and close-cropped hair under a jaunty hat. In front of the photo, a candle burns at all times.

A round woman with John Lennon glasses and a shawl sits on a chair with her eyes closed. I assume she is the teacher, but I wouldn't know because she doesn't introduce herself, which I find extremely pretentious. She also reminds me of Gail, and not in a good way. I promptly nickname this woman Jabba the Cunt, then shame myself. If this is good enough for Mickey and Jessica, I need to be humble, shut my piehole, and drink in what she has to teach. I'm here to learn how to win Oscars.

The days go like this: Lie down and wait until the teacher intuits it's time to speak, then accept her emotional prompt, which usually is something like a past event we are to vividly reexperience, maybe the first time someone showed us a kindness or shamed us or made us feel aroused or inspired. In these prompts we are told to embrace ourselves at the age when the event happened and to let our senses vividly reexperience the air temperature, sounds, smells. I gather the idea of this exercise is so you can use real feelings when acting. Like if you book a movie and have to be sad about, say, an alien eating a crew member on your galactic space station, you can conjure up your real dead dog or something similar.

From what I can tell, whoever cries the most during one of these prompts gets to "work" in front of the class with the teacher's undivided attention. If you do well in the work, a metric only she can track or judge, your reward is sitting in the carpeted area in front of the photo of the guru and listening to a tape of a heartbeat. During the tape we are told to repeat a mantra—"Om namah shivaya"—and concentrate as hard and intentionally as we can. This way the teacher, her guru, and our spirit selves, which are all invisibly linked somehow, can transmit additional information from our subconscious and make us even better actors. I give it my all and in no time my own heartbeat, inhalations, and exhalations merge with the mantra.

I find all of this very weird. But I keep my eye on the prize—a golden statue like Jessica Lange has and a better life full of love.

Next the teacher delves into the importance of "knowing your shadow," and the shadow is sometimes your exact opposite—the nicest people get paid to play bad guys, meek people play heroes, gruff people play sensitive characters, and so on. I embrace these sweeping generalizations with gusto. Following that logic, I posit popular actors Tom Hanks and Meg Ryan must be total assholes in real life.

But what about me? What's my shadow? What is the opposite of nothing, since I feel like nothing? Everything?

We are told to use our dreams to access our subconscious and identify our career-defining shadows. Each night before bed, we are to write a letter to ourselves: *Dear Inner Self, If it is your will, please show me in a dream tonight what my shadow is.*

You do this over and over until you can remember your dream. Depending on what your dreams reveal, you may be asked to "sign out" of your current astrological sign and "sign in" to another, until you dream a new sign to be or just decide to change back and "sign in" to your old self. I am struggling to adopt these confusing systems, yet they do feel somewhat familiar, because these ideas jibe with things Gail has taught me. Folks expect precisely this type of thinking from a Zappa, but I want no part of this freaky shit unless it delivers the results I want.

Finally, I have a dream. A ditz and I are hanging out in matching flirty pink outfits and blowing bubbles. Translation? My shadow turns out to be, surprise, a Valley girl type of airhead, the shopping-obsessed, dimwitted, insensitive, needy, can-you-just-do-it-for-me bimbo type. I am told I must seek out more of these types of jobs because once we are all sufficiently typecast in our shadows, we can *then* get the breakaway roles that will garner high praise and prizes. Or we can stay in our shadow lanes and work forever, "like Christopher Reeve as Superman."

I am devastated. I don't want to be a bimbo forever. Plus, bimbos are usually blondes with giant boobs. Am I supposed to bleach my hair and get a boob job in order to work?

I look around at my classmates—Laura Dern, Kyle MacLachlan, and Jennifer Connelly seem to be on board with their shadows. This makes me feel even less sure of myself.

Then fate intervenes and I get incredibly sick. I miss some classes. A sweet-faced young man, who is the teacher's assistant, takes care of me. He is fully enmeshed with the teacher's guru but I fall for him anyway.

I see my classmates go on to secure great leads. I decide I was too judgmental about the teacher's methods. I decide I should be more receptive if I want to be a movie star. I decide maybe I need to go to the epicenter of everything, to my teacher's teacher, the guru. The assistant offers to take me. I want to meet the woman my crush likes more than he likes me.

For better or for worse, whether by accident or on purpose, I've been primed to obey charismatic leaders and follow nonsensical rules in an effort to escape the arbitrary demands and chaos of fame and my family. I throw myself in.

MY CRUSH AND I ARRIVE at the ashram, a palatial Indian temple located in the backwoods of Vermont. I try not to be seduced by the intoxicating foreign smells of neroli and sandalwood and the impressive scale of the gold and white temples. My crush leads me through the gardens, past statues and the colorful and somewhat scary Hindu images of half humans and half animals everywhere. I take note of the signs around the property that say "God Dwells Within You as You" and "In Order to Lead You Must First Learn How to Follow."

We are led to a giant hall and told over a loudspeaker that the hundreds of us seated there on cushions or carpeting are to chant and meditate for several hours as we celebrate the guru's arrival and subsequent "darshan." We are told there will be a feast after.

At first, I resist joining in with the singalong to the strange, hypnotic, droning melodies in Sanskrit because I am afraid. I feel like an infiltrator, a spy working from the inside. All I want to do is save my future career and my crush and get out of there. But because there are many successful actors I recognize in the throngs—Phylicia Rashad from *The Cosby Show*, Peggy Lipton from *The Mod Squad*, Gary Busey—I think, *How bad can this be if they are here?* I look over at my crush swaying in bliss beside me. I look around at the sea of others devotionally smiling and participating wholeheartedly. I observe the theatrics of the light show and the dancing and music getting louder and faster as the guru arrives. The closest experience I've had to this is at one of my father's concerts.

Finally, the guru appears. She is luminous and gives a humorous and compelling talk about the nature of existence and the goal of seeing through all illusion. She chants, and her sincerity is greater than her singing voice, which makes the notes and melody all the more penetrating. Then she tells . . . parables. She closes with a personal story about her guru's guru and the lineage of "the guru's flash," reiterating "one moment of enlightenment is worth everything." Then the lights dim, and she guides us into meditation. I disobey all her instructions and refuse to sit up straight, but the strangest thing happens . . . . I feel myself floating. I feel like I am light and sound and vibration and effervescence. I feel a flash of terror, but the feeling of relaxation and euphoria is greater than my fear. I float. I relax. I fly.

Then the lights come back on and I am "me" again. I am totally freaked out. Am I making up my reaction or is this real? What. The. Actual. Fuck.

I tell my date. He says I have had a "mystical experience," that the guru has given me "shaktipat." Totally normal. Happens to him all the time. He tells me from now on she can protect me and speak to me whenever I want her to. That she is everywhere and in all things.

We head for a line that wraps around the property to wait for her to bless us by bopping us all on the head with peacock feathers on the end of a staff she is holding. We wait for hours. We can see her blessing everyone on the jumbo screens.

Standing in the long line, it occurs to me that my younger siblings are in school and Gail is probably helping Frank as he flirts with the idea of with running for president. And here I am under a banner of marigolds drinking my weight in cardamom-infused tea, hoping to fast-track enlightenment in order to have my name read from an envelope at the Oscars. This is the divide between myself and the rest of my family.

When we begin to get close, I see it's like meeting a ball of light in human form, but also like seeing my dad, because we are told by her many helpers not to take up her time and to keep it brief. I distill all of my questions into one and when it's finally my turn I simply ask her, "Are you my guru?"

She looks me straight in the eye as she smacks me in the solar plexus with the back of her staff. "Meditate."

🌑

INSTANTLY I REPLACE ONE NORTH star—my father—with another: the guru. I swap out one batch of chaos and confusing messages for another. Spiritual purity and superiority will become my new coping skills. I will be a cipher, a zero, for my guru, my family, my country, *and* my career. I will be the very best at becoming nothing to receive everything.

—

CHAPTER 39

Normal Life?

I put photos of my guru up everywhere in my house to remind me that everything flows from her to me. I invest in candles that burn for twenty-four hours to keep my flame of devotion going. I create an altar with a fresh flower in a bowl of water where I can pray to her. I have a japa ring on my finger so I can silently chant the mantra she's given me. By now I chant and meditate and contemplate my guru so much that I get a TV series.

Dweezil and I are summoned to pitch a show and offered a deal with Brillstein/Grey and CBS to star in a sitcom loosely based on our family called *Normal Life*. In essence it's our updated spin on *The Addams Family*.

We will be paid a five-digit figure per episode before taxes and agency commissions, which means I don't have to stay on Gail's payroll, which means I don't have to constantly be at her beck and call. No more driving my siblings around out of obligation, only when I choose to, for fun. No more grocery runs. No more dealing with her lawyers and accountants. No more owing her my time because she bought my plane ticket or paid for my hotel room. No more going where she wants to go or doing what she wants to do or sitting where she sits or staying where she wants to stay. No more waiting for her or being late because of her poor time management. I'll be my own boss now. At long last I feel a sense of possibility and the beginning of financial stability. I may not have a boyfriend yet, but I have *guru-given* success. Now I can just sit back, relax, and receive all of my guru's abundance, because I am acting for *her* now.

Even though I am not playing my "shadow" and I am still driving my trusty Subaru four-door, I'm feeling a little holier-than-thou in my God-pocket flow state as I pull onto the lot and into the spot with my name on it. Is this what everyone feels when God is on their side?

As I grab my purse and head for the soundstage to read through the pilot, Gail's voice is in my head telling me nepotism and Frank's last name are the reason I am here. I incinerate it with the mantra. My first stop is the craft service table for half a bagel with cream cheese and a handful of peanut M&M's. I wave to Christina Applegate, a Laurel Canyon neighbor doing *Married with Children*, and feel full and happy with a view of the sun settling upon the Hollywood sign in the distance. Then it's on to my dressing room. *My* dressing room on *my* show. Wow.

I grab a Mrs. Beasley's lemon muffin, and someone with a walkie-talkie hands me a hot coffee and the script changes for today's table read. I am filled to the brim with gratitude. I am shown to a large table where our names are on paper place cards. Actors are clustered together on one side, flanked by the writing staff, producers, assistants, and studio execs on the other. I am excited to show the world how fun my real life and TV family are to role-model how much fun real people can have in real life with their own families.

Hellos and welcomes are exchanged, and we all settle into our folding chairs, armed with Day-Glo highlighters and Bics for making notes in the script margins. I circle my lines and highlight any time I see "Tess," the name I have chosen for my character, after Nastassja Kinski's character in *Tess*. I am thrilled to see so much neon yellow.

"Action!" calls the director, the first AD reads the stage directions, and we are off and running, reading our very first episode aloud. Right away there is a tension, a feeling of deadness. Some of the writers laugh too loudly or too soon or too late to punctuate lines of dialogue that feel false and not at all funny.

They seem to have veered away from a family united in weirdness in a conservative world and embarked on a family story about weird kids sandwiched between tolerant, conservative parents and a conservative sibling who gets sucked into our shenanigans. A sort of who's-parenting-who show. To make things weirder, the chick who plays the airhead on the show is given all the funniest lines even though Dweezil and I are the stars. I no longer feel proud but feel embarrassed. Who do I complain to? How do I fix this?

I decide I will hang with the writers at lunch today. I tell our director my idea, which he promptly vetoes, explaining the writers will address the studio's notes. We are promised changes after lunch. Cool!

After our catered Cobb salads, we start blocking with the latest script changes. We start shooting in four days, so these new lines have to work, but they don't. Word gets back to me and Dweezil that Cindy Williams will replace our TV mom. There are other notes—for me. I am told my ass is too jiggly and that America doesn't want to see that. Also, I have to work one-on-one with an acting coach.

I am beyond insulted. It's *my* show. Loosely based on *my* life. Why do I need help acting like *myself*? Besides, I have already studied with the best of the best—from improv to the Meisner technique, the Method to scene study and shadow work. I have booked many jobs—not tons, but enough—*and* I have a guru.

I am livid.

But an order from CBS and Brillstein/Grey is an order. And since the guru blessed the show, maybe all that is happening is a hidden gift, even if I can't see the wisdom in it.

I MANAGE TO FIND A parking spot a few blocks up on the acting teacher's congested, tree-lined street east of La Brea, near Beverly. I lock my car and web my keys through my fingers like I always do in a place where I have never been. It is the habit of being a girl in the city as well as the daughter of a tall man who sometimes wears a bulletproof vest in public and travels with an even taller man called a bodyguard.

As I walk toward this Roy person's building, I think, *All the coaches I ever worked with were well-known, professional. It's bad enough I have been forced to work with an acting coach, one I have never heard of, but it's even worse that I am expected to meet this total stranger in his apartment. I don't even know anyone who lives in an apartment. Certainly no one who lives and works out of one.*

I climb some stone stairs, check the directory, and search for his name. Roy London. That doesn't even sound like a real name. It sounds like a stage name, like Veronica Lake or Winona Ryder. I press the buzzer. "Take the elevators to the left of the first set of archways to the penthouse," comes an enthusiastic male voice over the silver intercom. It's then that I notice the building's architecture—French chateau circa 1930—and that it is beautiful and ritzy as hell.

The lobby is as gorgeous as the façade and courtyard. Giant beamed ceilings, crown molding, a marble fireplace, and imported terra-cotta honeycomb floor tiles.

My fury turns into anxiety.

"Hello!" says Roy as the elevator opens into the foyer of his two-thousand-square-foot, all-white penthouse. He wears a navy T-shirt and khaki cargo shorts. Everything about him is round. Which I am mad to admit I sort of like. He is ebullient and warm, with penetrating intelligence and a confidence that could easily read as arrogance.

"Hello," I say back, withering against the backdrop of eighteen-foot vaulted ceilings, entryway skylights, hardwood floors, steel casement windows, and museum-worthy art.

"Let me show you around," says Roy with pride. I follow him into a beautifully appointed living room with just the right amount of comfortable-looking furniture. The space says "civilized adult," but it's warm. He points to a humongous bouquet of fragrant, globe-size flowers. "Those are from Geena Davis," he says with proud-parent enthusiasm. "They just announced her nomination for Best Actress for her role in *The Accidental Tourist*."

"Oh," I say, "you worked with her on that?"

"Yes." He nods, beaming.

"I loved her in that. 'You have to cluck every little minute,'" I say. I look around. Everything is tidy and sunny here, with natural light flooding in.

"This was a gift from Garry Shandling," he says, pointing to a coffee-table book the size of a dog bed. "Sherilyn Fenn gave me that wall hanging there; the rare, numbered print was a gift from Sharon Stone; that hand-blown glass is from Michelle Pfeiffer . . ." And on the tour goes.

The showstopper comes last: a typed and signed framed letter addressed to him from J. D. Salinger. "My rejection letter," he says, beaming, "when I asked him for the rights to adapt and direct *The Catcher in the Rye*."

I am officially intimidated.

◕

WE SIT AT HIS KITCHEN table and read through the pilot script. "Well, it's terrible writing," he begins, confirming my worst suspicions. "But no matter. I can always find something for you to act in any piece of writing." My stomach flips over. "Really, I can make sure you always come across well regardless of the garbage you are saddled with. That's what I do. Okay . . . What do you want?"

"What do you mean?" I ask.

"In your life. What do you want? I want you to ask for it in this scene but use these words here on the page to ask for it." I stare blankly at him. "What do you want? In your life. This minute."

I look around inside myself and draw a total blank. The sentences don't even compute. *What do I want? What do I* want? *Wait, I get to want something? In my life? The life that belongs to everyone else?*

"Nothing," I say finally. "I don't want anything."

"That's impossible. Everyone wants something." He is suddenly impassioned. "And you have to want it so much that the desire comes out of your vagina." He is trying to shock me with language, but he obviously doesn't know the house I grew up in. There is nothing he could say that would make me flinch or raise an eyebrow. "Are you saying you are completely happy in your life?"

Except that.

I struggle to answer. Then, out of nowhere, like we're in a scene in a blockbuster comedy, a blond, shirtless Adonis of a window washer lowers himself to clean Roy's kitchen window. "No . . ." I trail off, watching the window washer rhythmically soap up the glass with one hand and squeegee it clean with the other.

"Because if you are, you can teach me a thing or two . . ."

"No," I repeat, "I'm not happy."

"So . . . What do you want? Your family to always be safe? An end to world hunger? A friend to get off drugs? Babies to stop getting sold into prostitution?" Spittle lands in my eyelash.

When the chiseled David Lee Roth–alike raises his arms, I am transfixed by the tufts of his wet, darker blond armpit hair.

"What are you looking at?" Roy turns in the direction of the man suspended twenty-seven stories above the street and sees what I see: the hottest heaven-sent male supermodel with his pelvis thrust forward in a harness, balanced on a narrow metal platform. Roy turns and looks at me. A wide smile spreads across his face. "You want that?" he says, entirely pleased with himself.

My throat tightens. I blush against my will and burn with embarrassment. I feel caught, like a naughty toddler. The window washer keeps his gaze fixed on me.

"You want him?"

I blink, a deer in his headlights, the prey to his cheetah advances.

"You want HIM?" Roy says loud enough for the window washer to hear. Roy may as well be shouting from a pulpit. Or a courtroom. He's a judge and jury now, sealing my future fate on death row. "You want sex? You want LOVE?"

"No!" I stand and shout at Roy. A total lie. And we both know it. My face is red and wet and hot.

Roy's eyes are softer now, moved by the gaping crack in my façade that he's pried open. He digs his feet and fingers into the footholds. "You ready to work?"

I can tell he means more than acting. He is asking if I am ready to get totally real with myself and stop my lifelong practice of pretending in my family and in the world.

Hallelujah. I mentally kiss the hem of his cargo shorts. This man will become my teacher and chosen father figure. I will study all that Roy has to impart and never leave his side.

CHAPTER 40

One Fresh Raisin

The phone rings. I wait. I love screening calls. It rings again.

I pick up.

"Hey. It's Justine."

"Hey," I say from the coziness of my bed. "Hi."

"Hi," she says effusively, warmth spilling into my ears, "how are you?"

"Good, you?" I say.

"I'm great," she says, and means it. I marvel. "Mike wants to fix you up with a friend of his. He's suggesting we meet at a billiard place on La Brea."

"That's so nice of him," I say, sitting up. I am supremely touched. Even though he's friendly to me when I visit Justine on set, we aren't friends, and I don't think I could ever call Michael J. Fox plain old "Mike." He is always his whole name to me. But to him, I am Moon, not Moon Unit Zappa. "When is he thinking?"

"Uh, now?" she laughs. "I'm already down here. It's pretty empty, which is nice. It's more crowded in the VIP area on the second floor. Cool folks. Chill."

"Okay," I say, even though I am tucked in with one of my favorite Brontë sisters.

"Bye," comes her singsong voice, and like that, I have committed myself.

I dog-ear the page and hop out of my Robin Hood–green, queen-size sleigh bed and hurry past my pink and white striped wallpaper to my walk-in closet. I toss my Laura Ashley nightie into my hamper and throw on a skirt, my lace-up wrestling boots, and a baggy sweater.

Cruising along Sunset Boulevard through Beverly Hills with my sunroof open and the heat on is sheer pleasure. The perfectly paved, wide roads have plenty of streetlights that cast an amber hue, and the large homes with well-lit lawns and decorative fountains make for a scenic and pleasing ride. I have plenty of time to listen to great songs to build up my confidence. I check my reflection. I want to make sure my face and makeup look right in all lighting possibilities. I want to make sure my zits don't make shadows. I bet men never think about lighting for even a second.

I STAND ON THE SIDEWALK behind the velvet ropes and wait my turn to enter. Velvet ropes are obligatory. So are doormen. Even if you are the only one waiting to go in, you are made to stand and be granted access. LA is nothing if not a place to endure endless displays of the pecking order.

A bodybuilder finally lets me in. I find Justine and she gives my arm a punch. She walks me to the bar so I can grab a sparkling water with cranberry and lime, points the guy out, and tells me what she knows so far. "He moved here for a role on a show that shoots one soundstage over from *Family Ties* on the Paramount lot." My eye scans the room to see where she's pointing. Mike and his blond friend glance back at us. They appear to be halfway through a game that seems to have playfully, and loudly-for-our-benefit, escalated into psych-outs, good-natured ribbings, and minor threats. Mike is dressed like a slightly more casual version of Alex P. Keaton. His friend has a baby face and is as fair as the pale, foamy beer he's drinking. He looks like he raided the wardrobe department on set unsupervised—acid-washed jeans and a Cosby sweater, a neon-green nylon baseball cap, and round-toed light brown cowboy boots.

"Well?" asks Justine.

I do not say I feel sorry for this guy because he looks ridiculous. I do not want to seem ungrateful. Besides, both Mike and Justine like him, so maybe I am seeing things wrong. I second-guess my gut response, a classic move for me. Unsure what to say, I cock my head and throw in some solid people-pleasing. "Um . . . I think it's good he's not into fashion, because you never want to date a man who takes longer than you to get ready."

Justine laughs and takes a swig of her drink, one part tomboy, one part sex kitten. "Give him a chance," she coos as we sidle over to the pool table.

"Eight ball, side pocket," my fix-up says, lining up his last shot. His voice is pleasing, low, warm, and musical. He grins and grabs a small blue cube sitting on the lip of the table, then rests his stick across the top of his hand, smirks at Mike, and draws it back. Crack! Mike shakes his head, laughing, impressed. We all are. Mike turns and smiles at us.

"Moon, this is Woody. Woody, this is Moon," says one of America's most beloved actors. I give a shy wave and a smile to this blue-eyed stranger with an athletic build. Woody chalks the end of his pool cue again.

"You any good at this game?" Woody asks, a curious combination of cocky and polite.

"Sure," I say.

"Well . . . ," he says, motioning for me to help collect the balls. I dig my hand in a mesh pocket and send a few shiny ones down the table his way. "I'll rack 'em."

WOODY SPEAKS SLOWLY AND DELIBERATELY, like a drunk trying to lock in his words when a cop pulls him over, like his tongue is too big for his mouth. Woody has a lot of gaps between his teeth and a slight drawl when he speaks. "Wanna beer?" he asks, lifting his drink to his lips.

"No thanks," I say. "I don't drink."

"Oh yeah?" he says, half statement, half inquiry. He looks at his near-empty glass, sets it on a coaster on the edge of the head rail, then uses the triangle to corral the balls in place.

"Her dad fired people for getting high," says Mike, flashing his TV-show smile.

"Huh," says Woody. "What do you like to do to unwind?" he asks me.

"Read, hike, travel, dance, watch films, listen to music, make art, journal, cook . . . ," I say. *I also people-watch, compare myself to everyone, and criticize minor flaws in others to compensate for my low self-esteem, then hate myself and pick at my skin*, I think.

"She's a really great cook," Justine confirms.

"How 'bout you?" I ask.

Two blue eyes glance up, then return to the strike. "I'll tell you Friday when I take you to dinner." Woody splits the fingers of his hand resting on the felt field and promptly sinks two balls with one sharp hit.

Justine and I share a look.

Oh, will you?

ON FRIDAY, WOODY LEAVES THE car running as he steps out and holds the passenger door open for me. He wins additional points for being true to his word *and* for arriving on time. I feel pretty in black motorcycle boots and a flattering vintage dress in navy with a repeating feather pattern in pale blue as I descend my stairs. He's wearing jeans and a sweater. His web-thin strands of golden hair frame his smiling face. His expression is one of relief that I am just as attractive as he remembered, if not more so.

He moves in a loose, muscular way as he circles the back of his car and climbs into the driver's seat, confident. I am able to overlook the return of the cowboy boots because he smells freshly washed and because the solidity of his swagger has a calming effect, but it is impossible to condone the white Corvette and contradictory, full-throttle Cat Stevens. "Where are you from?" I ask, securing my seat belt.

"Texas," he says, securing his. This explains the boots. "You?"

"New York," I say, studying his face in profile, "but I grew up out here." My acting teacher Roy has taught me well. I can now apply all he says in class to work as well as life. "Anyone can fall in love with anyone," Roy had said recently when a student asked what to do when you're stuck with a love scene with someone you're not attracted to. "It's a skill anyone can learn—by noticing what makes someone similar and what makes them different from who we are. We can experiment with sensual curiosity about something unfamiliar, a flaw, something we'd push away."

Woody looks like he could be related to my fantastic cousin LaLa's sweet boyfriend Corey Haim, who I adore. There is something John Malkovich–y here, too, and I respect him as an actor. Woody's hands are soft, and he has nice eyes and a big smile. I practice using Roy's technique to dial up all these positive associations as Woody revs the engine and turns up the volume on "Moonshadow."

THE CINEPLEX ODEON IS LOCATED on the top floor of an enormous high-end mall and boasts the most theaters in one location in America.

Woody has decided we are seeing a movie instead of having dinner. He has chosen a foreign film neither of us have read about or seen a trailer for. It's risky but could be fun. Even though I am hungry, I keep applying Roy's thinking—a masculine man is making decisions for me to receive; receiving allows me to feel feminine. I remind myself foreign films are my favorite. I live for intimacy and subtitles.

Woody buys my ticket, so I buy the snacks. I don't want him or anyone thinking I don't pay my own way in the world. I never want to owe anyone anything. Plus, I overhear all the handsome men in my acting class say they don't like needy women, but they do want to feel like manly providers. Movies and TV and my guru seem to reinforce the same idea—want nothing.

Plus I'm peckish, so, yeah, I buy the popcorn and Dr Pepper.

Within a few minutes of the film starting, I can tell it is shit. There is no protagonist to care about, the film stock is ugly, the dialogue is trivial and acted in an unrealistic, melodramatic style. I do not care about this turn-of-the-century village priest's improprieties. I fear we are trapped in a poorly made farce about forbidden tits in a bountiful countryside.

"How long do we have to stay?" I whisper.

Woody looks at me with a sharpness in his face. "Are you joking?"

"No," I say in earnest. I am perplexed. Time is precious and we could be spending it differently, in a more productive manner—like talking. Doesn't he know that?

Woody exhales out of his nose, gives his head a disbelieving shake, and returns his gaze to the screen. I guess it's been decided. We will be staying.

When a horny priest takes advantage of a married woman in a tree with a pulley system, I repeat my request to leave. Woody just gets angrier and moves two seats away from me. I am so shocked I laugh. So do two witnesses seated behind us whom I'll befriend as a result.

I AM SURPRISED WHEN HE asks me out again. I am equally surprised I say yes. I guess he figured out what was obvious to me the last time we met—we didn't get to know each other.

He picks a romantic dinner spot, is affable to all, and orders for me with friendly bravado. He's fun to talk to and expresses ideas easily and on a wide variety of subjects; notably we both prefer organic food and avoid aspartame, we both love Scorsese and David Lean, and we both love to exercise. After dinner, while we wait for dessert and coffee, Woody takes my hands. Warmth floods my body. He turns mine over in his. "You like to keep your nails short? Not a polish person?"

"Not really," I say, "I prefer my nails short. It's European, and I write and cook and like to give massages." Woody's hands are clean, attractive, padded like a puppy's paws, with no visible scars. Everything about him seems perfectly proportioned in a pleasing way. If I am honest with myself, he's winning me over. "As for polish," I say, "I only like it on my toes, and I could never wear a dark color on my fingernails if my toenail polish was light. I'd feel like I was falling over."

Woody pulls my hands close to his lips. I am shy but enjoying the public, affectionate exploration. "You right-handed or left?" he asks.

"Right," I say, smiling demurely.

He selects the index finger of my right hand and begins digging around in his teeth with it. I'm puzzled.

"Got it," announces Woody, holding up a stringy piece of sinew.

Did he just publicly use my finger as a dental instrument?

I think back to the story about my father blowing his nose in Gail's skirt on their first date and how Gail was initially upset but soon realized it was Frank's way of merging.

Prior to this evening with Woody, I always hated that my mother turned that story into an act of love instead of seeing it for what it was: that my dad was treating what belonged to her as if it were his.

Tonight, with Woody, however, I can see the story as my mother did. Woody clearly likes me. You wouldn't put the hand of someone you don't like in your mouth. You don't use someone else's party dress as Kleenex unless you plan on joining bank accounts. We forgive a lot when we like someone.

Woody releases my hand. I tell myself to replace "grossed out" with "supremely touched." I conclude two things on date two: liking me enough to use me as dental floss is a good thing, and better still, Woody is a quirky, playful artist type, just like my dad.

I pay the tip so I can remain strict about not having sex until date three. If I contribute, I don't owe him anything sexually. I strongly put out the no-sex vibe when he pulls up to my teacup-size home.

"Would you like to come in for a little bit?" I say, void of seduction.

"Sure," he says.

IT'S ALWAYS WEIRD TO SEE your belongings through a stranger's eyes. Woody nods approvingly as he looks around.

"Who's that?" he asks, pointing to a framed photo of a tiny woman with an orange hat and matching dress. "A relative?"

"My guru," I say.

"Your guru?" he repeats, laughing to himself. "Why do you have so many pictures of her?" he asks.

I look around. There are several photos. "So I remember her and my real self," I say.

"Is that something you easily forget?"

"I guess so," I say. I hadn't really thought about how others might not have that same problem.

"Nice tub," he says as I show off my thimble of a bathroom with the tiny sink and sunken Japanese tub.

"This is my favorite room in the house. I wish everyone could shower in here," I say with 90 percent modesty and 10 percent flirtation.

Woody nods. "Maybe I'll take you up on the offer and try it sometime."

ON OUR THIRD DATE, I go for my sexiest look yet, with a red dress, red lipstick, and Egyptian-style crimped hair, because date three is a movie premiere on the Paramount lot.

"You look nice," Woody whispers. I feel butterflies.

On his set he introduces me to various actors, producers, camera operators, and others he works with. I recognize some of the folks from visiting Justine's. A pang of jealousy hits me—their sets and crews feel settled, united. Mine feels flimsy and hodgepodge. The vibe here definitely says "hit show." Next, he shows me around his palatial dressing room.

"Have a seat," he says. I opt for the squishy sofa from the prop house. "Want something to drink?"

"Water," I say brightly.

He hands it to me, then takes a long look at me.

"What?" I ask.

The phone rings. It's his assistant calling to let him know it's time for us to head for the press line.

We walk down the red carpet together, pausing every few feet. Photographers flash away. "Moon, Woody, Woody, Moon, over here." We freeze like statues as they shout for us to look the same way at the same time. This is my first time being perceived as part of a public couple, which is cool. But it's also confusing because we aren't a couple yet.

HIS APARTMENT IS ON A quiet street. Clean but not tidy, comfortable but not homey. The only pieces of personality in the place are a couple of movie posters and a bunch of books in his bedroom, ranging from Shakespeare to Vonnegut. Overall, it gets a passing grade for a location for clothes to come off.

Something on a lower shelf in his bedroom catches my eye, a clear glass rake with an extension cord attached to it. I've never seen anything like it.

"What's this?" I ask, picking it up.

Woody snatches it out of my hand, turns it on, and presses it against my forehead. It makes a buzzing sound and sends an electric shock to my face.

"Ow!" I jump.

He laughs. I stare at him and rub the place where he's zapped me. It burns. "It's a scalp stimulator," he says. He turns it on himself, scraping his head, partly to check to see if he has hurt me and partly to show me he hasn't.

I realize he's insecure about his hair and he uses this device to promote hair growth. I must have hit a sore spot for him to jab me in the face with it. I must try to be more sensitive about this. He flips the switch to off and sets it back down on the shelf. He looks at me in that weird way he looked at me in his dressing room.

"What?" I ask.

"Your face is only pretty when you smile." He says it like it's a fact. Not an insult. More like *Heads up, you left your gas tank open.*

As quickly as my brows knit, I try to soften the creases, to smooth and restore my face to adequate. "Pretty some of the time" still counts as a compliment, no?

He moves in close and presses his forehead to mine. I smell his warm, clean breath. He draws me in and begins kissing my neck and ear and jaw. Then his lips are on mine. He slowly urges me toward the bed. I lie back. I may not be pretty, but I can dance. His doorbell chimes as things get steamy.

"Is someone here?"

The doorbell rings again. He exhales and dismounts. "Be right back," he says with irritation in his voice.

I watch him find his pants and leave the room. I flop back down on his mattress, listening. When he doesn't come back right away, I try to meditate. My guru says only masters can meditate lying down; amateurs fall asleep. I let my mind drift like a kite without attachment, to simply observe what I can see, hear, and feel from his bed—watermark on ceiling, dappled light on glossy wall, my size-eight-and-a-half boot, car alarm chirping outside, clock . . . Soon, it's been another ten minutes. Worry creeps in. Maybe he's trying to tell me something by being gone so long—like *Leave already*. I look for my dress. I find it tangled up in the sheets. And something else. A stain. Dried blood. I pull the sheet closer, smell it, scratch it with my finger. It flakes off. Definitely period blood, definitely recent, definitely not mine. I feel humiliated. Stupid. Betrayed. He's having sex with me in the same dirty bed? Frantic, I throw on my dress and look around. I see his telephone. I dial my mother's private line, the one reserved for family emergencies.

"Gail?" I manage through muffled sobs.

"Moon? I can barely hear you. What's wrong? Where are you?"

"I'm at a guy's house," I whisper, "trapped in his back bedroom. I found period blood on his sheets, and I don't know what to do."

"Oh," she says dismissively. "Where is he?"

"I don't know. He left the room and hasn't come back. I found it after he left. What do I do?"

"Well, if you love somebody, that's the kind of stuff you put up with."

Suddenly I imagine all the silent injustices my mother has suffered for her to offer this terrible advice I am about to take. We say goodbye and I set the phone back down in its cradle. I wonder if I'm as strong as Gail. I put my clothes back on and head for the front door. As I walk past the kitchen, I see him and a pretty, moonfaced, athletic Asian woman passing him checks to sign. "This is Laura, my assistant," Woody says without looking up.

"Hello," I say.

"Hello," she says.

We share an awkward smile. I search her eyes—how many times has she witnessed these sorts of random lady exchanges?

"I'm leaving now," I say with a hair flip.

"Okay," he says as he signs another check, and I go home.

"WHAT IS WOODY'S DEAL?" I ask a mutual friend, twirling my finger around my phone cord.

"He's a weird guy," she says matter-of-factly. "You might be a little odd, too, if your dad was indicted for murder and you were becoming a huge star."

"What?" I yelp. "He told me his dad lives in Texas."

"I guess he left out the word 'jail.'"

I DECIDE I WILL GIVE him one last chance. I have plenty of time to do it since our show is "on hiatus"—read "tanking." I leave a message on his private extension at work: "Hi, it's Moon. Sorry I had to bolt the other night. Would you like to come over for a home-cooked meal this week?"

When he arrives, I have a fire going in the fireplace, candles burning, and a roasted chicken waiting for him. I want him to feel safe and loved.

"Wow," he says, "this is nice. Is it cool if I have some script changes delivered here?"

"Of course," I say. I know what that means. He's staying over. I can't be *that* ugly if he's back for more. Maybe I can get him to change his mind about playing the field. I cannot be like my mother. I feel certain I can get him on board with fidelity.

In the morning I wake before him to make him coffee and breakfast. He's all smiles and warmth. "Mind if I take a shower?" He grins.

"Of course," I say. "Please do!"

"Honey," he calls out from the steamy bathroom.

"Yes," I say, and run to do his bidding. I think this is why my father loves me. I am quicker, cooler, more cheerful, and more helpful than anyone else in his life.

"Can you get me one fresh raisin?"

"Sure," I say with music in my voice, but inside I'm thinking, *One fresh raisin? This guy is sooooooo weird*. But, hey, who am I to judge an artist's quirks and wants? Plus, I don't want to upset him, so I head for the kitchen. I have currants and sultanas, both organic like he likes . . . "Nope," I tell myself, "he said 'raisin.'" I cross my fingers and hope a blond one will do.

I open the shower door and let out most of the steam. I hold the small, dried grape between my thumb and index finger like it's an uncut gem. He looks at it, then at me, never stopping his circular soaping up. He looks at me with such disdain and confusion that in a split second I realize he said "razor," not "raisin." A fresh *razor*.

I turn and retrieve one from the medicine cabinet, where I have an ample supply. Our eyes meet.

"Here you go," I say, knowing this is the last moment we will ever share, and hand him one disposable, pink lady shaver. Like I'm the weird one.

—

CHAPTER 41

Three Teachers, One Test

When I am told *Normal Life* will not be picked up for any more episodes, I am very upset to be unemployed again but rationalize it as my guru's grace. She's given me Roy, after all. Besides, I'd rather have him in my life than bad jokes to try to make funny. I just pray I get more work soon. I never want to have to go back on the family payroll again. For now my time is spent pinballing between my total dedication to her and ashram life, Roy's acting class, my family, auditioning, and a new addition—therapy.

I keep trying with all my might to figure out which path is the right path for me. I have no idea I am a doormat in a people-pleasing tsunami. Therapy with June and Roy's class are compatible, with similar messages about putting yourself first, looking at your own needs, and heading in the direction of what you are trying to accomplish, but this contradicts ashram living and everything my family has taught me. Ashram life and my family both deliver the messages *I am the only way*; *do what I say, not what I do*; *desire nothing*; and *serve me to serve the whole*.

When I am around June and Roy, I wonder practical things, like: *Does success only happen by accident or through focus and intent? Or through the guru's grace? Was "Valley Girl" just a fluke? Was it my fluke or my dad's? Is creating from sincerity the answer? Or is doing an art form exactly like someone else wants it done the answer? Or is creating by only listening to yourself the way?* When I am at the ashram or with Gail and Frank, I wonder: *But who am I, really? If I am just an eternal spirit encased in a body, a fragile body, a body I was born with and didn't pick, a body that dies, and dies on something else's timetable, then what is the best use of "my" time and contribution? Ego-satisfying acts? Selfless service? Or selfless service to someone else who has power in the world to do good for the world, like my father or my guru? Both? Can I serve the world directly?*

Then I see the movie *Faces of Death*. In it is an autopsy scene. A dead person is having their skin and hair pulled back over their bones, like a wet suit. This truly frightens me. I can't believe a single one of us survives a day on planet Earth.

I journal like a motherfucker.

🌍

I LOVE THE ASHRAM BECAUSE I never went to summer camp. Where it gets wobbly is the "me" part. I only know that the more I am here, the less I desire to act, or rally on my own behalf. *Who is the separate me I am supposed to be fighting for if the guru says we are all one?*

Being an actress has reinforced my predisposition for taking orders; being told where to stand, what words to say, what to wear, and how to act; waking early; and eating what I'm offered. All of this is very similar to ashram life, where I get up before dawn, chant my guru's words, sit where I am told, eat what's served, and wear a sari instead of my own clothes. Performing selfless, urgent, and arbitrary acts for someone who rarely glances my way is exactly like the chaos of my childhood! It feels like home.

At night the guru gives "satsang" and "darshan," meaning spiritual talks and blessings.

Unlike at home, here I am "burning karma." The next time it is my turn in the darshan line to get bopped on the head with peacock feathers, I say to my guru, "Please, let me renounce the world, shave my head, and move to India to chop vegetables in your kitchen and make flower garlands!" Basically, I ask her to let me hide out in total isolation, indefinitely.

"No," she says.

I am caught off guard. "What?" I say in disbelief. I am ready to go all in, surrender my life to her completely.

She stares through me with eyes the color of onyx and flecked with the infinite, with love and clarity. "No," she says again, "you belong in the world."

I am shocked. I don't want to return to a place where I can't cut it. But I don't have a say.

I RETURN TO LA AND visit my family, wearing a bindi, smiling vacantly, and smelling like neroli and a wet hairy armpit. I haven't seen them in a while, and since they never visit or call or ask about my life, my appearance, demeanor, and new lingo must seem out of place. The house and my family all seem as frenzied as ever. Maybe my brothers are a little more girl crazy now that they are in a band together; Gail is a little heavier, gloomier, and angrier; and the house is definitely messier. I try to assess their doshas to cook balancing meals for them in ghee. I give my mother a meditation pashmina, and images of the Indian goddess Lakshmi to my baby sister, Diva, so she can pray to her. I figure that if Diva starts early, she can have her own money sooner. It feels good to be full of faith and willingness to help.

When my father gets wind of the fact that I am following a guru, he looks directly at me, pets my hair, and gives me this blessing: "If you are going to be a cabinet, be the best cabinet you can be."

His words sting me deeply, in a way I cannot grasp for some time. But I do grasp my family's newfound avoidance of me. And I pray for them to wake up.

🌐

IN THERAPY, JUNE TELLS ME, "To feel you belong is a human *need*, and needs are *nonnegotiable*. Met needs fill you up and motivate you to keep going."

I try to take this in. I can find no corresponding feelings. Anger revs in me. I survive every day without feeling that way. I do what is set before me simply because it needs doing. While June dips one of her homemade persimmon cookies into a cup of tea, I tell her what my father has often told me—"Happiness is not a goal."

June shakes her head in dismissal, shrinking his remark to the size of a dust mote.

"Draw your life story and goals on this piece of paper," she says. "I'll give you . . . as many minutes as this song." She pops in a cassette and I listen to Jane Siberry's song "Bound by the Beauty," a favorite of hers. My eyes flood with tears at the lyrics and the task.

"Haven't I already proven I can't take care of myself on my own?"

"Yet," she calls out from the other room as she changes out a Sparkletts delivery bottle of water for another. No matter what I throw at her, June tacks on "yet" to the ends of my sentences, flipping each doubt and lament on its head, soothing each fear with the idea of continuing to try.

🌐

IN CLASS, ROY SAYS, "THERE are only ever three types of scenes— love, power, and death." He explains that "women are always portrayed as a bitch or crazy" and how this is a crime. "They, too, should be able to stand in their power." I cannot grasp "power" at all.

I raise my hand. "Why would anyone want to get something from someone that isn't freely given? Why would they extract or steal or grab?" I am so puzzled by this, so he keeps assigning me "power" scenes from *Glengarry Glen Ross* and *Dangerous Liaisons*, and one from a screenplay he gets his hands on early, with two guys in a high-tension situation, a story that will eventually be reworked and re-leased as *Heat* starring Pacino and De Niro. Each week he blows my mind. Five scenes may be scheduled, but he only works with "what's alive," and if a whole class is taken up by waiting until just one student has a breakthrough, so be it. The whole process becomes cathartic for all of us. He teaches me that my peers' successes are my own. He teaches us to be generous and to "show the world how much love we need."

One week he reads a letter from Martha Graham to Agnes de Mille, explaining to us all that the artist's only job is to keep the channel open to fully answer one's unique calling in its entirety. Satisfaction is irrelevant. Another week, when someone hits a wall and can't find any fire, claiming they had a happy childhood, he announces, "I will not take your innocence, but once it's lost, come back and see me." I feel for the student and flash back to Roy catching me in my self-deception when we first met in his apartment and he showed me I *do* want things. I want a lot of things. Yet . . . I deny myself. In the name of my family. In the name of my guru. In the name of my father. To stay connected to them. But that doesn't make sense . . .

A deep unrest grips me. I wonder what else I might be hiding from myself.

One night, mid-instruction to some actors onstage, he wipes sweat off his neck and turns. "Moon," he says, seeing me furiously scribbling, trying to catch his brilliance as best as I can. "How high is your IQ, one seventy-two?" I freeze, having no idea if that's high or low. "You are a writer."

I AM IN MY BIG green sleigh bed reading through lines from a power scene Roy has assigned me when my phone rings. The sun is beginning to set. I pick up. Gail and Frank are both on the phone. My legs turn to jelly, my stomach tightens. I stand. It is the second time my father has ever called me in my life. My heart is racing. Before he even speaks, I know.

"Moon," he says, his voice cracking, "I have cancer."

The room is spinning. My throat tightens. My hand reaches for the hard surface of my headboard so I don't fall. "How bad?" I muster.

"Terminal," he says. "I've been given a year to live."

Crash Landing

1989-1993

CHAPTER 42

Healers

My father is forty-eight and he only has twelve months left to live. Last month he was getting ready to run for commander in chief, embracing his new role as Czech president Václav Havel's cultural ambassador, and preparing for his biggest, most prestigious overseas orchestral concert and finally being recognized as an American composer. Now he has stage-four prostate cancer. Out of nowhere. What is the universe doing?

I am struggling to grasp his illness. People don't usually die from prostate cancer. But here we are. *Soon I won't have a dad, soon I won't have a dad* is on a loop in my head. Though I don't have a relationship with him I can call satisfying, he is still my only ally in my family and in the world, and he's still the funniest, smartest person I know. He is my most favorite human ever, full stop.

And there's this: What will happen after he dies? What is a life? What is death? What meaning shall I make of his time here? He has so much more to say; I have nothing.

What about Diva? She is only nine. Who will walk me and my baby sister down the aisle? Who will teach Ahmet and Dweezil how to be men? Who will anchor Gail? Who will make us laugh? Why is no one talking about their feelings? Why is having a guru giving me zero comfort?

I am backtracking in my mind, trying to create the timeline. Was it a week ago or weeks ago that he was saying his kidneys hurt, that he had lower back pain, that urination felt like pissing glass? He looked uncomfortable walking. Using heating pads and wearing his baggiest sweatpants seemed to help. I just figured he'd gotten another STD or UTI, or a combo of the two. That maybe it was stress or the onset of shingles again. Then he mentioned blood in his urine, "blood work results," and "inflammatory markers." Then the phone call.

I know my father avoids doctors at all costs. Did he wait too long to do something about the blood in his urine or did he go right away, right when the pissing-blood thing started? Do you even get stage-four cancer that fast? Can you reverse it? Did he pick a bad doctor who missed it because my father is so young? Did smoking cause this? Too much fried food? Not enough water? Too much sex? Playing with mercury as a child? If we can all identify the cause, can the doctors stop it? Or is this just my brain refusing to accept the unacceptable?

Gail suspects it's "radio waves being beamed at my father from a radio tower" opposite my childhood home. "First our neighbor on the right, John Cassavetes, then our neighbor on the left, Barry Warshaw."

What I know now is my father doesn't want to do radiation. He doesn't want to risk losing his ability to have erections, extracurricular or otherwise. He has agreed to try alternative healing modalities first. I am enraged that sex is more important to him than life, but what can I say or do? It's his body, his choices.

Gail tells us we cannot say a word to anyone about his illness. She believes thought forms create illness, and if more people know, their thought forms will keep him sick or even lead him to die of the disease. She believes that if many people think the same thing together, they can create positive or negative outcomes collectively. Then it is suggested we move somewhere relaxing for a while, to destress my father. Doctors and healers alike all unanimously agree that stress makes illness a million times worse. I comply, but the inability to talk to anyone about any of this compounds my stress infinitely.

WE TAKE OUR FIRST-EVER FAMILY trip when our father isn't working and might interact with us, unless you count the time we went to L'Ermitage in Beverly Hills when the house was being de-flea'd. Ojai is a place I have never heard my father mention in his life. Maybe it was Gail's idea? She and I once went to a dieting "spa" there, one step above a jail cell, with a windowless room with two single beds, where we only ate a soup made of nothing but celery and parsley and a salad of raw shredded carrots, beets, and sunflower seeds.

Now we are installed at some sprawling hotel with a golf course. The oaky region an hour and a half inland is hotter and drier than LA. My father is unable to relax here and declares it a bust before the week is up.

Ibiza, here we come. Random as fuck, but okay.

There, Frank smokes in the sun with a blanket on his lap and hardly speaks, so I dance my ass off, try aioli for the first time, watch *Young Frankenstein* and discover it's just as funny in Spanish. I live for this uninterrupted proximity to my father. We take a chartered boat ride with Grace Jones and get bitten by mosquitoes, then we are all back home in LA again in under two weeks. It is healing in a way that has very little to do with physical health. But it is also incredibly fleeting. Then more tests to see if the time away helped. Nothing has changed.

⊘

I FIND GAIL'S REACTION TO my dad's diagnosis strange. No sadness, no tears, just a task-minded busyness mixed with a quiet glee—delaying his meals, letting his coffee get cold before she gives it to him, not showing him his mail, no longer letting him know about who calls him, not taking messages from them, postponing telling him his test results.

If I am honest, I find my own reactions confusing. I feel betrayed by his cancer. It is not lost on Gail or me that he has a kind of cancer that affects his sex organs. He has a kind of cancer that could stop him from cheating. Which means it could also stop him from filling up his well so that he can work and continue to tolerate Gail. If he can't fuck, then he's truly stuck with her, truly stuck with all he has been avoiding. It is hard for me not to wonder if this is cause-and-effect payback. I ask myself, *Is this what Gail thinks or what I think Gail thinks? Is karma even a real thing?* Another thing Frank is stuck with now is us, his children. Having a stay-at-home dad is our dream come true. If he's happy about family life, it doesn't show, since he now spends even *more* time working.

My brain is a churning cement mixer.

I was there as a witness to Gail's fake Zen-like acceptance of his cheating piled on top of her contempt for his chronic betrayals all these years, and as my understanding that he's going to die grows, so does my anger. I was there as Gail's backup whipping post when Frank didn't come home to her. I was there to be equally dismissed when he decided to stay wherever he had gone and have a five-star-hotel life with the latest mistress. I was there to fill in the gaps back home and take care of my siblings, who also got left behind. Are these my thoughts or Gail's or both?

"Zen" Gail rationalized that the price of genius is often a high libido that has to be quenched. When her spiritual pose evaporated, real-life Gail was depressed and compulsively binged on food and shopping to bury her rage and sorrow.

On his end, I often wondered if part of my dad's cheating involved the thrill of hurting Gail by not considering her at all and only satisfying himself. I'd feel bad for Gail, then they'd fuck, and I'd feel bad for the misguided other women who thought they could make Frank leave Gail for them. I was thrilled to move away from home. Now here I am, back in the Bermuda Triangle of their toxic love. Even still, I don't want my father to suffer or die. I want him to get well! I want a miracle!

I do not discuss my father's health or feelings with him. Gail is his mouthpiece. Gail shares information with me that she doesn't share with him about his medical prognosis. Gail explains Frank is incapable of dealing with disappointment. We spend a lot of energy as a family on taking his mind off of his current situation. Not on his feelings, not on my siblings', not on Gail's, not on my own. My father is not a talker. He has raised me to believe "feelings are irrelevant." But also, "anger is fuel." I sense something is off about all that. Without any outlet, I feel our family is in a pressure cooker. Do they?

Gail says the Western doctors somehow missed the prostate cancer because Frank is so young. But people aren't supposed to die from prostate cancer, so my father is dabbling in the realm of the woo-woo at Gail's behest. I know it is extra difficult for him to try this stuff because my dad has always made fun of "cosmic debris." But he wants to live, so he's doing the math, and if there's even a possibility these treatments can work, he will try them.

While he's unwilling to change his diet or quit smoking, he *does* let Gail take him to see many healers, including an older British woman who burps at you to remove your cancer. The more she burps, the more cancer she removes. He *does* let Gail take him to see the vitamin guy who lives off Olympic who seems like a carnival barker to me, and the Asian herb guy who sends energy at him with his hands, and a man with a special healing yogurt he makes in a sleeping bag under his floorboards. The man has wiry hair and rotting teeth, and he brings my father a jug of his rancid yogurt in a chlorine bottle that my father forces himself to swallow.

I hit my limit when my dad allows my mother to organize for a woman who removes the devil from your cells to come to the house. This woman believes there are angels and devils that live in each cell. And she knows how to remove the devils. I am there to witness this interaction. My father is lying on his bed with his eyes closed. He is under the blanket in his silk pajamas. This egg-shaped lady with thinning hair lays her hands in a triangle shape on my father's forehead, chest, arms, and belly. Then she looks up at me and she says, "I can't believe I'm in bed with Frank Zappa." I become volcanic. I politely excuse myself. I want to scream, *Get out! Enough is ENOUGH!*

But what if? What if what she's doing . . . works?

I PRAY FOR HIM AT the ashram with my guru. I ask her to protect him, and she says she will. Then I sneak and ask other people who trust their faiths to pray for him. I rub his feet and I make him soup. And I breathe with him and I keep him company so he is not alone when he's scared.

When a Reiki master comes to the house to massage my father in the basement, I begin to feel a warmth spreading across my lower back. It seems as if I, too, can feel the energy work and my father's burning bones.

"I can feel that," I say.

My father leaps off the table. "Stop, stop what you're doing. I don't want my daughter to go through this."

I am taken aback. It is the first time I have ever seen my father show real concern for me. He is suffering so much, and he does not wish this on me. This turning point in him is a turning point for me.

In that moment I dedicate myself to him fully. I would trade my life for his.

CHAPTER 43

Trials

My parents' bedroom is dark. My father's eyes are closed. "Do you want *anything*?" I say, removing his tray of un-eaten food.

"No," he manages to say.

I am twenty-two. My father is embracing Western doctors now, looking into clinical trials, being more selective with alternative healing routes, and doing radiation. Something is working, because it's year two and he's still here, but he rejects even the smallest meals. Nothing tastes good, or he is too nauseous from the medications.

Gail reminds us to keep our father's cancer a secret and to continue to picture that Frank will heal. How the five of us are stronger than everyone else on the planet combined is a lot to wrap my mind around. It's also a lot of pressure. I do what I am told, but it would be so helpful to have some relief or comfort or outside support from friends or someone or anyone.

The truth is, Gail and I are both hanging on by a thread at this point, enmeshed in twin mother/daughter magical thinking on overload.

Our teeny Siamese kitten Frank calls Bonecake hops on the bed next to him. Frank grimaces.

"Do you want some Dilaudid?" I ask.

"No," he says, "I want to work." The effort required for him to rise and rally hangs heavy in the air. I turn to go. Then, "Moon?"

"Yeah?" I say from the doorway.

"Never mind."

I CAN HEAR GAIL IN the kitchen as I return with the tray. Her voice sounds weird. When I round the corner I see she has the phone receiver pressed to her ear. She is braless and barefoot in a faded black slip dress. She looks tired. I check the phone closest to me—line three is lit up, so I know it's no one we are close to. Line one is inner circle. Eight-four-eight-five is reserved for outer circle, business dealings, telemarketers, the accountant, lawyers. Gail's voice is low; she speaks slowly and with deliberate calm. To an outsider she might sound fine, but I know her, her micro-inflections and subtle body language—clenched jaw and downcast eyes. She is not enjoying this call.

I inch closer to her, signaling my silent presence so she knows she's not alone in whatever this is and that I have her back. I eavesdrop as I quietly clean the dishes.

"You can ask him," Gail says into the phone, "but I'm pretty sure his sperm is probably no good because of the radiation."

I instantly burn with rage as I towel-dry my father's dishes. I'm the mother now. "Who are you talking to?" I demand in a loud whisper.

Gail puts her hand over the receiver. "Vicki," she says flatly.

My mind cartwheels. Vicki? *Vicki?* "Kiwi Vicki, the *groupie from New Zealand*?" I hiss. Gail gives a listless shrug. My hands ball into fists. I seethe. I pad over to her. "What the hell does *she* want?"

Gail puts her hand over the mouthpiece, waves me away. "She's crying. She wants to have a baby with Frank before he dies."

I blink in astonishment. She wants WHAT? What kind of maniac gets wind of Frank's illness, calls crying, and instead of offering help wants to *TAKE*? I explode.

"Hang up," I say loud enough for that bag of cunt to hear. "Hang up now!"

Gail rolls her eyes. "I have to go, Vicki, Moon needs me." She sets the phone in the cradle.

"What the fuck are you doing?" My voice is tight and shrill. "What the fuck is wrong with you?" I stammer with a choking rage. "Why the fuck did you even speak to her?"

"If she's stupid enough to ask, then she's too stupid to understand."

While I see Gail's point about the other person's capacity to comprehend, she should still *try* to educate idiots. It *is* still her job to set boundaries with injurious assholes. She needs to protect herself, us, and Frank from awful humans—that's precisely *how* they *learn* not to completely suck. "Where are YOU in this? What do YOU want? You don't have to put up with that," I entreat.

Gail takes a sip of cold coffee from a nearby cup.

"If you don't say something, you are condoning and even encouraging the bad behavior. If she calls again, just tell her to fuck off and die already," I command.

Gail sighs a weary "you don't get it" kind of sigh. I snort like a bull right back.

Outside, yellow jackets swarm plastic dishes of cat food, crows caw, cars speed on our quiet street, and the California sun beats down on fences covered in bougainvillea of every shade. I silently wish every groupie, every temptress and home-wrecker, every player and cheater, throughout all time and space, a never-ending boomerang of karma and kangaroo kicks to their overworked genitalia.

Except my father.

SOMEHOW DURING THIS TIME, I manage to book a role. A good one. It is my best job yet! Instead of playing a ditzy girl guys don't want with makeup on her teeth, I get to play a rape victim who gets to tell her story and be redeemed. It's only two scenes, but they are meaningful to me. I finally get to employ Roy's techniques and make use of some of the long-standing pain I carry around. I auditioned several times, and each time I used some actual pain from my own life and delivered exactly what they wanted—tears.

The show is *The Trials of Rosie O'Neill*, and I am working with Sharon Gless. I've been to hair and makeup and I'm in my costume. We already did the blocking on the diner set, and now I am trying not to trip on cables while I wait my turn to be on camera. As I start to do my prep—conjuring my unlimited supply of unhappy memories— what made me cry before is gone. All the hurt in my bottomless well is suddenly . . . dry. Did I cry it all out in the audition? How am I suddenly NOT sad about my life? What the fuck! I feel locked out of myself with no way back in.

Panic sets in. I have to deliver. I *need* to be sad. I need to be *very* upset in this scene.

I hear Roy's voice in my head. "Look for what is alive." What is alive and true in *this* moment is . . . I am happy to be working and getting paid to do what I love, on my own merit, in spite of my dad being sick. It is a reprieve. And I am proud of myself. But now I am hyperventilating.

Sharon Gless pulls me aside and says, "Moon, if I were you, I'd choose *not* to cry in this scene and I'd win a goddamn Emmy." Her generosity almost *makes* me cry. She is trying to help me grab on to *something* with confidence. Or she's trying to trick me into crying by giving me full permission to play it any way I choose, so I relax, so I can access my emotions naturally. Either way, I don't want to let anyone down.

The director gets an idea, asks if I am up for it. "Yes," I say, "anything! Help me. I am so sorry." She calls for a skeleton crew. Half the people on set clear out. To get a performance out of me she asks me to lie on the floor. She then does something generous and unorthodox in an effort to have me safely understand the physicality of being assaulted—she climbs on top of me to give me some sense of the violation. She half chokes me, lightly pulls my hair, then presses my shoulders to hold me down. Still no tears come. I am humiliated and in too much shock about being unable to deliver. I stand up and say I need a moment. I take a lap in the dark.

In the end, for time and money purposes, I have to shoot the scene just as I am. Numb. I say my lines without tears. It is the best I can do under the circumstances. It is "fine," but I disappoint myself. I call Roy and tell him I blew it.

But on my drive home, I realize something extraordinary about feelings. You *can* cry something out of you. When you feel pain completely, it can shift. I don't know why I am learning this now, but there it is.

Then the same nightmare occurs *again* when I book *another* job—doing a scene in a courtroom this time. An actor I know from Roy's class is on set waiting her turn to do her scene. She sees I am struggling and she, too, pulls me aside. Actors really can be the most generous, wonderful people in the world. Charlotte Ross stares me in the eye, gives me an infusion of her steely blue-eyed "you got this" gaze. She holds my shoulders firmly and tells me what Roy always says: "Show them how much love you need." My eyes instantly fill. My tears spill like water from a tap.

Someone yells, "Places," then "Quiet on set," then "Action." Then I stand on fake trial and I show the fake jurors how much real love I need.

CHAPTER 44

Debt to Be Paid

As we inch toward year three, I continue to hold my breath, grateful for each additional day my father is still here. Unbelievably, Frank starts feeling better. Then almost good. Good enough to take on a huge orchestral project with a modern ensemble out of Germany. Good enough to tell Gail he wants to leave her for German Gerda again. I am beside myself. Gail takes this moment to explain to Frank he will have to choose between us and his studio, and his mistress. Painted into an emotional and psychological corner, he grows more withdrawn. Then the cancer spreads to his bones. He is in agony. To raise my father's spirits, Gail instigates margarita nights on Fridays in the basement of my childhood home. This from my mother, who doesn't drink, for my father, who doesn't either. There are visits from Matt Groening, Roseanne Barr, documentary filmmakers, some Tuvan throat warblers, the bands Eleven and the Chieftains, Rutger Hauer, the musician Ravi Shankar, and some Tibetan monks. Even Bob Dylan manages a middle-of-the-night appearance.

Me? I feel batshit crazy.

I hide out in my home. Before powerlessness swallows me whole, my silver-lining defense mechanism kicks in. I think about how life goes in stories—how a bad thing happens that catalyzes a big, good shift. I keep waiting for the moment when Frank will stop everything to spend his remaining time with us and make up for all he missed. I picture Frank saying, "Oh fuck, what did I do? What *else* did I miss? Tell me everything." I let myself imagine him saying, "I am so sorry it's taken me this long to figure out what is so important—time with all of *you*."

I get honest. This isn't a movie ticking clock, this is a real-life countdown. What I really want is for my dad to stay alive as long as possible, for *us* this time, not himself. I want him to *want* to be *here* with us. *We* need him. His *family* needs him. It's *our* turn.

"It's *my* turn," I say, mouse-quiet, to my empty bedroom.

⬤

GAIL STOPS BY. SHE NEVER just stops by. Her hair is unruly, an eye-catching contrast to her oversized red Cartier eyeglasses and platform Robert Clergerie shoes.

I hug her at the door. She's given up her usual perfume for a cloying one that reminds me of rotting flowers. I liked her old, familiar smell much better. Green, bright, soft and feminine. But it is 1991, my mother is changing, and Frank isn't doing well.

Gail gently sets a newspaper article down on the counter next to her Prada purse and car keys while I boil water in my whistling teakettle and get to work preparing her a cup of Typhoo tea with milk and two sugars. Gail and I make what technically passes for mother-daughter small talk since I am finally accepting we are not naturally compatible.

"You should use more vibrant paint colors in eggshell instead of the chalky matte pastels you've got on your kitchen walls," she says, offering up unsolicited advice. My job is to nod and take it. Soon, she's on a roll. She roots around in the attic of her mind and offers her guidance on more-flattering clothing, home remedies for fresher breath, moving my TV away from the fireplace, and how the green sleigh bed in my bedroom would look better at an angle in the middle

242 \ *Earth to Moon*

of the room. I want to scream, *Who puts a bed in the center of the room, and at an* angle *no less?* But I don't. I just breathe.

I know this moment calls for longer exhales. I guess I am changing, too. My therapy with June, the meditative self-inquiry with my guru, and eight miles of geographical distance between us have softened me. I can simply notice the patterns at play between us, choose to disengage and not take the bait.

Then, out of nowhere, Gail tells me, "We need to sell your house. You cost us two hundred thousand dollars to raise, so we need to sell your house to pay for your father's cancer treatments because he has no health insurance." She says this so plainly and without emotion that I feel the wind knock out of me. I blink.

"Of course," I stammer. She knows I would do anything for my father. "Of course," I say again.

She stands to leave. I am frozen. She grabs her keys, heads for the door. "Gary and Owen will draw up the quitclaim papers so you can sign the house over to me."

I walk her to the door, then stand on my deck under the Chinese elm and watch her drive away in her black four-door Mercedes. I look at the scaly, peeling gray and rust bark of the tree. There is nothing else to do.

When I go back inside, the air has gone out of the rooms. The light seems a little dimmer. I have instantly begun the process of detaching from what I love. There it is, the tornado of impermanence my guru is always talking about—one day this, the next moment that. It is then that I notice the article my mother has left behind. A piece she's clipped from a newspaper, an article on how the madness and mental illness of one family member affects the sane rest of the family.

I am learning that nothing moves these people to be loving. I am a number to be spent, earned, lost, bargained with. We are not a family; we are a family business.

IT NEVER OCCURS TO ME I can say no or that their predicament is
theirs to solve. I do not react to the precise calculation of what it cost,
in her mind, to raise her child, as if I were a pet or a side business that
held no emotional connection. For her it is simply a given that I will
and must comply. The truth is, had she said nothing about what she
felt owed, I, loyal to a fault, would have likely done it anyway.

I consider how much more energy I will need to see this woman
with the eyes of love. I think: *I can do this, I can get up again, for him.
Fall down seven times and stand up eight.* I will honor where Gail and I
overlap on the slim sliver of the Venn diagram: we both want what's
best for my father.

CHAPTER 45

Transfusion

Frank is fifty. I am twenty-three. Living back at my childhood home, I feel happy to be able to be of some use to my father. I drive him to appointments, make him and my family food, rub his feet, and snatch any moment I can with him. I am a blood match for him and I donate it for his transfusions. It is good to be under the same roof with my siblings again, too, even though Ahmet and Dweezil are the close ones now, making music as a band, performing regularly on television, and touring. Diva is hilarious and precocious as ever. I love that Frank and my sister have their special time watching *The Simpsons* together.

I push open the heavy, soundproof door of my father's studio and peer inside. My father is working alone in his control room. He glances up from his knobs. Behind him I see the familiar framed family photo of my father, Gail, Dweezil, and me from 1971 hanging on the wall, reliably watching over his workspace as it always has. Now, twenty years later, his brown eyes are flat pools. His skin is loose and the color of faded fatigues. His black hair is turning Gandalf white. My father's terminal diagnosis pulls me in two directions: to neglect myself in order to help him in any possible way, and to hide out in a preemptive grief, catatonia telling me I need to give him space.

"Need anything?" I ask.

My interactions with my father have always bordered on telepathic. He gives a microscopic shake of his head, then raises the metal volume slider. It is an invitation. My cue to step inside and stay, to listen, to share a moment.

I stand beside him. He smells like him but metallic. His mug still has coffee inside. His lit Winston waits in the ashtray. I observe with affection a thinning patch of hair on his head. The awareness that he is playing me a song that will be among his last compositions hangs wordlessly in the room. It is my father's most transparent work. For this reason I immediately love it. There are no lyrics, just a melody with tight knots of rhythmic turns that pulse, spasm, fall out of step, then stretch into spaciousness. I can detect the whistling harmonics of the Tuvan throat singers he's recently befriended; their isolated mountain stories are braided into the covenant of my father's artistic journey with himself. I smile with pleasure. "Finally, a track I can dance to," I half-joke. His eyes smile back.

"You can do the artwork for the album."

"Really?" I ask.

He nods. "I'll tell Gail."

I am giddy. I already know what I'm going to create.

I paint my father in black and white acrylic on a small canvas with a dark gray background. Then I take fabric and sew two red velvet horns onto his head. My father, the fallen angel, calm, equanimous, triumphant, redeemed, his face relaxed after having defeated darkness, whole again.

CHAPTER 46

Dark Comedy

My dad and I both agree Lynda Barry is a genius. Each week our fun ritual is to read her hilarious and often uncomfortable *Ernie Pook's Comeek* together. It is something I treasure and look forward to. I clip the comics out of *LA Weekly* and present them to my father like a treaty to be signed between him and Death—pause, cease fire, let us remain in this tiny bubble of laughter and brief distraction from pain. A few of Lynda's comics stand out to us in particular—"Marlys' Guide to Weirdos" by Lynda Neptune Headed Barry, "Bats of Interest" by Lynda Winter in St. Paul Barry, and "OK, OK" by Lynda Sad as Hell in Luvull Barry. Her ability to be raw and real and funny and say so much in four panels is mind-bending.

With Lynda's comics, there is no uncertainty. Wherever she takes us, my father and I go there together. Nothing hidden, truth and reality in real time.

Another truth is it takes a long time to die. He was given a year to live, but so far, he has lived for almost four.

We discuss music. He tells me he likes the music of the Spin Doctors, and he thinks Amy Grant has a beautiful singing voice. We watch a snippet of *Fatliners*, an amateur porn with men ramming their penises into the folded flaps of skin of obese women, which made him laugh on a cultural-anthropology, human-response-to-its-own-extinction level. I roll with it. On bad days I prop up a bunch of pillows and curl up to read the comic alongside him in my parents' bed after I've rubbed his feet and hands. Today is a bad day.

The darkest thoughts I ignore.

My father's breathing is jagged from pain. I match it. Short inhale, short exhale, short inhale, short exhale. It is completely shallow. No air getting in past his clavicles. I am getting lightheaded from trying to match it for only a few minutes.

I hold a glass of water with a straw up to his mouth. He tilts his head forward to take a sip. He lets his head fall back into the pillow. He closes his eyes. I wait. His eyes stay closed.

ANOTHER DAY I ENTER HIS bedroom with the latest clipping and find my father leaving his bathroom, wiping Barbasol off his face and looking dazed. He has just shaven off his signature, trademark facial hair. Gone are his famous mustache and accompanying tuft. He is in shock. I am in shock about his face and in shock that he is in shock, but I don't want to let on. I say what's true: "Wow, I have never seen your whole face before!" He can't make eye contact or won't. I don't think he has seen his own, real, completely exposed face since he was a teenager. With the hair gone his lips look skinny and I see that we have the same soft chin. He looks frightened, not ready for his face to be out like this. "How does it feel? What made you do it?"

"I don't know." He looks stricken. Puzzled. Helpless. His wounded eyes still won't meet mine. My firstborn intuition tells me he doesn't want to be seen, by me or himself. I know this is a threshold being crossed. We both know, in fact. That threshold is the beginning of the end. No more Lynda Barry. The time we have left is meant for something else now.

When Gail sees his face, she says nothing. She stays busy. Goes into strong mode. Acknowledgment is admission, admission is weakness, weakness is failure, failure isn't an option. Ignoring is optimism.

Over the next days and weeks, time is measured in his hair growth, long studio hours, and bone pain. I watch him retreat into the caves of his creativity and the recesses of sleep until his stubble fast-forwards back toward a full beard, growing in almost entirely white. Each song is a last song, a race to the finish, a final riddle.

CHAPTER 47

Payback

I am twenty-five. My father's cancer is now very public. Life is surreal. I am booked on *The Howard Stern Show* to reassure the public my father is "fine."

Howard mentions he's always found me adorable and "very sexual" and suggests I should show off more of my body, wear bathing suits, miniskirts, and a "bippy top" to show off my stomach. Then he asks me if I have made enough money to never have to work again. I say I wish. He says he doesn't see me doing a lot of things, that I don't have a regular job. He razzes me pretty hard on this point, then tells anyone who is watching to hire me, that I'm a very qualified dropout and there should be zero problems having me as an employee, *wink wink*.

Then my dad calls in to the show and things get weirder. Howard gets my father to agree it would be nice if my siblings and I would stop leeching off of him, stop taking money from him, and get jobs. My father says, "There's got to be an end to it sometime, Howard."

This all feels doubly hurtful given my loyalty and sacrifices.

Then I tell my father I love him on national television and that I'll see him back at home.

BACK IN LA, I RESUME my caregiver role. Now when Frank calls out
to Gail, she seems to respond on a longer and longer delay. I recognize her coping mechanism from his touring days, a defense against
his leaving. I take this as my cue to try to achieve a true resolution
with Frank instead. I sit beside him in his bedroom. When I begin
to try to apologize to him for anything he might be upset about and
share my hurt feelings so we can both be at peace when he departs,
he musters low-voltage anger and says, "I am too sick to do this,
Moon."

I am truly taken aback. I had no idea someone you love could put
an end to how far a relationship could go—this is as close as we will
ever be. No negotiating, no mutuality. A stranger maybe, but not a
parent. Not your dad. Death is forever. Doesn't he know you don't
get a second chance at a singular exit? But there it is. A death before
a death, one he can live with and I can't.

. . . But he's the one with cancer, so I let it drop.

I try to resume my focus on generating peace for him. I rely instead on Ahmet, Dweezil, and Diva for laughter and hugs. I still have
Roy and June for the occasional infusion of sanity and creativity. But
on the day a sweet-faced, energetic actress named Catherine Keener
joins my acting class and sits beside me, Roy announces a surprise
sabbatical. Then Frank goes from a wheelchair to bedridden.

Gail makes my father give each one of us a letter she has him
write on Zappa stationery. Gone are his steady hand and beautiful,
perfect penmanship. In a shaky, black-ink chicken scrawl, my envelope says "Moon" with such effort that any lingering denial gives way
to the reality of all he has been reduced to, and I feel his agony, and
my own, viscerally.

I read my letter.

It says: "I love you, Moon."

I could not hope for more.

CHAPTER 48

December 1993

We stand by his bed. He is going. Gail, Diva, Ahmet, Dweezil, and I begin to take turns saying things to him. "It's okay to go." "Thank you for everything." "We will never forget you." "We are all here." "We love you." He makes a shallow gurgling sound. I lean in close and whisper, "Daddy, I am with you. You are safe because I love you. I'm so proud to be your daughter. I'm so glad I look like you. You are the most important person in my life. I love you and will always love you forever." We all have a hand on his thin, failing body.

I sing to him. I sing a chant I learned from my guru. It sounds like a magic carpet ride of peace. At least, that is what I hear.

But suddenly I am shaken when Gail snaps, "Moon!" Ahmet, Diva, and Dweezil stare at me. I am suddenly mortified. I had not considered I would upset them.

I shrink and fold into myself.

"Sorry," I say with downcast eyes. I look at my father. His eyes are closed. His mouth is open. My thoughts are swirling. *I'm sorry if these things I am saying upset you. I am sorry if I let you down. I am sorry for anything I have ever done that upset you. Find your peace.*

My father's chest is barely rising and falling.

I think to myself: *You are the funniest person I know and the smartest. I respect you so much. I hope you can hear me.*

His breathing becomes shallower and shallower, a whisper.

"Goodbye, Daddy." "Thank you." "We love you." "You can go now."

Then the warmth leaves his body, and he is gone. Gail, Dweezil, Ahmet, and Diva instinctively form a tight circle with one another. I watch them cry and hug each other. Even in my father's death I feel like an outsider. I cry and kiss his fingers. I blow my breath into his hands—the breath he gave me, I now give back. The light, too. And prayers for his peace and for our peace as a family.

Be at peace, be at peace, be at peace, I whisper. *But can you also watch over all of us, and maybe me just a little bit more?*

CHAPTER 49

There Can Only Be One

He died in the evening. Did Gail sleep beside his dead body? She must have. I remember they took him away on the gurney in daylight. Is that right?

Some things hurt so much they are put into a deep freeze to be remembered later or forgotten entirely. This memory stays out in the open, to be caressed and carried forward:

Gail and I washed his naked body with soapy water and sponges. He was reptile cold to the touch, with a cool looseness to his skin and a hardness underneath. I was careful with his mouth. The smell of interior rot lingered from the thick, black syrup of coagulated blood pooled around his tongue. I dabbed at his full salt-and-pepper, wiry beard, wiped his gray and yellow hollow cheeks. I cleaned what I could of his stained and crooked teeth, as if I were polishing ivory in a museum case. I kept thinking of how much he hated the dentist. I wanted to kiss those decrepit things, carved and brittle, made holy by his words and songs. We put him in black, silky pajamas and placed hydrangeas in his hands. I remember we set aside the supplies to pack in his coffin for his "final tour"—the pump espresso machine, cayenne pepper, guitar picks, his wallet, a pen. Notes of goodbye.

The next thing I remember is hearing the metal wheels of the gurney traveling down the hall toward my parents' bedroom. Security specialist Gavin de Becker arranged for the ambulance people to arrive without their sirens on. Gail has also organized a pre-signed death certificate. Everything is in slow motion. Straps are unfastened, a large, long bag unzipped, paperwork handed off between teetering laundry piles. Then we help two huge men lift my father.

"Wait," I say, "wait."

I pull the back of my dad's pajamas down so the fabric is smooth against his skin. I hate the feeling of fabric riding up, and I don't want him to feel that. As they pull at the zipper, I realize how pointless this pause was.

They move quickly, securing him to the gurney with the swiftness and familiarity of procedure. I try to imagine what these no-nonsense body movers must have seen in their careers as they raise one end of the gurney, lower the other, preparing for the steep descent with this latest stranger and chorus of onlookers. I watch their eyes scan the ground for obstacles, the calculations they make for leaving the house smoothly—width, depth, height, emotion, and other irregularities. The gurney slides past; I hear the sound of the ambulance doors closing, then the sour sound of metal clicking into metal as the doors close and they drive away. Forever.

WESTWOOD. MY DEAD DAD IS getting buried in *Westwood*. What is Gail thinking? A UCLA college student dead zone for falafels and unwanted medical procedures? I suppose that if things get too cemetery-y we can always walk forty feet and either buy a ticket to see a movie, get a root canal, or renew our passports.

Or was the appeal that he'd be in good company with Roy Orbison, Natalie Wood, and Marilyn Monroe buried nearby?

We huddle between a tree and a mound of dirt—Gail, Dweezil, Ahmet, Diva, and I.

Gail will not let my dad's family say goodbye or even tell them he has died. She won't allow us to tell them, either. "They can hear it from the press like everyone else." I am too sad about my father to argue.

His box is lowered into the ground. We each grab a handful of dirt and drop it on top, a small avalanche of earth the color of coffee grounds. Something feels wrong about this picture. I can't pinpoint what it is, until . . . it hits me. My mother has only bought two plots. For him and for her. What about the rest of us?

So much for a close family.

🌐

BACK AT THE HOUSE AN hour later, Gail says, "Gavin said the news will be released to Reuters soon. The phone will start ringing."

Sitting in the kitchen with a cup of Typhoo tea in my hand, I can see the steam, but I can't feel the heat. I feel drained. My head feels enormous, heavy, vacant. Gail will sleep in their bed alone from now on. No one will ever hold her, hug her, and kiss her or tell her she's beautiful. She's now wearing her widowhood like a badge. I don't see her cry, I only see her dressed in black, receiving visitors with a strange demurring solemnity. Twenty-seven years of devotion. Twenty-seven years of her history have been swallowed up, gone forever. He has crossed over. All that remains on this side is her resentment and their shared debt. And us.

"It would be nice to have a headstone," I say. "He wanted it to say, 'Too little too late,'" I remind her.

"I don't want people knowing where he's buried."

"I'd like to know where he's buried. I'd like to be able to visit him."

"I don't want his brothers or sister or mother to know where to find him."

Or his girlfriends, I think. I look down at the table. "Why?" I ask. "Why don't you want his family to be able to go to his grave?"

"They'll leak it to the fans!"

"So? That cemetery is small, pretty hard to find, you need to sign in, there's hardly any parking, and they have a guard at the entrance. It would be nice for people who love him to be able to visit him."

"I lost my best friend!" she bellows with a bitterness and intensity so tangible it almost leaves a mark.

I blink. My sorrow turns to retaliatory fury, matching her pitch for pitch. "I didn't realize this was a contest," I hiss. "We just lost our *father*. Are we really going to play 'who has the greater loss'?"

Gail's face and jaw settle into a corrosive pout. I look into her eyes and see her anguish and helplessness. I drop my own pain, postpone it, bury it. I rally strength instead. I speedily find my center. "I'm sorry I yelled," I say in my softest voice. I wrap my arms around her. "We are *all* sad. I was hoping we could all be sad together."

She pulls away and gives me her back. Bare feet slap across her painted floors. The king is dead. The queen exits *her* castle.

🌍

STILL, I CAN FEEL THE collective grief and collective compassion as the news travels from one continent to another. I can feel people thinking about us. I can literally feel their love. I don't want to move. I don't want that love to stop pouring in on us.

———

CHAPTER 50

Unfathomable

My father is dead. At fifty-two.

Roy suddenly dies next. AIDS. I didn't even know he was sick.

June shortly after. Cancer. She kept it a secret.

Within a year my hero and my chosen parents are gone.

All I have left are my three younger siblings and Gail and my guru.

I am the most lost I have ever been.

PART II

Moon

Ground Control

1993-2015

CHAPTER 51

One Small Step

I smell my father's lingering scent, commingled with the stale air of his palpable absence, everywhere—his studio, the kitchen, his bedroom, and the living room. The void is substantial, a photo negative, a vacuum of nothingness, but also solid, a heaviness. My father, the genius, is truly gone. Only now can I begin to feel what that means for me. Before, I just wanted him to not be suffering. The release was good and necessary. Now it is not.

Gail, the self-proclaimed business guru, tells us Frank died millions in debt. *How?* I wonder. "Did he leave a will?" I ask Gail.

She is furious with me for daring to ask such a thing, and so directly. "Earth to Moon, he left no *will*," she says bitterly. "And even if he did, there is *nothing*."

"Okay, Gail," I say, treading lightly and thinking about our survival. "That's okay, we will all be okay." I have clearly pushed it too far. She storms out.

I make a cup of tea and let her mood blow over. Later I rub her feet and shoulders and say sorry some more.

Years from now Ahmet will remind me we went to a softball game later in the day, which I have no recollection of.

What I do remember is Paddy from the Chieftains stopped by with a Paramahansa Yogananda book I adore, and that saint Jamie Lee Curtis brought a photo of her daughter swimming with dolphins—the antithesis of what I was feeling, the exact right medicine. A reminder that joy still existed and that it wouldn't always feel this awful forever. The image still burns bright in my mind's eye.

What I also remember is that Gail put black fabric over all the mirrors in the house, sold my father's catalog, and went shopping. I don't begrudge her. I accept this is how she's processing grief. Buildings, homes, chandeliers, art, furniture, spiral staircases, high-end appliances . . . Then she's writing huge donor checks to the Democratic National Committee and buying tables at fundraising events in support of her favorite candidates. I'm happy for her. I figure she'll get around to her kids losing their father and to their needs sooner or later. My assumption is Gail will eventually provide for all of us equally, because that's what the legal document she has us sign every year always says.

But with Frank gone, Gail changes the rules. She has no one to answer to except herself now.

IN THE BASEMENT WITH A hundred license plates with my father's initials hanging on the wall, Gail gathers us together.

"Dweezil gets all the guitars," she says.

"But, Gail," I say, "that's not fair. I'm sure we *all* want one of the guitars. I am sure we *all* want something he touched all the time." I certainly want something he chose over and over again instead of spending time with me.

"I am the only one who can play them," says Dweezil.

I can see his point, but I disagree. "Take your favorites then!" I blurt. How does my sweet brother not want *all* of us to have one? Later Dweezil will give me an acoustic Ovation Frank played that he doesn't seem all that interested in. I am grateful.

"Diva gets Frank's record collection," says Gail.

"But, Gail," I protest, "Frank gave them to me, and I reminded you because they are what I grew up listening to. Can we at least split them equally?" Diva's face contorts. I remind myself she's *twelve*. I had him twelve years longer. I let it go. She *should* have a turn getting to know Frank in some form.

"Ahmet gets the Rolls-Royce." I start laughing. We all do.

"That thing doesn't even drive!" says Ahmet. Gail seems to have it in for Ahmet *and* me. I feel some relief. Now it's not feeling so personal. I *know* he has done *nothing* to deserve this weird move.

"And, Moon, you can have Frank's black piano you want so much."

Par for the course. An enormous instrument I can't even play, that I didn't ask for and I have no place to even store.

I TAKE A LONG DRIVE. Maybe time away from Gail and her money and ego will be good for me. I visit my guru, hoping to find equilibrium again.

A second time, I humbly ask my guru if I can shave my head, move to India, and become a renunciate. She looks at me with her big brown doe eyes, pools of infinity and compassion, and says, "No, you belong in the world."

I want to say, *Check again*, like the scene in *Lost in America* when Albert Brooks's wife loses their nest egg and he begs the casino owner to make them whole again.

Then the guru calls me "Chandra." Now I am certain there's been a mistake. She's given the wrong answer to the wrong person! But my assigned swami, who escorts me away, explains: "She's just given you a spiritual name. It is a gift and a great honor. 'Chandra' means 'Moon.'"

Great, I think, *I don't even get a different name, just my same old annoying one.*

MANY YEARS FROM NOW, I will connect the dots and realize the guru has given me back to myself. It will coincide with the day I find out that my father *does* in fact have a will. In a drawer, in Gail's desk—a will that says sell everything, divide it equally, and have a great life. An instruction Gail ignores. A will that becomes void the moment she dies.

CHAPTER 52

Controlling the Narrative

The whole concept of reincarnation troubles me now. I don't believe in it, which makes me question my whole guru path. I don't want to think my father is now suddenly off waiting to get born and cavort with another family somewhere. Fuck that. I want him to be an angel or a ghost and help me and my siblings out from the other side. We didn't get him in real life. And Gail won't let us have him in death. So I don't care if it's magical thinking, I need to believe I finally get his love, help, support, and protection, forever, from now on.

When I get a job interview to work for VH1 in New York, I believe my angelghostdad had a hand in it. They are looking for on-air hosts for this new, more adult-skewed music channel, and I am to sit down with k.d. lang for an hour and ask her questions off camera.

The west-facing midtown Manhattan hotel room that Viacom has rented for the interview is large but feels stifling. "Keep your hands at your sides and don't speak over her, we need clean edits," says the director, a mealy apple of a man in a black turtleneck.

"Okay," I say, adjusting my mic on the nonthreatening cream-colored blouse the wardrobe lady has selected for me to wear.

"And don't ask the questions in fragments. Try to sound natural." I shouldn't be scared. The questions I am supposed to ask have been preapproved by the subject ahead of time. I look down at my cue cards as a refresher.

"Okay," I say, tugging at my wedgie-inducing weird gray business-lady pants, which are itchy as fuck. It's one thing when a costume designer picks out clothes for a *character* you'll play and another when they pull clothes when you are yourself. Instead of complaining or speaking up for myself, I make a Roy adjustment and just roll with it—I *am* a character today, in the lead role of "on-air journalist."

"Keep your arms at your sides and don't talk with your hands. This is an over-the-shoulder and you must never obstruct the camera's view of her."

"Okay," I say.

"And don't interrupt her."

"Okay."

"And don't turn your head. Or nod. Or laugh. And do *not* ask her anything about her relationship."

I've been told all of this before and more, so I am not sure whether this barrage of last-minute reiterated instructions is from this controlling dude or the higher-ups are having doubts about me. "Okay," I say. In my research I read that she's just recently gone through a rough breakup. It must suck to be emotionally raw and then have to be on the hook to promote something at the worst possible time.

I wonder what this hired-gun director has directed before. He's certainly not an actor's director. He's certainly not making sure the talent is comfortable. Maybe only k.d. lang is considered talent today.

I appreciate myself as a journalist. Having been on the other side of the microphone for so long and been interviewed the wrong way over and over again, I like to think I know how to have a proper human interaction. Even though I am here for VH1, my allegiance is with the subject and their art form. My goal is to get the subject to open up.

VH1 could be a big deal and a big break for me. If it goes well, I'll get the gig, move to New York, and become a real actress with a job by day and the chance to do Broadway by night. Hollywood will have to pay attention to me if I become a legitimate stage actor.

"And don't ask her anything about thumbs. Or hitchhiking," he says, hastily riffling through the notes he's written on the production sheets. The camera/lighting guy adjusts the reflectors illuminating the waiting, empty chair.

"Okay."

Maybe I am not supposed to ask her about her relationship because the network does not want to hear about girls dating girls?

"Or motorcycles. Or Uma."

I want to say, *Seriously?*, but it's my first day on the job. Instead, I nod in a way that I hope says "Got it" and makes me seem professional at the same time.

THE INTERVIEW IS STILTED AND tense and lame. Halfway through, k.d. is so harsh with me that I have an out-of-body experience imagining myself at home on my couch watching this interview and cheering for how she destroys the lame interviewer. Except the interviewer is me! I persevere, but barely, and hope they can scrape something together in the edit. The interview finally ends, and before the sound man can remove her mic, k.d. leans in and says to me,

"What are you doing?" I take it to mean *You are a Zappa and this job is so beneath you*. She says it with such strength and with such a look of pity and disgust, I am scarred by it.

Back in my hotel, I consider maybe she meant I am a bad interviewer or that she didn't like how the director was speaking to me or *Hey, aren't you that chick who started a whole cultural movement with "Valley Girl"?*—the ponderances rattle around inside of me like a virus.

I get the job. It is not what I expected. I can't go on auditions in New York like I planned because they phone me each night to give me my call time for the next day. I can't plan anything, not a social life, not exercise, not to travel back to LA to see my siblings and my friends, not to hang out and try to make local friends, not to plan a vacation, not to go to the ashram, nothing. They choose my wardrobe, my hair, my makeup, the food that gets ordered in, the random people who pick me up. There is nothing stable about this gig except predictable chaos. Of course, this feels familiar, and I stay with it because the good parts are: I am away from home and I feel like everyone else. One month's salary equals rent for my studio apartment plus a small sum for savings and a small sum for play. Trying to find the silver linings is difficult, and chaos is chaos no matter how accustomed to it I might be.

I'M TWENTY-SEVEN. IT HAS BEEN one year since my father's passing. I have no idea I am grieving. How would I know? My father, an icon, had a ten-minute funeral with the handful of us who happened to be at the house the night before. There was no celebration of his life, no discussion, no swapping of stories, no shared grief, no tears, no extended family that day or any day since. What came next was Gail released a record to mark the one-year anniversary of his passing. And she didn't use the cover art I made at my father's request.

I feel really depressed. Maybe a trip to the ashram would help, or at the very least a chat with my assigned swami. I put in a call. When I am patched through, my swami thinks I am still the switchboard operator. "Tell her I'm at Temple of the Dancing Shivas. No, tell her I'm in Lakshmi's garden. No, tell her—" I hang up. Swamis lie? And instruct the operators to lie? The swami is one tier beneath the guru, a right-hand person. If she lies, who else lies? Does the *guru* lie? The floor falls out beneath me. The spiritual betrayal devastates me. I lose my shit.

I call the switchboard operator right back: "Lying is wrong. Lying for the swami is wrong. Lying is not spiritual seva, lying is lying—you tell that to the swami and anyone else you speak to." I am shaking when I hang up.

In my all-white one-room studio apartment, I pace. I stare out my window. Then I hug my knees and sit in the corner sobbing uncontrollably.

My phone rings. I screen the call. It's the swami. "Hi, Moon, there's been a mistake. You must have heard me wrong and misunderstood."

My eyes widen with pure rage. *Oh no you don't, you gaslighting cunt. You do not get to pull a Gail on me.*

I am instantly up on my feet. I feel trapped. I pace some more. I open my window, sense the air on my face twelve stories up. I listen to the frantic city sounds and recognize my isolation against a backdrop of too many buildings and windows and cars and people to count. Internally I am spiraling out of control. I can't find me or recognize what I am feeling. Then I do. It's the S-word. I am feeling suicidal. I call my boss.

"Sorry to bother you, but I feel crazy and I am contemplating leaping from the twelfth floor of my building. I don't know who else to call."

"I'll be right over," she says. And she's there in ten minutes.

THANK YOU, KAREN, WHEREVER YOU are.

SHE TELLS ME TO HANG in there and changes my schedule around so it's more predictable, and because of that I finally start to become social and begin to make friends in my new city. I root myself in the burgeoning comedy scene with the cream of the crop of those just starting out. Soon I am seeing comedy four or five nights a week. Janeane Garofalo, Marc Maron, Louis CK, and a gal named Amy Poehler from a little group called the Upright Citizens Brigade shine brightest. I am watching them grow and learn. All the while, k.d. lang's admonishment haunts me.

GAIL GETS A CALL THAT my father is to be posthumously inducted into the Rock & Roll Hall of Fame. She calls me venting because they've asked Lou Reed, a mortal enemy, to induct him. She tells me we are boycotting the event as a family unless they get someone else. Lou apologizes for the old injury via fax and Gail ignores him and still refuses to attend. I tell her I think Frank would have loved getting recognized and that I want to go.

I ASK FOR TWO TICKETS. My awesome friend Frankie is dating the lead singer of the Spin Doctors and loans him out to me to be my date. I am hugged by a weeping Jeff Buckley and told I am "quite funny" by Robert Plant. I swoon. I take my father's statue home.

WHEN I HEAR JANEANE GAROFALO has quit *SNL*, I easily muster the courage to quit VH1. My two-year stint in NYC is done.

When I return to LA, Gail says I can move into a property she has purchased, her fourth investment with the proceeds of her sale of my father's catalog. The three-bedroom two-bath is down the street from my childhood home. I am an adult child again, but that's okay, because I feel she owes me a house, and anyway I am a fancier, wiser baby this time around.

My father's piano is delivered.

I have no guru, no boyfriend, no job, no home of my own, but I feel the beginnings of happiness. At 8071 I tend a little cutting garden and jog the three-mile loop I used to enjoy and cook my own food and hang with my siblings and daydream about writing my own stand-up material. Then a new neighbor moves in across the street, into Carole King's old house.

I cut some roses from "my" garden and put them in a mason jar for her. "Thank you for waking me up," I say, then I smile from ear to ear as k.d. lang warmly returns the grin and accepts them.

CHAPTER 53

Engagement

arry me!" Paul shouts out his car window, driving south on Lankershim. I'm in my car, also driving south on Lankershim. We are driving beside each other. I love this man, but that's not how you propose to someone. You don't propose to someone three weeks into dating them. You don't shout it from a car. In the San Fernando Valley.

I tell myself if this were a movie, a rom-com, I'd absolutely think this was adorable. What's wrong with me that I *don't* think it's adorable? Because this is my life and I want something real. I want him to ask my brothers for my hand because my dad is dead. I want a ring. I want something different from what my parents had. I want something different from a scream by a freeway on-ramp.

"Ask me again after you've known me a little longer!" is what I shout back. I hope I haven't blown it. He deflates. "But can we go get promise rings?"

"Yes!" he says enthusiastically, but something in his face says otherwise.

I'd taken Janeane Garofalo's advice and started doing stand-up. I was getting good feedback and finding my voice and style. A mutual friend of ours brought Paul to one of my gigs. We clicked.

Paul is in a band called Matchbox Twenty. I am a Zappa. His band is popular. All I know is AM radio. All he knows is playing arenas. All I know is flying under the radar. All he knows is the red carpet. All I know is crickets and saloon doors and making lemonade out of life's lemons. He knows saloon girls and snake eyes and cherry cherry cherry.

I am scared. He is the sweetest, kindest, most handsome, most successful, most loyal, most faithful, most generous person I have ever known. He could have anyone. What's he doing with me?

CHAPTER 54

Dum Dum Da Dumb

It's 2002. I'm thirty-four. Paul and I have been inseparable for the last three years. We have weathered meeting each other's families, travel for his work, travel for fun, a death, a friend's wedding, a disappointing election, a long engagement, couples counseling, construction on his house, alternately living together in his place and "mine," and the day I was alone in New York City when my debut novel was released on 9/11 and the towers came down.

Diva, Gail, and I are standing in the kitchen of the brand-new five-bedroom six-bathroom Malibu house my mother has purchased and is now renovating. Even though I have created a life for myself away from her, I am angry she has not put any of the properties she has purchased in her children's names so we *all* feel security and we *all* benefit from what we *all* invested in—Frank.

Instead I try to enjoy watching Gail's creativity blossom as my father's widow. Nowhere else is it showcased more beautifully than here, nestled under a eucalyptus grove on a cliff with an infinity view of the Pacific Ocean.

"I was thinking you could have white terry cloth bathrobes with pointy hoods made for every guest that they could wear for the ceremony," says Gail. She means every guest at our wedding, the wedding between Paul and me.

Diva spits out her tea, laughing at the joke, then searches Gail's face to see if she's serious. Gail's face doesn't change. Gail is not laughing. Gail is genuinely suggesting an updated Druid ceremony. "But . . . that sounds like the KKK!" says Diva, who keeps laughing.

I am not laughing. My brows knit. "The bride wears white," I say, genuinely concerned. Gail's face hardens into anger; she's deeply offended that her idea has been shot down.

"I'm just trying to do something nice for the guests," she says bitterly.

I gently put a hand on Gail's arm. "Gail," I say sweetly, "I don't need you to do anything other than provide the location. You don't even have to pay for anything, not the food, nothing. Not even my dress. Paul and I don't want to burden you with a single cost. I would just like for us to get married in your yard because it's a beautiful setting and it would be wonderful to make a wonderful memory here all together."

"Well, anyway," says Gail, pulling her arm away, "I'd have to do a geological to find out if people can even stand on this cliff."

Diva peers over the top of her teacup, eyes tracking the topography of the Malibu bluff.

"Huh? What do you mean?" I say. "You've had bulldozers here for construction." I was not expecting any pushback. Especially with the date fast approaching. Especially as her firstborn and the first to get married.

Gail explodes in anger. "Why would you make me have strangers in my yard!" she screams. Diva's eyes widen over her milky brew. Gail is in my face now. "What happens when you and Paul drive away, and I'm left here with everybody?"

My chest tightens. My face momentarily contorts in disbelief. "Well . . . if we drive away . . . other people will also begin to leave because the wedding will be over. Throwing rice as a couple leaves and everyone watches signifies the end of the wedding. And none of them are strangers."

"What if they don't leave?"

I blink, dumbfounded. Diva sets her cup down, unsure whether to stay or go, assist in some way or stay the hell out of this one.

"Uh . . . someone could say the party is over?" I suggest. "Something like *In case you missed it, folks, the bride and groom just left*? Could that work?"

Gail snorts and keeps her gaze fixed on the distance.

"I thought this would be something you'd want to be a part of." I'm suddenly a two-year-old having a tantrum in the body of a thirty-four-year-old.

"I said I could do the dress," says Gail.

"I already bought the dress," I say. "You told me you would buy the dress after I bought the dress. The thing I'm asking for you to contribute is the location."

"There's no parking here."

"I'll happily pay for the valet. I am pretty sure the public works people in charge of Malibu parking make exceptions for weddings. They shoot movies and TV shows here all the time. They have workarounds."

"Wouldn't you rather get married in your own backyard? Wouldn't it be nice to have that memory at your *own* house?" My temples throb—Gail owns the house I reside in and she knows it. My face burns. My throat constricts. Hot tears come. I slide my plate of food away.

Gail picks a piece of bread off my plate and silently butters the toast and takes a bite. My disbelief is incalculable.

Outside, a vast sea, the sound of birds, and a low-flying plane. Inside, the sound of Diva sipping, Gail crunching. Inside, deeper still, my ragged, shallow breathing and my equally vast hurt.

I look at the two people seated beside me. I try to see them simply. We are three different generations of women in one family—a boomer, a Gen Xer, and a millennial. Three females in a giant world that makes things hard for women. If no collaboration exists here, how can it exist anywhere? We are all we have.

Pull it together, Moon.

Gail licks her glistening, buttery lips. "Did it ever occur to you that you hurt *my* feelings by not taking me with you to buy the dress?"

I can only stare. I want to scream, *No, of course it never occurred to me! You are the mom! The mom takes the daughter to buy a dress, not the other way around! I didn't want more power plays with money. I thought I was doing us a favor by transitioning to a peer-to-peer, adult-to-adult relationship that you CLEARLY don't want.*

What is it with the endless double binds and victim/martyr dances with her?

Back on earth, I breathe. Inside, I calm the fuck down. I tell myself, *I will let this anger go and will myself to find other options.* I go against myself and ask Gail, "Would you want to accompany me to pick up my dress?"

"I'll think about it," she says. "I'm going to Portland with Diva. We have to get her kitchen put together. We found her a place in the heart of the Rose Quarter."

Breathe, Moon.

Right.

My maid-of-honor sister, Diva, age twenty-two, has decided to move to Portland to go to college there after a seven-year hiatus from being enrolled in a formal education. While I am extremely disappointed that she's jumping ship on me and her wedding duties, I am also very proud of Diva for her courage in taking this step as the baby of the family. I am extra proud that she will be the first of all of this band of Zappas to attend any college. I can live with the bad timing and hard feelings if in fact Diva is finally seizing *her* own dream. I never knew I was smart enough to attend college. At least Diva got another message.

I PARK ON ROBERTSON, AND we enter the atelier. We are seated in elegant chairs and offered bottled water while we wait.

I gasp when I see my dress the second time. "It is gorgeous," I gush. Clean lines; narrowing, square Flemish collar; Italian; modern in every way. It says I am capable and confident, an equal to my partner. It is just so me.

I look at Gail, whose eyes have narrowed behind her giant eyeglasses. Her fingers rest on her chin. Suddenly she's Marlon Brando at the end of *The Godfather*. "It's too white for your skin tone. You should do something in a creamy, slightly yellow white."

The salesgirl's face plummets, as does mine.

"What is the most princess-like dress you have?" Gail asks.

"Gail, I really don't feel like trying more stuff on."

"Humor me." Gail glares at the salesgirl, who wasn't expecting to be put in this position.

"Gail," I say, "anyway, there isn't time. Appointments must be made. And there's not enough turnaround time for alterations."

"If you find one that doesn't need alterations . . . ," says Gail, weary from having to explain how the world works. "There's no one else here in the shop! Of course she can help us."

"Well," says the salesgirl, looking at the clock, "I suppose I have a few minutes before the next bride."

"It wouldn't hurt to at least *look*."

The salesgirl and I peer at each other helplessly. Then she sets my dress on a rack and disappears into a back room.

"It's one of those things you just *know* when you see it," says Gail. I sink into the chair, wishing I could vanish.

"There wouldn't be time to alter it here," says the salesgirl as she places a few dresses in a dressing room. I slowly stand and look at the price tags. My eyes widen. They are twice as much as my dress. Paul will shit himself if I spend like this. I will shit myself. I try on several dresses too wide to walk through doorways, with trains as long as fire hoses. With each dress I try on, I can feel myself panicking. Second-guessing my other dress. This one is better than my dress in this way, this one is better than my dress in that way. At last, one straight out of a fairy tale, with a pale clotted-cream-colored satin corseted bodice and a billowing skirt littered with a Milky Way of hand-sewn beads. It fits like a second skin. My cheeks flush. I feel lightheaded and utterly radiant.

"It doesn't need a single alteration," says Gail, beaming.

Then I see the price tag. Sixteen thousand dollars!

Gail hands the salesgirl her Amex.

Out the door we go. Gail has provided her version of an apology for refusing to let me use her home for the wedding. I am consumed by a confusing mixture of joy and despair, but mainly full of superstition and worry, wondering if my marriage will fail because I have two dresses in my hand.

When I drop Gail off at my childhood home, Diva trots over to my car to inform me that she plans to wear prosthetic elf ears the day of my wedding. She is giddy with excitement. I look at her with love. She will always be my little sister.

"That's great," I say, "sounds great."

"I will do a makeup trial first to get the skin tone, hair, and look right," she says, twirling in the sun.

A MONTH BEFORE OUR WEDDING, Paul and I receive an invite from Gail. She's throwing a fundraising event for two hundred people. At the Malibu house. Because I'm me, and because I am so flabbergasted, I attend. I'm even pleasant to the guests and to Gail as I walk around. This is not a wham-bam thrown-together thing. This took planning. Gail's paid for everything—catering, tables, linens, bartenders, valet parking, the works. I roughly calculate the costs. After

California governor Gray Davis's plea for campaign contributions and a warm thank-you to Gail for a six-figure sum, plates of food and drinks continue to circulate while small talk and party laughter drone on for hours. When I finally leave, I congratulate myself on not letting my hurt show. *You are getting married. Your life is starting. That's all that matters.*

OUR WEDDING DAY IS PERFECT. Paul is perfect. My brothers walk me down the aisle and give me away. Everyone there understands the significance of this brotherly gesture and feels the weight, absence, and blessings of my father. I cry. Diva cries. Gail even seems to have a good time getting attention as the mother of the bride.

As a wedding gift, Gail surprises Paul and me and offers to sell us the home we have been living in at $200,000 below market value. We leap on it. I replace my anger that she didn't just give us the house, since she can certainly afford it, with gratitude. We'd never be able to buy a house on this street without it. I let myself see it as Gail giving me her blessing *and* finally compensating me for when we sold my house to pay my uninsured dad's hospital bills.

And, better, I am no longer an adult child beholden to Gail Zappa. I am thirty-four, a woman, a grown-up, a wife.

CHAPTER 55

Showered

"Surprise!" they all yell. My system freezes. My eyes automatically drift to recognizable objects for some sense of safety—the chipped, Egyptian-blue soup tureen from my childhood on a familiar shelf, a shadow box containing a taxidermied fruit bat bleached white from the sun, and a watercolor portrait I painted of my family when my father was alive that hangs in the foyer. Little by little, I take in the room, the friendly faces. Ohhhhh, Gail and my friends are throwing us a baby shower.

We are at my childhood home. Gail has sold the Malibu house and moved back into the Hollywood Hills house. There are raucous laughter and contagious smiles and the smell of tuberose candles and slow-cooked duck with cherries and prunes. I see my type A, outgoing friends and my shy, Catholic mother-in-law, who has flown in from Florida, and my mischievous siblings, and Gail. I see catering staff passing miniature hors d'oeuvres and alcohol-free spritzers. I see them filling silver serving trays and arranging cheese on giant wooden boards and a Jenga tower of tea sandwiches.

I SQUEEZE MY HUSBAND'S HAND as we are guided into my mother's kitchen, which is festooned with every form of pale pink decoration heralding, "It's a girl!"

It is the first time my mother-in-law has ever been to my mother's home. Even though it's a celebration for a mom-to-be, i.e., me, my emotions are divided in equal parts—extreme happiness, extreme discomfort, extreme worry about Paul's mother being comfortable, and my fear of what Gail might do. I'm hoping Paul will mind-read my signals to be ready just in case.

AFTER THE SHOCK OF A room full of people shouting "surprise" wears off, I'm left confused. This is the house that I have been historically discouraged from filling with "outsiders." Not to mention that I do *not* love being the center of attention. I tell myself to take this all in, to see this as a marker in time denoting my mother's efforts.

Gail taps a wineglass and asks everyone to cluster around me and Paul. I look for Paul's mother. She moves slowly, positions herself in the back; her face looks pinched. I know the look: part curiosity, part survival mode. I try to make eye contact. My mother has a ribbon in her hand. She holds one end and asks the people on the outside of the circle to pass it behind their backs until she holds both ends. Now we are all inside a giant circle she has made. "As we stand here together," Gail begins, "we will use our combined energies to create a room in outer space where we will send our best wishes. This little space station at the farthest end of our galaxy is for Moon and Paul and Mathilda and can be accessed at any time by them when they need a little support."

I scan the faces of the guests. Some look bemused, some teary-eyed, some envious that I have such a fun and loving mom.

"The firstborn daughter of the firstborn daughter of the firstborn daughter is a witch." Oh. My. God. I look over at Paul's very

Catholic mother—her smile looks pained and plastered on. Gail continues, "Today I have asked you to gather twigs because we are going to make the newest witch a broom." My mother looks pleased with herself. She's on a roll. Everyone's eyes are on her. "Please pass this branch around and put your energy into it. This will be the seat."

Part of me doesn't want to ruin Gail's moment. Part of me wants to scream out, *Fraud! No one is buying this shit.* I look around again, vowing to stop talking to anyone who is dazzled by this display.

Then I look at Paul. He eye-rolls with me in solidarity. He was onto her at their first meeting. He astutely and compassionately said, "Your mom is a very sad and insecure woman." It made me trust him and love his inability to be corrupted or manipulated. I decided to see Gail through Paul's eyes. I listen and hit my invisible decoder ring and translate her theatrics: *This is her version of love.*

I take a breath.

Maybe Gail is truly turning over a new leaf and her broom is a literal olive branch, because she is becoming a grandmother and that is a life-changing event.

Eventually everyone gets to touch the broom-branch-seat and channel their wishes into the bark. When Gail says, "After you all leave today, I will assemble the broom with the sticks that some of you gathered," I actually laugh.

"Moon," she announces, "I hope you have a daughter who is just like you." She is smiling. I stop laughing. All eyes are brimming with tears. Except mine. And Paul's. And Gail's.

There it is. The double wish. Plausible deniability. She has witnesses. Everyone would agree it sounds kind, only I *feel* it as a curse.

Then again: what if I'm seeing her as wrongly as she sees me?

I search her eyes. She holds my gaze.

CHAPTER 56

Mathilda

Paul and I are in the exam room. "She's in what's called a 'Frank breech,'" says my doctor. She explains to us that the baby's head is basically under my solar plexus with her spine pressed up against my spine. I picture her like a little spectator on my lap. Except I don't have a lap. I have ballooned from 120 pounds to 216 between six months of bed rest and all of my "pregnancy cravings." "We will need to schedule a C-section. Her due date is technically December twenty-sixth, so . . . ," she says as she hovers between two calendars.

I am crushed. We have tried everything to get her to turn, from massage to acupuncture to energy work to headfirst plunges into swimming pools, but here we are. I don't want to play God and decide, but if I have to . . . humorously I am thinking Jesus's birthday—finally having a daughter is certainly my second coming, plus I love Christmas more than anything since even the shittiest people tend to be the kindest then, *and* our doctor is Jewish and doesn't celebrate it, so . . .

"Before you say Christmas, I'm traveling between then and New Year's, so how about the twenty-first?"

I'm torn. I whisper to Paul: "The twenty-first of December is my father's birthday. Gail will be furious. What do you think?"

Do *I* want to always think of him when we think of our kid, or let her have her own day to herself? I love him more than anything and miss him terribly, but must *everything* in my life always be connected to him and Gail? But wouldn't any day that close to his birthday be a reminder, and wouldn't it be weirder to have consciously missed it by a day or two?

Paul whispers back, "It's also the winter solstice."

I perk up and beam. He's right! The twenty-first was a pagan holiday before it ever belonged to my dad. Druids and oak trees, I can do.

But my water breaks on the morning of December 21. It *is* her real birthday. And a *real* blessing from my father, who isn't alive to meet her. The weird thing is, I am suddenly allergic to the M-word—"mom." I cannot hear what I've never been able to call my other parent. Maybe I could tolerate the British word "mum" . . .

As soon as she is born and I see her and she cries and I hold her and she calms, I know I was born to do this.

"Welcome to the world, Mathilda Plum Doucette."

CHAPTER 57

Empathy Training

Mathilda brings us overflowing happiness; so, too, does being new parents. Since Paul's mom and dad live in Florida and Gail and my siblings are here in LA, my husband is concerned that our daughter will be closer to my family than to his. Paul grew up with doting parents, and Tom and Jane can't wait to be doting grandparents. I have to laugh. "I promise you your mom and dad will still see Mathilda way more than Gail, who is just down the street."

I am proven right in no time.

For starters, Gail announces she is to be called "Grand Gail," never "Grandmother." "Paul's mom can be Grandma," she says, as if the title is lesser and hers to bestow. She also makes it abundantly clear she is finished raising kids—meaning unavailable to babysit or help unless we "drop the baby off at the house" while she works.

Paul says, "I've never seen someone with so few maternal instincts and so little interest in her grandkid, and her *first*!" I'd be upset, but I am more pleased to form an even tighter bond with my husband over her total lack of interest.

Every day of watching Mathilda discover a new skill or take in the world around her is heaven. For the first time in my life, I wake up happy every single morning, excited to give everything I have to this tiny human. Life finally makes sense to me, and so does my body—I am a food source! Even my past struggles make sense to me—I learned everything *not* to do so I could do everything right for our child.

I love watching Paul show up for Mathilda in a way my father never showed up for me—reading to her, taking her on neighborhood walks, playing with her. I love seeing him fall asleep with her on his chest, both of them wrapped in a bubble of deep calm.

Another marvel is seeing nearly everything Gail ever told me is fucking untrue—a baby doesn't pick a family to be born into before it's born, any more than it chooses its hair or eye color. No. People make babies with their bodies and then it's their job to care for the glorious consequence they created—rub two pieces of flint together, you get fire. Two bodies? Baby.

And I have a witness who can back me up on reality: my husband.

☾

MY FRIEND MOLLYE POPS OVER. We lovingly gawk at my angelic, sleeping child.

"Get on the list at Pacific Oaks *today*," whispers Mollye.

"What? Are you serious? Apply her for school *already*?" I ask as we tiptoe out of the room. Mathilda is six months old.

"Yes. If you get on the wait list today, maybe in two years, by the time she is ready to go, they'll have a spot for her."

"Wow," I say, suddenly overwhelmed by a future stress and a fresh fear we won't get into a place I have never heard of.

"Quaker values plus converted Craftsman homes plus nature plus Steiner method plus Magda Gerber's foundational RIE . . ."

"I have no idea what you are saying. Are you even speaking English?"

"Go take a tour ASAP and get on that list! You'll understand when you see it all. I'll wait."

Mollye and her husband have a great marriage and great kids. I look up the phone number that second and do as I'm told.

Paul and I are completely impressed by the school—the kids look happy and dirty in the best way—and parents are invited to observe all that the teachers model. The idea is to foster confidence, curiosity, and self-trust as our kids explore their authentic feelings free from parental projection. Mathilda can't get enough of this place and this loving environment. It has a curious effect on me, but I can't quite put my finger on why I also feel so good here. The answer will be empathy. For today what I know is that with each smile and discovery our daughter has, I feel I am getting a second chance at being parented for the first time, too.

WHEN MATHILDA TURNS THREE, THE school offers a special six-week class series called "Nonviolent Communication." I sign us up, assuming it's about talking to one another better. Paul and I have started fighting. Now that Mathilda is in school for longer stretches, he wants me to go to back to work instead of being a stay-at-home mom like we originally discussed. He met me as an author, stand-up, and director he put through film school. He grew up in a family with two working parents. I did not. My desire to nurture and be fully present for our child in a way my parents were not there for me overrides all my previous ambitions. His financial concerns in a fickle music business outweigh our previous arrangement. Our differences and updated needs are coming to the surface, and they are highly incompatible, as are our strategies.

The class turns out to be heart-centered parenting lessons based on the work of Marshall Rosenberg. Our teacher, Brian, is a dad and a musician, tall and affable, with curly black hair and a little soul patch. He and his wife and mother-in-law teach empathy with a capital E. A whole course on one word and an accompanying heart opening, tectonic-plate-shifting mindset? It's impressive and inspirational to me. Brian breaks out a giant tablet of paper. He asks us as a group to name the qualities we want our children to have. He writes down what we call out:

"Autonomous," "kind," "compassionate," "fun," "funny," "generous," "gentle," "patient" . . . and so on.

"How do you think you actually teach this stuff?" he says innocently, baiting us. No one answers. "Children become what they experience. You have to demonstrate these qualities. You have to live them and your values yourselves."

Wow. It's so obvious. Of *course* that's what you do. He goes on, explaining empathy's definition—"It is the *other* person feeling felt," not fixing or educating or consoling or commiserating. Repairing a rupture isn't taking turns being miserable or agreeing to disagree like what Paul and I do. Another wow. Then Brian gives us a reading list about brain development, attachment, and emotional intelligence, along with a handout with a list of needs and what happens to the body and psyche when they are not met. All of my suspicions about something being very wrong with Gail and Frank's parenting are being laid bare.

We learn about boundaries and a "connected no," and collaboration instead of "power over" another human or manipulation through punishment and rewards, neglect and shunning. I want to start my life over from the ground up. How easy it is to give love. How easy it is to say sorry and be patient.

I feel angry at my parents all over again, but also soothed—here is a practical, tangible, constructive way out. As we stack the folding chairs into neat, upright rows, I look at Paul—he liked it, too, but probably won't read the books. Me? I'm all in.

CHAPTER 58

Someone Else's Birthday

Mathilda's breath smells like nail polish remover. Our three-year-old is in our king-size bed, dwarfed by a tufted headboard and matching pillows. Her blond curls are wet and matted to her temples. She's too hot in her nightgown but her teeth chatter.

I wipe her forehead with a cool cloth and check her temperature with the back of my hand. Still crazy hot with *both* Tylenol and Advil in her system. Paul's been away but he's coming home late tonight. I'm starting to freak out.

It's day four of this bug. Violent surges of fever, diarrhea, and puking, followed by nonproductive coughing fits, and sleeplessness for both of us. I brace myself each time her face goes pale, signaling she will now convulse like a cat with a hairball. I hold a metal mixing bowl under her chin and have a second bath towel standing by. A dry heave chokes her, then three rapid-fire tsunamis of projectile vomit hurl out of her tiny body. This time it looks like raspberry jam. A deep, dry, scratchy, persistent cough follows. Her dull blue eyes fill with terror and plead with me to make it stop. I'm scared but can't let on.

I clean her up as fast as I can, grab another towel from a nearby stack, and craft a new bib across her rib cage. Then I run to the bathroom to rinse the towel, pour the puke down the toilet, and give the metal container a speedy rinse for the next round.

"Mama!" she calls out through choking spasms from the other room. I rush back to her side.

"It's okay, honey," I say as calmly as I can. "I'm right here." I pick up my cell phone and dial the pediatrician.

Mathilda and I have been to the office twice this week. Both times her pediatrician said, "Her lungs sound clear." Both times her doctor ruled out meningitis, strep, and pneumonia. "It's likely just a standard, winter, garden-variety virus. Croup or a rotavirus or a combo." I felt some small relief then and I try to feel some now, remembering those words. As though naming what this thing is or isn't will tame it. After yesterday's second visit in three days, they even drew blood. "To be extra sure." And now I am calling in the middle of the night to be extra, extra safe.

The voice message says the office is closed but gives instructions about the numbers to press in case of an emergency. I press all the buttons. Then I second-guess myself. *Is* this an emergency? What I do know is: she's still burning up with a very high fever, she's barely eaten, and she takes in almost no water, then throws up twice over what she's ingested. None of this seems remotely normal to me.

"Mama-mum-mum," Mathilda whispers. She is both weak and restless.

"I'm right here." I kiss her forehead to reassure her and to check her temperature with my lips. Then I touch her feet to check if they are hot, the way Gail taught me to check. "That's the real sign," she'd say. "Hot feet means a very high fever." Mathilda's feet are lava. An adrenaline rush of panic floods my system. My legs buckle.

I tell myself, *Don't panic, maybe you have it wrong, try the ear thermometer.*

I insert the bulky thermometer into my mumbling child's ear

canal. I look at the readout. My hands start shaking. I look again. A hundred and four. Can that be right? I check the clock. Nine twenty-seven p.m.—it's gone up more than a whole degree in under thirty minutes, she's being cooked alive in her own skin, and I can't give her any more medicine for two more hours.

Fuck fuck fuck, this is bad.

Don't let Mathilda see your panic, I tell myself.

"Mama," she cries as I briefly leave her alone in our bed to rush to the bathroom to run her an ice bath. I quickly wet a fresh washcloth while the tub fills. Temperatures this high can cause seizures.

"I'm right here, honey," I call out. I squeeze excess water from the compress, then rush back to Mathilda's side.

"Mama," she moans.

I place the cool terry cloth on her head. I grab for the cold chicken soup on the bedside table. Is it "feed a fever and starve a cold," or "starve a cold and feed a fever"? I scoop a spoonful of broth and hold it up to her mouth.

"No," she whimpers.

"You have to eat!" I scream.

"Mama," she cries out pitifully.

We are both scared of my sudden angry command. But then I hear Brian's voice in my head: *Give yourself empathy so you can give her empathy. Put your own oxygen mask on first.*

I recognize and name that I am terrified. Without my husband I feel completely powerless and alone. It comes out as panic and anger. After seven years together of constant connection, I am intertwined with Paul in a way I never was with my family of origin. I feel I can't make a move without him or do anything solo without doubting myself. Paul and Mathilda are my everything. I don't know how to handle this level of anxiety in my happy place.

I get her in the tub. I'm only able to give her a quick rinse before her face gets ghostly white. I get her out of the water and onto the toilet in time for a river to pour out of her. She's shaking. I clean her up. I wrap her in a towel. I put the toilet lid down and take a seat with her on my lap. I hold her tighter. Willing my life force into her, willing health into every cell of her being.

"Mama," she moans.

"I got you. Everything's gonna be okay," I say as I rock her.

I hear the front door click. "Hello?" Paul sings out. Thank fucking God.

"We're back here!" Paul enters and I watch him adjust the situation from "this is worrisome" to a reassuring "we got this."

He smiles at the two of us and scoops Mathilda into his arms. "Hi, Bug! I'm sorry you don't feel so good."

My cell phone rings. It's the doctor. I head for the hallway to keep Mathilda out of earshot.

"What's up?" he says.

"Uh . . . her temperature is at one oh four and seems to keep rising with *both* fever reducers. She can't keep anything down."

"Is she crying?"

"Yes."

"Do you see tears?"

"Yes."

"That's good, that means she's still hydrated."

Mathilda barks a hearty, dry cough.

"Any news on the blood work?" I ask. "What about that cough?"

"Monday," the doctor reminds me. "But if you are still concerned tonight, drive her to Cedars with the windows down, and if she's still coughing when you get there, take her in. If she stops coughing by the time you get there because she's had some cool air to calm her lungs down, we'll know it was just croup, so just turn around, go home, and try to get some sleep. And as always, if she's not improving over the weekend, call the hotline again, or wait until Monday and we can try to squeeze you in."

"Okay . . . ," I answer weakly. From the other room Mathilda punctuates the end of the call with a thin, dry, mucous-less wheeze.

🌐

I RETURN TO WHISPER-DEBRIEF PAUL in our master bathroom. "She looks wrong," he mouths.

"Her breathing isn't right," I mouth back.

Paul adjusts the humidifier. I prop more pillows behind her to elevate her head. Paul puts Vicks on her sunken chest. I put a cold compress on her forehead. He dims the lights. I rub her hands. Paul rubs her feet. Her breathing sounds like my dad's did just before he died. *Drive her to the hospital now*, urges the voice in my head. But I second-guess myself.

I match Mathilda's breathing. Short inhale, short exhale, short inhale, short exhale. Her breathing is completely shallow. No air is getting in past her clavicles. I am getting lightheaded from trying to match it for only a few minutes. How is this happening again? *Drive her to the hospital NOW*, screams my inner voice.

Paul and I lock eyes.

As if one person, we leap up and wrap her in a blanket. I grab my purse, he grabs the car keys. Paul carries her down to the car and we strap her in the car seat. I jump in the back with her. Paul drives. He rolls all the windows down. The winter night air blasts us all as he speeds. She is gasp-coughing when we park and carry our limp, molten child through the emergency room entrance.

🌐

"TWO WHITE-OUT LUNGS," SAYS THE emergency room doctor as he taps on the X-ray he's just taken. "That's a BIG pneumonia." Mathilda is in a hospital gown with a faraway look on her face. "We need a urine sample," he says, holding out a plastic cup. I pick her up and position her so I can catch the flow. A trickle of drops . . . and blood.

I shakily hand the lidless receptacle to the attending doctor, who says, "We are admitting her right away."

"Now?" says Paul as two attendants arrive with a gurney and begin loosening the straps and pulling back the bedding.

"I don't understand," I say. "*Yesterday* the doctor said her lungs were clear. Tonight, he said wait until Monday. Did the doctor get it wrong?"

"Well, it's a good thing you *didn't* wait until Monday."

"She's gonna be okay, though, right?" asks Paul.

A pause. "We're gonna try to do everything we can."

MATHILDA IS IMMEDIATELY TRANSFERRED TO a small, private room and given an IV bag of fluids and broad-spectrum antibiotics. Our parenting classes have taught us to shield Mathilda—one of us will step into the hall to hear the up-to-the-minute information and one of us will always stay with her. So far, we know that if it's viral pneumonia, the antibiotics are worthless; if it's bacterial, we've already got the ball rolling and the blood tests will determine the right antibiotics. "It's okay, Bug. You're safe. The doctors are going to get you better," says Paul.

"I love you, honey, we're right here," I say.

Paul secures Mathilda's favorite bedtime toy, a squishy mermaid, under her arm.

"Dada," Mathilda says in a small voice.

"I love you," Paul says. She closes her eyes. I stand and dim the lights.

"Be right back," I whisper. I pick up my cell phone and step into the hallway. I dial my mother's number. Diva answers Gail's cell phone. I can hear laughter, holiday music. "Mathilda is in the hospital," I say through tears. "Can you put Gail on? I need her to come down here."

"What? Why? We just got to a Christmas party."

"Pneumonia. Two white-out lungs. Can you please put Gail on?"

I hear Diva repeat what I said to Gail. I hear Gail and Diva cheerfully say hi to some guests, then Gail jumps on. "Mathilda's in the hospital?"

"Yes. Can you come down here?"

Hesitation. "Isn't Paul with you?"

"Yes. We're at Cedars. Can you come down?"

"Well, is she in intensive care?" she asks. "I'm at a Christmas party with Ahmet and Diva. We took one car. We just got here."

"Mathilda is in the *hospital*," I repeat, urgently enunciating the word.

"Moon!"

"Are you saying . . . you'd come if she was admitted to intensive care? Whose party are you at?"

"A friend of Melanie's."

"So . . . a stranger." I am blinking with confusion. "Can one of you come down at least? Take a taxi or something?"

"Well . . . ," says Gail over festive music and distracted hellos, "what time are visiting hours over?"

"Never mind," I say. "Can you please put Ahmet on the phone?"

"We just got here. It's rude to just walk in and walk right out. Maybe we can come by in an hour or so. We are all in the same car."

"Forget it."

"Jesus, Moon, I said I can try to come later. Or tomorrow. I don't really like hospitals."

Nobody likes fucking hospitals. Hot tears sting my eyes. "Forget it," I say again.

I CALL DWEEZIL. I KNOW he can't come now because it's late and he's got teeny daughters of his own at home.

"Maybe you can come tomorrow?" I ask.

"Is it contagious?"

His question is a slap. I mean, I understand it, he doesn't want his kids to get whatever my kid has, but we are in a hospital. Wash your hands. Wear a mask if you are concerned. "I don't think so," I say, "I don't know. I haven't gotten it."

"Let me know when you have more information," he says. "I hope she feels better."

I hold the phone in my hand. I am beyond confused by my family's reactions. Don't you just automatically show up to help, bring food and supplies and flowers and hugs, and stay and keep watch, too? A wave of anger and hopelessness overwhelms me. *When it comes to your family, you are on your own.* Would my dad come if he were still alive?

I wipe my face on my sleeve, then reach out to a few friends, who surprise me and express the exact *opposite* sentiments of my blood family.

"What can I do?" they all say.

"What can we bring?"

"When can we come?"

"What does she need?"

"What do you and Paul need?"

They reassure me that even though Mathilda is seriously ill, we are in the best possible place for her to get better, and they spring into action.

I dry my eyes and shore myself up for the next onslaught with a little more fight in me. As I head back to her hospital room, another miracle. I see Ahmet's girlfriend Shana standing at the nurse's station. I burst into tears.

"Shana!" I say.

"Ahmet and I broke up."

"What? When? Oh my God, I am so sorry . . ."

"It's sad but it's gonna be fine, but he called to tell me. I was around the corner. How scary."

She hugs me tight. Her ultra-soft black leather jacket smells like safety—musky and warm and heavy with her good-smelling perfume. In her embrace I realize Paul didn't even hug me when he got home. Her blond hair, round face, kind eyes, and warm smile are such a relief to me.

"I will not cry in front of Mathilda," I say.

"That's good," says Shana. "You can show her she has a rock— you are a mama bear, full stop." She bores this truth into me, then leaves. I feel it in my core—I am not just a rock, I am a mountain range.

BACK IN THE ROOM, I climb into the bed beside Mathilda and say good night to Paul, who will attempt sleep on a portable cot. Moments later, four doctors enter dressed in hazmat outfits. At first I think I am dreaming—they look like aliens or astronauts. "We are from Infectious Diseases," someone says. They hand Paul and me the same plastic jumpsuits and face shields they wear and instruct us to wear them, too. I refuse. I am not going to let my daughter think anything is wrong. If she has something that contagious and deadly, I will gladly have it, too. "We need to transfer your daughter to a special room in intensive care."

I look at Paul with pleading eyes—*Not in front of Mathilda.* "Can we please speak in the hallway?" Paul asks the team as he leads them outside.

As we are transferred upstairs, I think, *Gail got her wish— intensive care. Maybe now she'll come visit.*

BY MORNING ROUNDS WE HAVE a diagnosis—bacterial strep pneumonia and hemolytic uremic syndrome. We are told what she has is as rare as getting struck by lightning twice and that Mathilda will be "staying in intensive care for a while." In addition to a team of infectious disease doctors, she now has twenty-four-hour nurses, a pulmonary team, a cardiology team, a nephrology team, and round-the-clock doctors in residency who have to have everything explained anew with each changeover. "Usually, it's caused by exposure to E. coli bacteria, but sometimes the wrong antibiotic can set it off. Her body sees itself as the enemy. Given her age and the severity, both of these infections are life-threatening on their own; together . . ." I feel faint.

I look at Paul. "If anything happens to her . . ."

"We will do everything we can."

Next thing we know, we watch helplessly as a straw and a balloon are inserted into her urethra. After that, an emergency surgery is performed to remove the pus and fluid that's collected around her lungs. They insert a Broviac into her heart so they can draw blood twice a day and give her round-the-clock medications and transfusions more easily. She is attached to a suction machine on the wall that is changed twice a day. She has X-rays taken twice a day. She is put on a series of high-blood-pressure medications. Then someone from Physical Therapy comes along to pound on her back and get her to raise three Ping-Pong balls in a plastic breathing apparatus. All day long, every day, different teams of doctors make their rounds, confer, and calibrate the next plan of action.

We white-knuckle every day and every night. Paul and I never leave her side, except to take turns to shower or speak to a doctor or receive a meal from the online meal train that's been set up by loving friends and strangers. Ahmet and Shana get back together and become champions, showing up almost every day with infusions of big, loving energy, humor, and Spanish lattes from Urth Caffé. I am beyond grateful to Shana for being normal and a wonderful influence on my baby brother, who truly steps up during the worst possible time. When Gail and Diva finally visit, Gail tells me, "Mathilda doesn't look that bad." As though I exaggerated her illness, as though everyone hangs out in intensive care for no reason, as though the doctors who say it's life-threatening have it wrong. I tell her I need her support, not judgment. She takes offense. I don't have time for her antics. I just keep paddling the rapids.

The second week it is still touch-and-go. Groundhog Day with no respite. Then she has a reaction to vancomycin and puffs up to the size of a sea lion, which prompts an emergency surgery for her to be put on dialysis. Now she also has to have blood *and* platelet transfusions, but we need to find a true platelet match ASAP. We put out the call for everyone we know to donate blood and platelets. By some miracle, Shana's brother is dating a woman who is a perfect match. We nickname her Super Platelets.

Even weirder is that Super Platelets has my kid's and my father's same birthday.

Angelghostdad, are you here?

Week three. Our child stops being potty trained and reverts to a diaper. She loses the ability to walk or talk or draw. She misses school and socialization. She starts to squeak like a dolphin and use hand gestures and facial expressions only Paul and I understand. As she mainlines *SpongeBob SquarePants* on our family laptop, I force myself to make peace with the shrill, nails-on-a-chalkboard voice that has become the soundtrack for the clockwork urine samples, X-rays, and blood draws.

With every setback and obstacle, I train my brain to shake off fear and doubt and banish it in every form the moment I detect it. I will myself to picture Mathilda healthy and happy and home again. Now that I am a guru-less atheist, I only have my focused mindset to rely on. And an imaginary friend called my dad. When trusted friends offer prayers from their faiths and a visit from some Buddhist monks, I reconsider. The moonfaced holy men in orange robes speak no English as they turn prayer beads and chant a powerful song that makes the hair on my body stand on end. Then one of them pulls a plastic bag out of his pocket, blows his breath in, and pops it. It is startling. We deeply bow, then they bow and depart. I can't help but think of my father, of course, but when you are confronted with total powerlessness and fighting for your child's life, rules are bent.

When it's my turn to shower, only then do I drop all the way down to my core and allow myself a fat cry. I was devastated when I miscarried earlier in the year, and now I am flooded with gratitude to not have a newborn *and* my firstborn in the hospital. Under the water, I wail.

The next day, a small improvement allows us to be moved out of intensive care and back onto the main floor. We are one step closer to going home. Then we hear rumors of a potential discharge within twenty-four hours with a home nurse option and regular return visits for additional procedures and tests. A total reversal. It will be difficult but manageable and a better environment for Mathilda. Nurses bid their farewells; Paul begins loading the car. But then a doctor rushes in. Something was spotted on an X-ray, a collapsed lung. Popped plastic bag much? Instead of a departure, an emergency lung surgery is immediately scheduled.

By lunch we are signing scary paperwork indemnifying them against outcomes I still can't say out loud. We are sent back to intensive care. Then a sharp, steep decline in her health. My stamina is starting to slip. Our marriage tether is starting to fray. Our coping skills are starting to diverge—my tightly wound hypervigilance grates on his trust-the-experts, chill, all-is-well vibe, and vice versa.

It is week four now with no end in sight. There is a tube connected to a wall unit that makes a rhythmic sucking sound; the other end is hooked to Mathilda. The hospital room is cold. Mathilda weighs half of what she did when we first arrived. She is turning four today. When Paul returns with balloons, he joyfully announces, "Happy birthday, Bug!" I take a walk down the corridor and call Gail.

"Are you coming down?"

"Down where?"

"To the hospital," I say, "for Mathilda's birthday."

"Moon, it's someone else's birthday, too, you know."

I stamp down a surge of explosive rage. "Do you mean my *dead* father?"

"Moon," Gail clucks. "Anyway, Chloe's kids are here jumping on Mathilda's trampoline and having a wonderful time." *Is this real? She has healthy children over, jumping on my sick kid's trampoline?*

A doctor approaches me. It's Mathilda's lung surgeon.

"Okay, Gail," I say calmly, "I need to hang up now."

The surgeon shifts his weight from one leg to the other. "We want to transfer Mathilda to Children's Hospital. We are very sorry, but there is not much more we can do for her here. The good news is each regular room there is the equivalent of intensive care here. We've arranged for an ambulance to transfer her tonight."

My breath becomes ragged. I look around at the hospital where I gave birth to my daughter on my father's birthday, the same place where I sometimes brought my father. I feel the intertwined history, the roller coaster of diagnosis, suffering, treatments . . .

Daddy, I pray on the spot, *please intervene. Please, please, please save my baby.*

OVER THE NEXT FOUR WEEKS at Children's Hospital, Mathilda's medical care is nothing short of harrowing and miraculous. Our child remains mute and fragile. Paul is able to surrender, stay as relaxed as possible, and catch up on cop movies from the seventies, while my only defense against terror and overwhelm is to be on high alert. I try to fast-track our daughter's healing by connecting with others globally who lived through similar illnesses, comparing notes and researching alternative therapies and medications. His strategy is distraction and trust, mine is immersion and sheer force of will. We cannot seem to give each other any comfort, which only makes him retreat and me more frantic.

There are more surgeries and complications. The next infantry battalion of friends shows up for Mathilda, including Debbie Lee Carrington, an actress we barely know from *Total Recall*, a favorite film of my father's. Ahmet and Shana continue to be the MVPs, with Diva and Dweezil close behind now. When a friend's mom gives Mathilda the softest pink blanket in the history of soft, there is a new glimmer of light in our daughter's eyes. On the day Mathilda asks for paper and a pen and draws for the first time in almost two months, I feel my first genuine ray of hope. It is a snail she draws. It is Gary the Snail, SpongeBob's pet. I interpret this as meaning she is coming back to us, and to herself, slowly, slowly, one inhalation and exhalation at a time.

Meanwhile my marriage continues to disintegrate in inverse proportion to Mathilda's recovery, as if our unity is a source that must be depleted in exchange for her recuperation.

One morning on my way back from the lobby coffee cart, I hear a man howling outside the X-ray waiting room. It is the piercing, unmistakable wail of a father who has just lost his child. His tidal wave of grief slams my body. My eyes fill for him. I return to Mathilda's hospital room with extra softness for her and for Paul. Whatever suffering we have, it isn't that, not today.

🌐

MATHILDA IS RELEASED A WEEK before Valentine's Day. "This is a huge trauma for her and your family," says the kid-centric hospital social worker readying us for our imminent departure. "Whatever you do, don't make any sudden changes. Give her and yourselves a year to recover." Paul and I nod in full agreement. Then Paul, Mathilda, and I pile into our car on a crisp, sunny morning, the reverse image of the night we arrived in early December a few miles away. We drive away from the hospital shell-shocked. "Goodbye, hospital!" we say. "Thank you for getting Mathilda all the way better!" Mathilda gives a wave, then closes her eyes, settles into her car seat, and strokes her cheek with her blanket, which she has named Softy Pink.

When Mathilda is safe at home in our big bed, I have a long bath and an even longer cry. I silently thank the doctors, my family, my friends, God, my friends' gods, everyone, and my dad.

By the end of the weekend, Paul asks me for a trial separation. Within a month, he moves out and takes half the furniture. Yes, Mathilda is home and alive, slow and fragile, but our marriage hangs in the balance, divided into two homes, dying a fast death.

CHAPTER 59

Righteous Anger

I help Paul find a nearby rental, knowing he'll be back—our kid needs him. I need him.

The place is a tiny, magical spot a mile up the road. I reassure myself that time away makes the heart grow fonder. So does a shoebox. Anyway, we've been through too much; we have a daughter to raise, under one roof. We are a family. We can weather this.

I take Mathilda to physical therapy and to "play therapy" twice a week. Mathilda's body is an entirely different shape now. Gone are the openness and athleticism; her shoulders slump forward and her spine is now curved, as if to guard her heart. She has no stamina and very little range of motion in her neck, so the PT tosses all sorts of things high in the air for Mathilda to look up at and run after— stuffed animals, balls, Frisbees. The running helps her strengthen her lungs to deepen her breathing, and the element of surprise makes new brain grooves, so she'll begin to heal psychologically, by seeing some surprises are safe, even fun.

At play therapy, Mathilda interacts with a kind, soft-spoken British woman named Liz who has a homey office with thick rugs, furry sheepskins, and many pillows to roll around on. There's a toy doctor's bag, art supplies, and a dollhouse full of tiny beds, like a hospital. After months of play, Mathilda begins to create small scenarios that Liz translates as integration of her experience at the hospital and home life without Dad around as much. Liz suggests a pet. Mathilda wants a kitten. We find a little Tonkinese rescue she names Seasons. I am crestfallen when Paul suggests switching his visits to his new place because of allergies.

In spite of Paul's move-out, life sort of gets back to a kind of normal—school, friends, birthday parties—but with regular doctor check-ups. Mathilda's post-illness anxiety also includes refusing to eat anything other than what I cook at home. It's more work for me, but I would do anything for her. After reading all the empathy books, I've become a black belt in being present for our kid. I watch how slow healing is, how it has its own timing and process, Mathilda's and my own, but the PTSD is real.

One day when Paul is visiting Mathilda outside at our home, I accidentally see a text in his phone. Someone named "Angel" is just getting out of the shower. Now Paul and I both picture her naked. Thanks, Angel. I am in shock. It never occurred to me the separation meant fucking other people. I thought it meant healing and regrouping solo, not so low.

When I ask him about it, I see his mouth move and hear the words but can't find their meaning. "I want a divorce" rises like steam from a kettle. My husband has just said my worst fear out loud. I shatter and scatter in every direction.

"But . . . ," I stammer, "didn't you hear what the woman at the hospital said? What her PTSD therapist said? What our friends, our couples counselor, and literally *everyone* has said?"

"Yeah, but I can't do this. I feel a weight pressing down on my chest and I can't live like this."

I want to scream and throw up at the same time. "You think I don't feel that way, too? So what! It will pass." He says nothing. "Did you . . . already . . . talk to a *lawyer*?"

"Yes."

Terror and rage braid together and loop around my throat. I can't breathe. Who is this? He wants to get away. From me. All this time all in and now he wants out? These years mean everything to me, but apparently not to him. This far in and I am just *starting* to heal from my childhood. Our daughter almost died and now my have-your-back-forever partner and best friend wants an exit.

I OPT FOR MEDIATION. I refuse to provide an attorney with a summer home. I want to be able to afford to send our kid to college someday. When he says, "You can stay in the house until Mathilda is eighteen," I lose my shit and hear the old, internalized choir of self-hate.

I boil over with a surface-of-the-sun fury I will come to know as "righteous anger." I reject his offer. I will bet on myself.

Paul gets his wish. I must become an earner when my confidence is at an all-time low.

The cord between us unspools. I am the discordant sound of metal grinding on metal in an unending free fall. *How could he?* repeats on a loop in my head. *After everything we've been through? After everything Mathilda's been through? After everything I've been through?*

After we tell our families, I learn the German word "schadenfreude"—glee at someone's misfortune—when Gail tells Paul, "If there's anything you need, just call me. Moon has no idea what we know, no idea what it's like to come from nothing and make your own way in the world." I want to scream, *If those ingredients are missing from my pot, blame the chef!*

But I don't.

I have to be strong for that little girl. I have to accept that Paul and I were dealt a hand that's too much to come back from together. Then I move me and Mathilda to where I can afford to live, the San Fernando Valley.

Bag my face, bag my whole world.

CHAPTER 60

Insurance Policy

My siblings and I are in a fancy, top-floor conference room in Beverly Hills with a NASA-like view as far as the eye can see, along with Gail, her accountant, and three of the attorneys she's had since I was a teenager. The nine of us are seated around a large, honey-colored, surfboard-shaped table. Each of us has copies of legal paperwork and pens within reach. I'm used to this "no pressure, just sign it right now" drill, so why do I feel preemptively off-kilter?

I notice Bob, the bespectacled attorney I've always trusted more than the others because my dad liked him, is squirming. Gail begins, fingering her rings and studying the grain in the wood: "I am five million dollars in debt." Her voice is uncharacteristically soft and girlish, with overtones of forced calm. "The insurance policy I put in place after your father's death was supposed to be one I could borrow against." I see this is hard for her. She sounds small and weak.

My spine straightens. She has my full attention. Something doesn't sound right.

I think, *You? The brilliant businessperson made a business mistake? How?*

"I am asking you to sign over your rights and forfeit your shares of two point five million dollars apiece so I can dissolve the policy and take the remaining money that's there to use it to go toward my debts." I am confused. Gail *did* set a substantial sum aside for us when she sold my father's masters? There *is* a legal document with my father's signature on it that outlines an equal split that Gail wants us to dissolve?

"What do you mean?" I ask, leaning forward.

"When we dissolve the policy, the ten million dollars liquidates to only seven hundred and fifty K. Two hundred K of it I have to pay back to the investor. The rest will go toward a deal I owe two million dollars on. If I can't find the rest of the money in the next few months, Universal will get Frank's catalog. But this small infusion of money could stall them, show good faith, and give me time to get the rest of the money. The first step is to take Bob off the document as the trustee and assign all the rights to all of you so you can all assign all the rights over to me. It would need all four of your signatures. It must be unanimous."

I look at the faces of all the men in the room on Gail's payroll. Her employees are silent, each face more impossible to read than the next. I look at my siblings. Ahmet looks resigned; wide-eyed Diva knits. Dweezil chews the inside of his cheek, indicating he's formulating questions. Bob shifts in his seat some more.

"So . . . wait . . . ," I say. "I don't understand. This money won't even solve the problem?"

"No, but it will help," Gail says with a razor's edge of impatience. Do the lawyers also see me as an ignorant, annoying question-asker? Gail is so strange with them—deferential, feminine. Do they see her denial? Delusion? Her overspending disease? Do they care?

"What's the rest of the debt?" asks Dweezil.

"Money I owe the lawyers for defending Frank."

A wave of anger sweeps through me. *Frank told you to get out of the business and live happily ever after.*

Wait, I think, *why can't your lawyers just forgive their debts? You've been paying them for more than thirty years. I can't begin to imagine how much they have made off of you and Frank. Why can't they bail you out as a courtesy for all your loyalty to them? How does this even happen?*

"I don't understand. Why can't Bob just sign everything over to you?" I ask.

"It must be unanimous with all four of you," Gail repeats, man-tralike.

Bob continues to thrash in his seat.

"I want to hear what Bob has to say," says Dweezil.

Bob pipes up, twitching. "Look, I made a promise to your dad. I have a fiduciary responsibility to you kids and this situation does not make me feel comfortable. I think it's best if I am relieved of any responsibilities here. What you four decide after I am gone is up to you."

Another lawyer chimes in, "I think what Bob is saying is Gail has laid out a reasonable plan that will positively impact all of you if you all decide to move forward together."

Wait, are we a *family* of stooges? I study Bob, who avoids looking at us.

"I don't feel comfortable being put in this position. I have a fiduciary responsibility to you kids," Bob reiterates.

I don't know what to think. I don't know what to do. What does a normal person say to someone who has a serious debting problem and then encourages them to take on more debt? What does a child say to a mother who asks her children to agree to be left with nothing? Why is Bob fighting for us and Gail isn't?

What kind of a mother even asks her kids to *not* receive the *only* gift they are only *just* finding out their father intended for them? Do I let go of the money I didn't even know I'd receive? Do I take a spiritual leap of faith and hope maybe Gail gets it right this time? Or do I fight to still receive a gift from my very absent father?

I get an idea. If we can be a real family, united in helping her, united in betting on each one of us, working together shoulder to shoulder, united in earning, and equally invested in rebuilding Frank's legacy . . . Would Gail be open to *all* of us finally thriving emotionally and financially in real time, together?

I take a chance.

"Okay, Gail," I say, "yes. I say yes on the condition you let us *actually* help you. From this moment forward, if you agree that we *all* have the ability to *finally* make Zappa projects to generate income, if you agree that we don't have to wait for you as you stall and hold stuff up, if you agree that *all* of our ideas will be green-lit so we can *all* begin to actually generate income and help you and ourselves, together, in our lifetime, then I am a yes."

Her mouth tightens. She won't make eye contact.

"I will say yes, too," says Dweezil, "but on the condition that you also pay me back all the money you owe me for T-shirt sales and that you uphold your end of the bargain we already made with my touring. I get to keep my own income for what I do."

Gail's face twitches.

"Yes," says Diva, "of course, Mama."

"Yes," says Ahmet, "I don't need your money. I'm doing well at my job, and I love you, so no conditions."

Gail stays silent.

Bob is on his feet. "Sounds like you have what you want."

IN THE END GAIL IS insulted by the parameters Dweezil and I propose. She sends an email letting us know she will "find the money some other way." I am flabbergasted "equal and united" is not a real thing to her even though she has us sign legal paperwork every year at tax time with that all-for-one, one-for-all framework. Bob still removes himself as trustee.

I send her and her lawyers an email back saying she's an embarrassment to our last name, that Frank wanted all of us to be happy at the same time. For me it is a normal everyday argument, same as any other we always have. I have no idea I have crossed an invisible line with her. But I will find out soon, and so will the public—*after* she dies.

WITHIN A YEAR, GAIL IS diagnosed with lung cancer. Our relationship changes overnight, I think, for the better. I suddenly have unlimited energy to be *kinder* to her because it occurs to me there is now an expiration date on her cruelty and self-serving manipulations. When she goes, my siblings and I will finally be free from her undiagnosed mental illness, chaos, and manipulations. I think of the Ram Dass quote about how in the end we are all just walking each other home.

I can do that. She is mean, but she is our mother.

CHAPTER 61

A Change

"Moon, can you do this?" asks Diva. She means change our mother's diaper. Gail has—metaphor not lost on me—literally shit the bed. Gail appointed my sister to be in charge of her medical directives. It makes sense; she still lives at home, and let's be honest, she will always be the "baby" and the favorite. I am just so glad our mother has finally lightened her load post-medication side effects. Plus, years of changing my own baby have taught me not to care; it's just a bigger diaper.

"Sure," I say to Diva, who rushes past me flapping her hands.

I survey Gail's messy bedroom for what I'll need to help my very overweight mother—new diaper, pee pad, new sheets, trash bin, wipes. So many wipes . . .

"I'm going to change you now," I say to Gail, "so you can feel better." As high as she is, her face is set in rigid defiance against this pending humiliation. "Bend your knees," I say, "and open like a butterfly."

I actively see her as a giant baby and start cleaning, getting into the nooks and crannies of her whole nether region. I see this opportunity as a gift, tending to the holy place where she conceived me and then pushed me out. After several minutes of this process, Gail finally surrenders and relaxes her muscles. There is simply nowhere to hide, no place in her, on her, and around her I cannot plainly see.

"I'm gonna change the sheets now," I say.

I support Gail's back with my hand and roll her away from me to position a large blue doggy pee pad and an enormous diaper underneath Gail's white, flat bottom. Her large, rigid back looks like a block of marble. "Now roll toward me," I say. She grunts as I wriggle the other end of the pad and the diaper in place. I ease Gail onto her back, pull the diaper and the plastic padding between her legs, and tape the flaps. Then I use the same rolling technique to change the sheets.

"There you go," I say, the way I'd coo to my tiny daughter drying her off after a bath, the way Gail must have spoken to me at some point early on in my life. "You're all clean," I say, adjusting her pillows and giving her elbows some height. My restorative yoga training is coming in handy. It gives me pleasure to make sure my mother feels cared for.

Then something remarkable happens. Gail, the all-white puzzle with no edges or clues; Gail, the unquenchable mother this firstborn daughter could never please; Gail, the destroyer, speaks: "What if you were always this nice?" she asks.

She says it as if she's solving the riddle of the Sphinx. She says it so matter-of-factly that I almost miss it: Gail is *seeing* me.

I think back on the guru's flash—*One moment of enlightenment is worth everything.* For the first time in my life, Gail truly sees who her daughter really is. "I *am* this nice," I say through tears. "I was, and I am, this nice." I beam at her and squeeze her hand, so struck by the total full-circle role reversal. I just feel so grateful for this briefest recognition. Then her face contorts as if she's glimpsing the magnitude and foolishness of her lifelong projection of me. I hold her water glass underneath her chin and position a straw at her lips. Her eyes flicker with childlike desperation and raw vulnerability.

"You think I am a failure!"

"No," I say. "You did great. You are a great mother, and you saved the day. In the hundredth hour you pulled off the Universal deal that meant so much to you. You have secured something meaningful all by yourself. I love you."

"Do you forgive me?" she blurts, looking pained, a featherless bird with patches of soft tufts for hair.

"Yes," I say, "of course I do." I stroke her face with deep affection.

She pulls the breathing tubes out of her nose, panicked, like there's something she's forgotten to do. She is loopy as fuck on the strongest tarry capsules full of marijuana, but there is a stampede of wild horses rushing through the body of this dying woman. "Give me a piece of paper and pen," she says, grabbing at her bedside table. I hand her a Uniball and a book to use as a stable surface. She makes several wavy marks and dashes on the back of a used envelope, then hands it to me imploringly before falling back into her nest of pillows with worried eyes.

"It's okay," I say, setting her masterpiece down. I massage her fingers. "I'm right here. I got you." She thrashes a moment more before taking me in and allowing all her earthly tension to briefly be carried downstream.

When I report the tender, transformational moment to my siblings and show them Gail's important chicken scratch, Ahmet and Diva share a look, then shrug, nonplussed.

THE MOMENT GAIL BEGINS TO leave her body, I am at a yoga class in savasana. In corpse pose, I feel her spirit departing her body. I just know. I leap up, grab my mat, and exit before the meditation bowl is rung. As I rush to my car I see I have missed several messages from Ahmet and Diva—fuck. It's really happening. Or it's happened. Fuck, fuck, fuck. Where the hell is Dweezil? Can we get him there in time, too? "Pick up, pick up, pick up," I say aloud as I call them and speed up Laurel Canyon. The cell service is choppy.

"You're on speakerphone," they say, "she's going, Moon!" They are crying. "I love you," we all say. "Thank you!" we all say. And then she's gone.

CHAPTER 62

Slide Show

I am standing in my mother's ostentatious kitchen. I am washing my hands in the sink with a chip of yellowing muguet-scented soap she uses. Rather, used. Gail is dead.

I am numb.

I am looking out at the familiar view of jacarandas, palms, and Chinese elms outside the south-facing window, but internally I am seeing Thanksgivings, Christmases, birthdays, in this gathering space, along with the normal days. I am seeing my mother's slim, willowy, sturdy form in her twenties taking messages and writing phone numbers on the wall. I am seeing her older, lumpy, limping, more recent figure pacing on endless legal calls or ignoring collection agencies. And I see her beauty all the years in between. Always barefoot. Always in action. Always a force.

I picture Gail shuffling a well-worn deck of Bicycle cards and dealing herself a winning hand in solitaire or hunched over her laptop replying to emails. I see her filling bowls with dry food for a cadre of dogs and birds and rats or using her foot to drag a dishrag over a splatter of cat puke. She is forever in my mind's eye folding laundry or reading or making tea or crossing a thousand tasks off a list of thousands more. And I am seeing my mother's giant, Cheshire cat smile toasting me and Paul and yet-to-be Mathilda.

Memories like these become precious, transparent slides.

Now a crow swoops past the bay window, startling me back to the present. Again, I take in the view—the trees in our garden that have grown alongside our family's evolution, the low hills beyond, and farther still, a vast sky. I burn this last image into my mind, like a snapshot, singular, and the caption: *The war is over and we survived.*

I am shaking. Like refugees, my siblings and I made it. My eyes are wet. My teeth chatter. My system floods and shudders with relief. I hear the cackle of a coal-black bird echoing through the canyon. I wipe my face with a tea towel and laugh back.

At the end of her life, I can finally say the M-word. Because she can't hurt me anymore. I say it and I mean it. It feels wrong and weird in my mouth, but I see now she has earned it. She never deserted her post as our leader in battle. Even if she helped perpetuate the war.

"You did good, Mom, you did good."

Going Gigantic

2015-2019

CHAPTER 63

Trust

I am seated at my kitchen table. I thumb through the legal documents but cannot take in the words. A high, tinny droning buzzes in my ears. An invisible fist has my heart in a stranglehold. The room vanishes. So . . . Gail *never* loved me?

My probate attorney tells me the legal term here in this case is "unnatural disposition." Dweezil and I can *never* be involved in any decision-making about our family home and our father and our last name? An eternal unequal distribution of my father's legacy for me and Dweezil *forever*? A lifetime of signing legal documents where we are all equals, a lifetime of a shared definition of and commitment to family I thought we all possessed, a lifetime of saying one thing reduced to a tectonic-plate-shifting doing another, eternally. I am so blindsided I cannot think or speak. Then I zero in on an additional particularly hateful clause that my attorney says he's never seen in any will before, a clause that feels extra targeted at me—whoever has a faith will be cut out of the will entirely. Gail over God or you're out. *This* from the fake-Zen, lifetime-psychic, scarf–from–the–Dalai Lama–having, Transcendental Meditation–ing, mantra-repeating, spell-casting witch?

I am in utter disbelief.

From beyond the grave, Gail is *still* pulling power plays. It's the perfect final chess move. She didn't give me and Dweezil *nothing*, so *technically* she can be seen as beyond reproach, generous even. Bravo.

WHAT PARENT DOES THIS? WHAT *mother* does this? What the fuck did I do? What mother chooses some kids over others? What mother wishes unending love and peace and belief and resources and creativity and total empowerment and divides a family into a *them* and an *us*, into a hateful before and an even worse after? What siblings *allow* that? Who *are* these people?

CHAPTER 64

Wishes

G ail is buried in Westwood. On top of my father. The funeral is an open-casket celebrity circus.

As people drive away, Ahmet looks wild-eyed and exhausted. "I had no idea," Ahmet says. "I was just as surprised as you." His dark suit is clean but creased. Shana is beside him, somehow managing to look natural and casual in Chloé. We are standing in the cemetery, close to where our parents are buried. "I looked into making the situation right in terms of the financials," says Ahmet. "I talked to Diva. I was thinking to offset five percent of my thirty to you, and Diva could do the same for Dweezil, but my hands are tied and Diva really wants to honor Gail's wishes."

"She really wants to honor Gail's *evil* wishes that you both get more than us and that Dweezil and I can *never* be in charge of *any* decision-making about *our* father's legacy *ever*?"

"I'm not in charge of Diva and it's not my responsibility to fix your relationship with our mother. I already told you, my hands are tied. I really tried."

"He really did," says Shana.

"My hands are tied," says Ahmet.

"I don't understand. Did you say, 'Hey, how can I fix this whole thing so that it's completely fair across the board?' Did you ask about creative solutions?"

"What difference does it make? I told you my hands are tied."

Ahmet turns and starts walking away.

"Where are we going now?" I call after him.

"*I'm* going home," says Ahmet without looking back.

"Moon, Gail loved you," Shana says, tucking a strand of her long flaxen hair behind her ear. "Tensions are high right now and everyone's hurting. Ahmet's a good man." My sister-in-law smiles and half hugs me before running to catch up with her husband, my brother, my dead mother's statement ring on her finger, glistening in the sun.

—

CHAPTER 65

Walk with Me

A hmet and Diva file a petition against me and Dweezil in probate court over a myriad of complicated issues including Dweezil's rights to perform our father's music. This sets off a cascade of additional undesirable, lopsided financial burdens and outcomes on *top* of the stress and anger that already exist regarding my baby siblings, leaving me to wonder, *How is inheriting nearly everything not enough for Ahmet and Diva?*

How did we get here? Because I set a boundary with Gail and asked her to make the family business fair for all of us in her lifetime? Because I offered Gail help and honest feedback?

The probate horror drags on for almost three years, with the back-and-forth only occurring between lawyers, in the press, in Facebook posts, and through family friend Steve Vai kindly acting as self-appointed mediator.

As hurt and angry as I am at my flesh-and-blood siblings I helped raise, I search my soul, dig deep, and ask myself, *What do I want?*

I answer: *I want Ahmet and Diva to stop their legal proceedings against me and Dweezil.* So I can keep what remains of my nest egg to live and pay for Mathilda's private school and eventual college, and to give myself the time to write and do my job well, instead of being crushed alive under the weight of grief and stress. What I want is to feel the same peace and closure they get to feel, the same power and decision-making, the same creative freedom and financial security. What I want is restorative justice for Dweezil and me, and for all of us to be made whole, like they had been.

I have given up hope we can ever be a family again, but, in Rumi style, I return to myself and my core values: love and family over gold. I remind myself we all grew up feeling robbed and owed, but I have had a thirty-year head start in yoga and therapy, and at least ten years on them actively practicing the spiritual principles of yoga, mindfulness, and trying to rewire my brain for empathy.

In an effort to create harmony, I email Diva directly and ask her to take a walk. Now is *not* the moment to ask her to hear *my* grievances, so my thinking is to give her my ear and my support and just remain silent. Maybe I missed something. Maybe I will learn something. Maybe I can apologize for some mysterious thing I don't understand that she feels I've done to warrant taking legal action against me and Dweezil. Maybe if Diva feels totally heard and seen and understood, she will soften and become reasonable. If she becomes reasonable, maybe she can open up to heart-centered solutions. If she can access her heart, I will ask her to drop her end of the legal action against us. Maybe she can be my sister again and we can become allies in teaching our brothers how to be collaborative and kind, like us. Maybe we can unite and role-model family fairness.

Diva's reply to my request for an in-person stroll and talk is "Yes."

I instantly feel, dare I say, excited and brimming with hope.

We select a time and local, neutral, public place to meet, then I get to work to get into the most impartial headspace I can, so I can show up the way I intend.

To prepare, I kick and punch my heavy bag, do some ashtanga yoga, sit still, and try to cry out as much hurt as I can before I see her. I call my closest friends. I name my fears and talk out all the possible scenarios that could go right or wrong and how to respond. "Here for you," says Justine. "Ask for what you want no matter the outcome," says Amiira. "Trust Spirit has your back and all is happening *for* you," says Julesy. "This or better," says Stephanie. "Breathe," says Clio. "Yoga, yoga, yoga" is Joan's offering.

I call my wise eighty-year-old friend and writing teacher. When I call her to report my latest heartbreak, Claudette always says four funny things I love to revitalize me and make me laugh:

1. "Metaphors be with you."
2. "Don't worry, dear, it gets so much worse."
3. "Bring 'em to their feet or their knees."

And 4 is a little inside joke when we go too long without speaking: "All is forgiven, come home." It could be an hour or a month. I melt and laugh every time. I'd like to be the kind of person who can say that and mean it. Oh well.

I PARK ON A SIDE street. When I see Diva's beautiful face, I feel an overwhelming surge of love for her. It has been almost three years since we last saw each other in person. I smile with my whole heart. She smiles her gorgeous smile back. In the mutual beaming I see there is also mutual wounding, fear, warmth, and anticipation. Though twelve years apart, we have roughly the same height, weight, and proportions, and now we are both blondes in bright colors and flattering hats. In the time that has passed, I know she has bought a house near me, made art, started an online tarot-reading business, and taken up running. It shows. She's radiant. I am happy to see she looks fit, rooted in herself. I see the strength she has acquired and the defenses and boundaries she has built up. I am proud of her.

I think if we two sisters can resolve something and make some progress, there is hope for our fractured family.

We make small talk for almost two miles. We try to do a bit of catching up about pets, little work wins, and why we are single—boys are dumb and our dad set the bar too high. It goes as well as it can possibly go until we hit a big rough spot about Mathilda.

"You've weaponized your daughter," my sister says. "You never let me see her." I am taken aback—how would that have worked exactly? She'd pick my kid up and hang out with her but not me? Tell my kid stuff directly, but I'd keep speaking to Diva through lawyers? Or they'd just make small talk over ice cream? Would Ahmet feel comfortable dropping his kids off at my house and driving away?

"What makes you think she'd want to know someone who is hurting her mother? This is her choice as much as mine," I answer.

"She can't choose if you won't let her. She's always going to do what you want."

I take this in. It stings. This was certainly true in our house. We always made Gail's choice become our choice. Have I done the same to my own child?

Fuck no. We know the difference between right and wrong, fair and unfair. We have the ability to feel empathy and we know how to look out for family—our *whole* family.

"Will you drop the legal stuff against me?"

She summons invisible fortitude. "I can't do that, Moonie." I can't read her face. Is she sad about this or feeling justified for causing me pain? "But if you needed a kidney, I would give it to you."

"The kidney I am asking for is that you drop the legal actions. This *is* the kidney I need."

Her face contorts in anguish. Her sorrow-filled, dark chocolate eyes—my father's eyes—say that what I am asking for she will not give.

We part ways with a half hug, our energies already withdrawing from each other, back into survival mode. "I love you," she says.

"I love you, too," I say.

Even as I walk back to my car, I feel the emotional hangover coming on, the sadness creeping back in.

I CALL MY FRIENDS, MY chosen family. The choir sings: "Find your feet." "Hand it over." "Dance it out." "Keep moving." "Healed people heal people."

Right.

Walk away, I tell myself.

—

CHAPTER 66

Stipulation

In March 2019, the longstanding legal battle with my siblings ends when a judge signs a stipulation saying I am not bound by the terms of the agreement Dweezil accepted from Ahmet and Diva. It is a Pyrrhic victory because it does not end the estrangement, nor bring restorative justice, nor foster goodwill, nor repair ruptures, nor equalize financial disparity. It does not generate harmony or collaboration or insight or peace. I would rather have my family, but at least I have my voice.

What is freedom worth to you? Your artistic expression?

I am my father's daughter after all.

Earth to Moon

2019-NOW

CHAPTER 67

—

How to Heal in a Hundred Steps

I move to Taos. I hike and cry.

I read many books, including: *Breath* by James Nestor; *The Body Keeps the Score* by Bessel van der Kolk; *How to Solve Your People Problems* by Alan Godwin; Chris Voss's *Never Split the Difference*; *Attached* by Amir Levine; *The 5 Personality Patterns* by Steven Kessler; anything authored or coauthored by Gabor Maté, Esther Perel, Stephen Levine, Marshall Rosenberg, bell hooks, or Nayyirah Waheed; and, for fun, everything by Denis Johnson and George Saunders.

I watch the entire series of the American *Office* with my daughter. We laugh like hyenas. I cry some more. She disappears into her room to be productive and make art.

I can't stop making and freezing soup.

I order a cord of wood. I buy an axe and chop the wood into smaller pieces. I make a lot of fires.

I commit to podcasting regularly for the Writers Guild. I lean into every aspect of writing and storytelling. I feel so proud of being a member of this auspicious group. I volunteer to speak to other writers. I feel uplifted when they all describe their tenacity to stay with a dream despite slammed doors. And they *all* have a stick-with-it, turn-no-into-yes, right-place/right-time, trial-by-fire story. Then I lose my membership status because I haven't sold anything in a while.

I use my jealousy as fuel to transform my inaction into my next steps.

I pay attention to my daughter. I do yoga.

I turn longing into words on paper and art.

I turn anger into curiosity.

I get a really excellent business coach. I try what the smart people who have what I want tell me to try.

I love on my teen. I hike and cry some more. I make more fires. I pay attention to nature. I run. I grieve. I let go a little more. I love on my teen some more.

We funyak rapids on the Rio Grande.

I take a tantra class to heal my sexual hang-ups. I grieve. I take guitar lessons. I grieve. I do a gestalt workout called the Class online. I get seriously fit. I grieve. I make more soup. I get sourdough starter from a friend. I focus on making crackers. I take Ryan Heffington's dance classes. I take Kate Shela's classes. I do 5Rhythms. I try dumb stuff that works for a little while, like the Marco Polo app and posting stuff on Instagram and Facebook like normal people. I give them up. I try again. I lose interest and write a newsletter. I love on my kid more. I am thawing out.

I lean in to treasured friendships. I cry, a lot.

I drink a lot of tea, so much tea that I start a tea business, a buried lifelong dream.

I fall in love. We break up. I cry harder. I grieve again, more than I thought was possible.

I start teaching yoga and meditation online. I start making art again. I continue to love my daughter all the time. I take more online courses. We get a shitty president. The planet gets COVID. The world changes. I make more fires. I observe. I listen. I breathe. I teach. I study. I anchor down with my child. We paddleboard on a different river.

A friend suggests I try her amazing therapist. I speak to her. She says that if we meet once a week, starting today, she can reparent me in three years. I think, *FUCK THAT, I'll get three therapists and do it in one year.* I get a super-smart, super-loving Jungian analyst, an ultra-nurturing cognitive behavioralist, and an empathetic master in polyvagal theory counseling for PTSD recovery.

I get a book deal.

I start to heal. With care, I start to heal. With the company I keep, I start to heal. With self-love, I start to heal. Finally, I start to fall in love with myself.

—

CHAPTER 68

Anatomy

Two small forms lie on metal gurneys with white blankets draped over them. Two former humans who have given their bodies to science. The people who run this place name the "donations" alphabetically. "Wanda" has been with them awhile, "Gerda" is the newbie. Seriously? *Gerda?* What are the chances.

This nonprofit school of anatomy is housed in a hexagonal building it shares with a massage school. It is located in Colorado Springs on a university campus. The space is clean and well lit, with clear cabinets with "clean" reference books you can look at without gloves when you aren't working and "dirty" ones you can flip through as you dissect. There are boxes of fresh gloves and spare lab coats and tables with dishes full of scalpels and scissor grips and other instruments for slicing and separating.

There are fourteen students, most of them in their forties and fifties. Half of them have dissected together before. They greet each other with smiles and twinkling eyes. They are a collection of medical body workers, yoga teachers, hospice caregivers, palliative nurses—all experts in their fields, all loving, deep, kind-eyed, and present, all anatomy nerds.

At 9 a.m. we arrive and circle up in our street clothes and sit on folding chairs. Our instructor is warm but no-nonsense, ferocious with integrity, and holding the highest respect for our "teachers," who wait for us in the other room.

In the center of our circle is a small altar with feathers and smudge sticks and tea lights, small heart-shaped stones, and chocolate in the shape of body parts. Our other instructor is the resident dissectionist. He is welcoming, down-to-earth, and playful but serious as he explains the lab rules to the newcomers like me.

Our other instructor reads an excerpt on grief that describes the importance of giving the act its full due and what distinguishes grief from sorrow from disappointment. The passage she reads is also about praise and how grief and praise are entwined gifts that invite us to live with the vitality of openhearted aliveness. What she shares is very moving. No one has dry eyes. We all understand that journeying inside a human body is a sacred endeavor.

In the same way that I needed to go to Burning Man to experience firsthand the amplification of the field of love and unconditional giving, I now find myself desperate to know the fullest extent of what it means to be and have been a person. I want to understand from the inside out. The corporeal part. I want to actually look inside and see who we all are underneath our personalities and stories, possessions and achievements, talents and preferences, shortcomings, failure, pain, and genius.

Then our instructor asks us to pretend she is our fairy godmother. She asks us to say our names and what we hope to see in this process. The hyoid and insertion points of arteries and meeting places of optic nerves and heart chambers are some of the options said aloud, but all acknowledge that whatever shows up is welcome. I say I am new and know almost nothing even after a few anatomy classes. The words don't stick, and the concepts seem elusive, no matter how much I study. Still, I tell them, "I just felt a strong pull to come and see for myself. I'd love to see and hold and feel the weight of as many organs as I can, like the kidneys and lungs. I am also hoping to see a vagus nerve in real life and maybe the little Florence Nightingale helper organ in our abdomens—the greater omentum."

The male instructor is kind and reminds us all that a beginner's mind is the best kind of mind for adventures. I feel genuine acceptance and I deeply accept in myself that I may not be able to keep up with my peers, but I am a keen observer and trust something valuable will be here for each one of us. We then smudge ourselves, apply some scented oil to the interiors of our disposable masks, change into scrubs and rubber boots for easy cleanup, and choose our lab coats.

I overhear a discussion about Gary the Snail. I remember that my daughter is one of the main reasons I am here. The reason I want to see the kidneys and lungs. I want to see what got so sick and what got all the way better. I am here to heal old wounds. I am here to heal fresh ones too. I am here to look at what we are all afraid to see.

When Mathilda finally drew Gary the Snail that day in the hospital, I knew we were out of the woods. I thought we were safe. I did not see the rest of what was to come. We humans wouldn't be able to go on if we could see what comes next. I don't think I could. Who signs up for this much heartache? I guess we all do, unknowingly.

"Wanda" looks like a cross between a dog's dinner and homemade jerky. Her eyes are closed. Her arms have been "examined" down to the muscles just below her wrists. It looks like she's wearing white driving gloves. Her feet have also remained untouched. So has her face. Her hair has been removed for cleaner access to her skull. "Tomorrow we will try to see her brain," says the male instructor. In medical anatomy classes, hands and faces are covered so students can focus on specific areas. But we are voyagers and explorers charting our own expeditions, with total access to gather our own data, then interpret what we see for ourselves.

Today "Wanda"'s rib cage is lifted off and set beside her, showcasing her organs. Her uterus was removed long ago during her living life. Her gallbladder also appears to be missing. The heart is enormous! We watch the lungs inflate and deflate when our male instructor inserts a tube into her trachea and pumps air in. We look at the relative positions of the organs during the breathing process, check for the evidence of her emphysema, note how pockets of the lungs remain inflated after the exhalation, and imagine how this would have caused discomfort not just in her lungs but in other organs too.

Since I am new, I ask where I might begin. I am led to "Gerda," who is being explored at the other table. After an hour of peeking over everyone's shoulders and getting used to slicing and peeling back tiny sections of her lower leg, arms, and breasts, I feel compelled to give her eyes a look. As I carefully begin slicing into her eyelid skin, I am suddenly mentally and emotionally catapulted sideways. My brain is flooded with images. Like plugging into a light socket and receiving a sudden shock, making contact with her eye plugs me into a barrage of images—a ranch home with a view of mountains, ribbons, antiques, horses, grandchildren, church . . . the pictures come and keep coming . . . I feel her unexpressed grief is still looking for a place to exist, is still very palpable and asking to be acknowledged. There is life force here with no body to animate. Are these her thoughts? Mine? Real? Imagined? Remembered? Projections? She was a mother. A daughter. A grandmother. A lover. A sister. A little girl. She was a woman, like me. She was a spicy mama.

The female instructor takes me by the elbow, walks me outside to get some air. I didn't realize I was crying and hyperventilating. I had not anticipated losing my shit. "That's what happens," she says, "in a room full of empaths working together." She guides me through my reaction and waits for me to land back in my own body.

"Smell the air, look at the trees, sky, birds . . . feel your feet and take some belly breaths."

I'm having a paroxysm of deep understanding I can't verbalize. Grief, love, healing, it all lives on. It is a gift to be alive. If my own mother's death had gone the way I hoped, I would have lived out my life and become an expression of ego, forever in my father's shadow, running a lesser version of his life instead of finally living the fullest expression of my own. My mother's acts set me free. Free to be in my own art form. To be a creator and a beauty maker. To tell my own stories. To have agency over my life.

Soon it will be six years since I last spoke with Ahmet and Diva. Dweezil has been absent for two, for reasons only he can name. I let myself feel the deep sadness, the loss.

I hear "Gerda," I hear Roy, I hear my angelghostdad, and I hear myself.

And what do I choose today?

Today, I choose to see how we work. To lovingly hold the human body in my two hands. To see what we are made of.

Grief, love, healing, and *I* live on.

CHAPTER 69

Freedom

For my birthday I have custom noise-canceling earphones made, the professional type musicians wear onstage. "In-ears," they are called, made from a mold in the exact shape of your ear canal. Mine are clear with red sparkles. It is sunrise. I start strong with a steep hill and Miss Janelle Monáe to get in the zone. I breathe rhythmically to Kate Bush and take in the view—towering trees and mountain laurel in full bloom. Because I'm fancy. They are perfect for my current favorite indulgence—running in nature.

It is time to set things right. To name the truth, to name what hurts and run it off.

Gail, you were pathologically unrepentant and constitutionally incapable of and uninterested in being accountable or changing your behavior. Still, you gave me your tenacity, your attention to detail, your sense of color, and your love of tea and books. You taught me how to care for sweaters and make the greatest Caesar salad and make holidays extravagant with holy beauty.

Frank, you were peerless and as selfish as you were creative, with a talent and body of work that were limitless and still remain un-matched. You loved me and got me, you gave me my work ethic and my integrity, my taste buds and my fashion sense, my humor, my hair, my good mind, and my ability to reason.

Together, the two of you taught me the hard lesson that you can die before you die and live beyond your death. As a duo, you created the map and destroyed the key.

Ahmet and Dweezil and Diva, no one makes me laugh harder or knows how difficult it truly was. No one can take away the birthday parties and holidays, time in the pool, boot camp in that shitty bank building, walks past Patsy Vinegar, home leg waxing, knitting to crime shows and *Dr. Who*, cooking together, being kids together, then briefly raising our own together. I will remember you all singing, doing the worm, playing the guitar, and making art, so much art.

I alternate between running on my toes and a solid heel-to-toe strike through a section of my route that resembles a cloister walk. This has been a truly terrible time in my life, a time that has stretched on with an intensity and a duration that may have destroyed some. Still, I have seen beauty. The ballet performed by the fly fishermen wading in flowing rivers in summer and the stillness of the ice fishermen outside their January tents when the water is hard enough for a tractor to drive over. Attuned to the world around me, I've learned things like what to expect when certain trees tremble in the wind and the undersides of their leaves curl (rain) or what the thickness of stripes on a fuzzy caterpillar signifies (a long winter).

In the land of salamanders and voles, deer and foxes, snapping turtles, black bears, and turkey vultures, I am shedding my old skin and my old life. I've seen an amanita in person, smelled linden and wild azalea, gathered trumpet and oyster mushrooms, and nibbled blueberries off a bush. With novelty, new brain grooves, new memories, new possibilities.

I break into a full-fledged run now, sucking in clean air like my dad swallowed his cigarette smoke. All I ever wanted was a loving family. I wanted to give my kid the stability I never had. I wanted to give that to myself. I have always had a sense that love is something that can beat back pain, even death. That if you are loved by someone, truly loved, you can internalize them and their deep well of emotion for you, and it will live on through you. Death is still sad, of course, but *that* grief has a completely different quality. That's not the grief I got.

Every day I make a decision: To walk through the hurt I've felt at the actions of my parents and my siblings. To remember that each of them was operating from the bank of their own learned behavior, that each of them was navigating the world as their hearts and minds told them was right. Their decisions were not in my control. My reactions were. And my reactions have ranged from anger to grief. I have always remained utterly loyal to my parents and my siblings. But I grieve relationships that could have been, or never were.

Oh well.

For now I'll just keep on breathing and running.

It is here, in the gobsmacking greenery, that I begin to make a kind of peace with my past, with what has come and what can never be, with all that was lost and all that remains, and with myself. Like Björk once told me, you make an energetic double of yourself, and when they match, relief comes. My outsides finally match my insides. At last, I am committed to myself, no matter what.

I slow down. I even out my breath. My eyelashes glisten.

How do you heal? You make a decision. Mine is this: no more bullies allowed.

Mean people suck. Everyone makes mistakes. But I don't have to keep welcoming them with open arms.

I turn the music up. Led Zeppelin's "Whole Lotta Love" for the last mile and final push. I run like I am shot out of a cannon, like I'm fireworks. Free-ish at last, free-ish at last.

CHAPTER 70

—

Text

I compose a group text. I add contact, add contact, add contact, knowing I don't require a reply. Even though Frank never had a cell phone and Gail's old number's been assigned to another user, I mentally add my dead parents as I thumb-type five words to my living siblings. Before I press send, I picture them all healthy and happy and whole. I see Dweezil and Ahmet and Diva receive these words and smile. I say the words out loud to myself and press send.

All is forgiven, I say. *Come home.*

Delivered, it says back.

ACKNOWLEDGMENTS

A humongous all-caps, boldfaced, underlined, exclamation point THANK-YOU to the following humans for your vision, path-cutting, and vital contributions on this juggernaut of a memoir:

Carrie Thornton, you are both a goddess and a human acropolis. This book would not have been possible without you. You were the perfect editor for this book. You saw the literary way to pull it off, distilled the story to its essence so I could always find my hand- and footholds on the ascent, and kept me elegant. In so doing, I am a different person now than I was when I first began. I will especially treasure the in-person times with you reading aloud and discussing all things music, family, and art. I am finally at the top of the mountain with you, speechless and complete.

I also want to thank the behind-the-scenes team at Dey Street who also put in the long hours and helped made this book possible: Drew Henry, Allison Carney, Sarah Falter, Heidi Richter, and Rachel Meyers. I infinity thank you, too! Thank you to Suzanne Mitchell, Jessica Kaye, Skyler Kilborn, and Tanya Orlov in audio land. An extra fireworks thank-you to June Cen. Your US cover art is pure magic. It infused me with fresh energy and inspiration and served as an engine to give me the push I needed whenever I ran out of steam. And a special mention of lasting appreciation for David Wiener.

In the UK, I wholly thank my incomparable editor Lee Brackstone. You are a champion and a gentleman. You were my distant constant, my lighthouse, and my touchstone. Your notes shaped the structure of this book and let me separate my life from my story about my life. Thank you for loving what you do and doing it so well, and for the books on your reading list for me—they were psychic transfusions and brain candy. They and you made me a better writer, though this sentence seems a bit iffy. Thank you to the incredible team at White Rabbit/Orion Books—Aoife Datta, Alice Graham, Sophie Neverkla, Leanne Oliver, Clarissa Sutherland. You all also made and continue to make all the difference.

Now for the group hugs and extra unending love for my global cheer squads. As corny as it sounds, you have been a light in the dark for me in some small or enormous and unforgettable way. When I needed you most, you tangibly took action and helped me by hugging, hearing, housing, humoring, healing, grounding, feeding, reading and reading and rereading me. You listened, stayed silent, stayed present, stayed over, stayed the course, held the space, found spelling errors, took notes, nourished, nurtured, advocated, endorsed, advised, encouraged, brainstormed, checked in, helped me check out and reset, hiked with me, sent memes, sent flowers, sent backup, watered my plants, fed my cats, rummaged, researched, ran errands, ran the bath, and/or made me laugh, and my heart is overflowing with gratitude and joy for:

Claudette Sutherland, queen of queens; my besties, Justine Bateman, Stephanie Fein, Kate Luyben, Jules Blaine Davis, John "Handsome Jack" Lovick, Adam Paloian, Brigid, Chris and Alexa Grant, Aris Moore, Anastasia Thompson, Chelsey Goodan, Melissa Bushell, Rebecca Cammisa, Jessie Deeter, Joanne Winstanley, Carisa Hendricks, Emily and Berthold Haas, Jaqueline Lopez, Karen Ahmanson, Heidi Miller, Rosie Carnahan-Darby, Lisa Sall, Susan Morris, Rhoda Lawrence-Harris, Jennifer Bell, Michele Vicary, Lori Echavarria, Rhys Darby; my A-plus foreverettes in our online writers' room,

Amy Alkon and Stephanie Willen; goddesses Carolina Goldberg, Annalynne, Kimberly, Helena, Cindi, Deb, Rosemary, Adriana and the Reiki crew; Joan Hyman; Clio Manuelian; Christy Lynn Hicks; Jennie Powell; Jennifer Elliott; Dawn Stillo; Emi Fontana; superhero Kathy Kaehler; fire tender Nikki Hainstock and Canyon; Blaire Embrey; the inimitable Martha Clarke; David Grausman; the indispensable Reyna Lopez; the well-dressed Nastassia Lopez; Nick and Bélen Coleman; and a flash flood of love for my extended family Paul and Erin Doucette. I also thank Tom and Jane Doucette; Gwyn McColl; the hilarious Jackie Kashian and Maria Bamford; Chris Manson; Chrys Johnson; Marissa Cummings; Courtney Holtzclaw; songbird lovebug Jimmy Demers; Yuriko and Hiriko Sakamoto; Megan Adell; my beloved Miss Pamela Des Barres; Jo Cobbett; Kate Shela; Jessalyn Maguire; Therese Balagna; Marianne Ronis; Stanley Siegel; Eileen J. Kenny; Vicki Saikali; Marjie Royalty-Ward; Mariel Tourani; Paul Pascarella; Marci Kipnis; Sandeep Bollia; Sadie Mestman; Tamar Kaloustian; Pamela Wynn; Chichi, Chloe, Coralie, and Crystal Barthelemy; Victor Lewis and Lloyd Douglas Wynn; Kristin and Michael Heming; Gregg Mitchell; Brian Gary; Steve Trautmann; Jackie Burt; Jensen Fairchild; Jennifer Bunting: Mallory, Nathalie, and Taryn from The Class; Maura Smith and Theophilus Donahue; Antoinette Peragine; Norman Seeff; Kim Max; Randall Slavin; Tina Scmelzer; Dana Blaire and the tea.o.graphy dream team; Isa Stewart; Susi Stone and Russ Barton; WeTransfer; Jamila Musayeva and the Avocado Toast team; and my East and West Coast dance fam.

Additional high-voltage love for Gail, Colin, Ruby, and Hart Campbell; Jamie Lee Curtis; Brett Goldstein, Flannigan and Michael at Largo; Orna and Matthew Walters; Annabelle Gurwitch; Laurie Metcalf; Boise Thomas; Solina Kwan; Bellina Logan; Nathaniel Lowe; Genevieve Oswald; Gurmukh Khalsa; Land Romo; Greg, Mighty, and True Behrendt; Christina Stone; Lynn Goldsmith; Al Malkin; Catherine Ingram; Karl Saliter and Liz Macaire; Heather T. Roy and Learka Bosnak; Tina Smith; Wendy H.; Massimo Bassoli; Alessandra Izzo;

Cheo Martinez; Claire Kellerman; Robert Downey Jr.; Gina Cook; Nate Rubins and fam; William Monasse; Judy Auchincloss; Laura Milligan; Joe, Sam and Juliette Sehee; Stanley J. Zappa and Sarah Beadle; Lala and Lula; Brendan Smith, Richard and Goti; Kate Bush; Sinead O'Connor; Björk; Bowie; Dennis Johnson; John Hughes; George Saunders; Nick Murphy; Bon Iver; Martin Scorsese; David Lean; Dalai Lama; Thich Nhat Hanh; and Fiona Apple. You all said or did or sang or created something that made all the difference.

An honorable mention thank-you to my professional badasses and day-to-day team: Bianca Grimshaw, Craig Cohen, Jerry Kurlak, Josh Rothstein, Gavin Kim, Steven Giammichele, Dan Coleman, Debbie Gower, and Maria Speth, with a special shout-out to Wolf Wallace, Jennifer Ramirez, Emily Collins, and Jonathan Kramer.

A deep and heartfelt acknowledgment to those of you who do the difficult work of healing yourself and/or mending broken connections in friends and family lines. My love and respect for those who endeavor to repair all ruptures. The tool kit is total honesty, empathy, capacity, willingness, integrity, humility, humor, timing, stick-to-it-iveness, kindness, shared values, boundaries, forgiveness, and smarts. I send you luck and patience and carrot coconut smoothies from Beverly Hills Juice Club.

Special squeezes to these dear ones:

Ahmet, Shana, Halo, and Arrow Zappa

Diva Majika Zappa

Dweezil Zappa, Zola, and Ceylon Zappa and Mia Marsicano.

Eternal gratitude for my writing secret weapons:

Elena Seplow-Jolley at New Moon Editorial. You are a true genius and genie in a bottle. Your talent and abilities are gobsmacking. From macro big picture to micro attention to detail your comprehensive overview, creative suggestions, prowess, attunement, thoroughness, true care, mirroring, and encouragement are everything.

The peerless Ruthie Ackerman, who performed triage on 146,000 words. You saw me better than I saw myself, made firewalking seem fun and easy, and helped me spot my personal and professional blind spots. You also taught me the joys of a shared Google doc, renewed my faith in my own abilities, and helped me stay true to my original seed and vision.

Allegra Huston, writer and reader extraordinaire. Thank you for teaching me how to ride the rapids literally and metaphorically, for being my sister-friend, and for helping me find my ending.

Ariel Leve, full stop. Uncut diamond. Amplifier. Lightning bolt. Literary emergency contact. Vanquisher of PTSD. You get it and you name it and you do it.

Amiira Ruotola-Behrendt, my all-hands-on-deck soul sister in all the trenches. I literally could not love you more, yet I do every day. Tears. Laughter. Smarts. Style. Fall down seven times, stand up eight. We cross finish lines. Blood until the end of time, and time is infinite.

To my true blue, Molly Stein. So much laughter, so many cookbooks. Thank you for loving me, reading me, recovering the treasure in the wreckage, and thinking I am funny. Thank you, thank you, thank you and Kevinstein and French Toast and Miranda, too.

Aaaaaaaand lastly, Jett. I am happy at you. You are my teacher, my hero, and my friend. No one makes me laugh harder or is more fun to talk to about stories and storytelling. Thank you for your work ethic. Thank you for the hugs and the reminder on the kitchen cabinet. Thank you for your honesty and courage. Thank you for the art and music and walks and popcorn nights. A forever love without beginning or end, you are my favorite and my best. Who's Youmore?

ABOUT THE AUTHOR

Moon Unit Zappa is a writer, yogi, mom, artist, nature lover, podcaster, and tea baroness. Find her at moonunit.com